'Place is everything. Place is terribly important . . . There's got to be some sort of place, particular places, holy places. Once you get there you know you're kith and kin. The stones start to talk.' Colin Middleton

The accelerated changes and dramatic events of the late 1950s to the mid-1970s – the dawn of the space age, the birth of rock and pop culture, violent clashes between conservative and revolutionary politics – profoundly altered our view of society. And in Ulster, as elsewhere, the arts mirrored the galvanised tensions of the late twentieth century, displaying the same expansion of knowledge and technique that dominated the non-art world. But whilst Ulster's artists diverged from inherited precepts, eschewing traditional media, their art still found itself underpinned by a 'sense of place', engaged with the 'mystery and melancholy' of the Northern Irish landscape.

Structured around four broad thematic sections – landscape, figurative and non-figurative art, sculpture, and the art of the Troubles – Mike Catto's *Art in Ulster 2: 1957–77* takes an intellectually penetrating look at the new colours, new media and new visions of Ulster's artists. Arresting in its scope, this study ranges from the 'innocent vision' of Neil Shawcross's fine 'colour essays', the dark humour of Gerard Dillon, the stylised structures of Brian Ballard's work, and the spare but energetic Abstract Expressionism of Deborah Brown to Jack Pakenham's savage metaphors, displaying the full confidence and panache of Ulster's modern art.

'a fascinating guide to a wide group of extremely distinguished artists'
Tom Paulin, *Times Literary Supplement*

Front cover painting: *Fruit basket* by Neil Shawcross.
From a private collection.
Back cover painting: *Fish Eaters* by Gerard Dillon.
Courtesy of the Arts Council of Northern Ireland.

ART IN ULSTER 2
1957 – 1977

MIKE CATTO

with biographies of the artists by
THEO SNODDY

THE
BLACKSTAFF PRESS
BELFAST

First published in 1977 by
The Blackstaff Press Limited
in association with
The Arts Council of Northern Ireland

This new edition published in 1991 by
The Blackstaff Press Limited
3 Galway Park, Dundonald, Belfast BT16 0AN, Northern Ireland

This edition has received financial assistance under the Cultural Traditions Programme which aims to encourage acceptance and understanding of cultural diversity.

Printed in Northern Ireland by Nicholson and Bass Limited

ISBN 0-85640-129-3

CONTENTS

ILLUSTRATIONS

COLOUR PLATES

BLACK AND WHITE ILLUSTRATIONS

ACKNOWLEDGEMENTS

The author, the Arts Council of Northern Ireland and the publishers wish to thank the artists whose work appears in this book for giving their permission for its use. For permission to reproduce work by artists who were no longer alive when this book was written, we thank the following: Heinz Hammerschlag for the work of Alice Berger Hammerschlag, and for the work of Gerard Dillon, his family and the Ulster Museum. Thanks are also due to the Imperial War Museum, Faber and Faber, Appletree Press, *Punch*, the *Irish Times*, the *New York Times*, *Introspect*, Ferranti Ltd, Seamus Heaney, John Hewitt, Kenneth Jamison and Michael Longley for permission to reproduce illustrations and extracts, which have been acknowledged in the text.

INTRODUCTION

In the context of world art, the contribution of those artists who were born or have worked in the North of Ireland is inevitably minor. This in no way invalidates a project which seeks to examine the work produced over the last twenty years by Ulster artists. In fact it gives an impetus to it because the very lack of outside documentation and critical analysis given to artists here has been misinterpreted to mean that there is little worth examining. Far from it, and the time is right to erase the self-deprecation felt by some and to examine the art of Ulster alongside the art of the rest of Ireland and that of the international art scene. My intention is not to inflate artistic reputations; neither do I wish to denigrate achievements because they emerge from a small corner of a small island. There *are* some older artists, such as William Scott, F E McWilliam and the late Gerard Dillon, who have had international acclaim, and there are those such as T P Flanagan and Colin Middleton who have established credentials which are as recognised in Dublin as they are in Belfast. That being said, there are also other artists producing work which is qualitatively comparable with much that is exhibited and recognised in the rest of the British Isles.

This book is a companion volume to John Hewitt's *Art in Ulster 1* but unlike the majority of the artists discussed in the pages of his book, most of those found in this short survey are not only very much alive but are also, hopefully, only part way through their careers. So it is intended more as a mid-term report than as an end of term assessment. The last nine years have been a time for collective soul searching. It has also been a time of intense publicity for almost every facet of life here except the *visual* arts. Yet during this period, as in previous ones, artists in Northern Ireland have seen and reacted to their environment with perception and compassion. To write of them is not chauvinism, merely a recognition of their worth. It is never easy to practise as an artist in any society and Gerard Dillon once said it was impossible here in the North. This short survey of artistic endeavour takes as its starting point Michael Longley's introduction to *Causeway: The Arts in Ulster* (1971) where he discusses the implications of Patrick Kavanagh's definitions of the words 'provincial' and 'parochial'. Kavanagh claims that the provincial looks to the metropolis for guidance while the parish inhabitant trusts the culture of his own environment. It is up to the reader to decide whether the artists of this part of Ireland are provincial or parochial.

While it is recognised that the use of the word 'Ulster' means all things to all men and that its connotations even beyond this little island are calculated to raise partisan passions, this writer has to start somewhere to define the locus of his study. For the purposes of this survey of the last two decades I have restricted myself to the political unit of the six counties which constitute the modern Ulster or Northern Ireland.

Even so, it can be contentious to go further and nominate someone as an Ulster artist when the individual concerned considers he has either an Irish dimension or an international identity. Thus it is with caution that a non-Ulsterman such as myself states that within the context of this short work an Ulster artist is one who was born in the six counties and has spent a relevant part of his (or her) artistic career here or else is one who had the misfortune to be born elsewhere but has made up for it by working here for a period of not less than five years. Five years may seem like too short a time to qualify for Ulster adoption but as the time scale of this survey is only twenty years then it will be seen that five years is sufficient time to practise and have some influence (particularly if the artist is also a teacher) on other artists.

Sadly, there are some native born artists who follow the great Irish tradition of emigrating and I must perforce only mention those who have kept up some connection with Ulster either by producing Ulster influenced subject matter or by continuing to exhibit here. I apologise therefore to any artist who considers himself an Ulsterman through and through but whom I have omitted because he is now established in Kilburn or Kentucky and no longer shows here. While on the subject of shows I have further restricted myself to those artists whose work has been seen in exhibition (either in commercial galleries or else in public collections such as those of the Ulster Museum, the Arts Council of Northern Ireland or An Comhairle Ealáion) during the past twenty years. Such is the nature of the art world, even in a small geographic area like Ulster, that art must not only be done but also be seen to be done. My apologies to those who may be prolific in output but who have not shown to the public except perhaps in local art club annual shows. I can only write about what I know or what I have seen and even then, to avoid producing merely a catalogue of names, I have included some names and excluded others. This decision was not arrived at arbitrarily but as the result of a desire to produce a narrative and a thesis which is concise.

The reader will notice at the back of the book the biographies of just over thirty artists and while it is not intended to represent a Top Thirty it gives fuller details of those artists whose work and/or influence may be said to have contributed significantly to the condition of the art scene in Ulster today. In the main they were born after 1927 but some older artists are included who are discussed in John Hewitt's companion volume. Just as 1957 is merely a convenient time for this volume to begin (it was the year that John Hewitt left the province for a time to go to the Herbert Art Gallery in Coventry) so too 1927 is only a rough starting point for the artists in this volume. Some artists such as William Scott, Colin Middleton, George Campbell, Gerard Dillon and F E McWilliam were born before that time and no-one would suggest that their work or influence ceased on 1 January 1957. Thus there need be no apology for including their biographies and their later work especially where it can been seen to have viewed afresh not only their own oeuvre but also the nature of Ulster subject matter.

Objectivity and systematization in history and criticism are the twin foci of much contemporary writing, especially that of the structuralists and semiologists, but while I have great sympathy with their aims and objectives this present study is more modest in scope. It is an empirical analysis of certain themes and trends exhibited by certain artists over a period of only two decades. My reading of this corpus of work is based upon criteria which are inevitably subjective in origin. It is not based upon a study of the art works alone but also upon the artistic, social, cultural and political factors which have guided artists of and in this society and its culture. And since this reading is a personal one it may differ from interpretations of the same artists, themes or phenomena arrived at by other writers.

The works discussed and the artists who created them are all part of an artistic *zeitgeist* and any discussion of it should include the related artistic traditions which manifest themselves in the work of craftsmen and designers in the fields of ceramics, silversmithing, jewellery, textiles and the like. A lack of time and space are reasonable excuses for this omission from this book but the main reason is that I lack the specialist knowledge to do them justice. As a result, the bulk of the narrative will consider only painting, sculpture and fine prints. That being said, the materials and techniques used by artists of today are such that many media will be mentioned that were unknown to and undreamt of by the generations of artists discussed by John Hewitt. My task is to reconcile and explain media as traditional as oil paint and as unconventional as Ordnance Survey maps.

Just as it is not possible to mention every artist here in the North, I must equally restrain myself from cataloguing every single person who has helped me in the preliminary research and final preparation of this book. Theo Snoddy, who contributes the biographical section, has been a constant and infallible source of material to me and has lifted much of the burden of cross-checking references from my shoulders. I am also greatly indebted for the help provided me by Ted Hickey, Keeper of Art at the Ulster Museum, at a time when he and his staff were heavily involved in their own work in the same area. Indeed I must record my gratitude to the

Ulster Museum for invaluable photographic material and for permission to consult and quote from the manuscript of the scholarly catalogue *Irish Art from the Ulster Museum*. I am grateful to *The Irish Times* for allowing me to quote from several interviews, and to Faber and Faber for permission to reprint in full the two poems by Seamus Heaney on pages 13 and 31. I have happy memories of the time and hospitality offered me by many of the artists mentioned in the following pages; to all of them, many thanks. Thanks also to the various organisations and individuals who supplied me with good quality photographs and original works and who granted me their permission to have these reproduced in the book.

My sincere gratitude goes to the Arts Council of Northern Ireland for having confidence in me, and my gratitude extends to its Director, Kenneth Jamison, and its Director of Literature, Michael Longley, who have allowed me to quote from critical essays and catalogue introductions written by them. Above almost everyone else I wish to thank Brian Ferran, Director of Art/Film, Arts Council of Northern Ireland, who has devoted so much official and personal time and energy to this project. With his knowledge, he should have been the one to write this book! Particular thanks to Bill Porter, Bill Kirk, Tony Feenan and the other photographers who have always provided the goods, even at disgracefully short notice. And of course, my greatest appreciation goes to my wife Valerie who has put up with my hermit-like existence while this manuscript was being written.

Reproductions

Dimensions are given in centimetres and height precedes width. The majority of illustrations are taken from works in the collections of the Arts Council of Northern Ireland and the Ulster Museum since this will allow the reader a greater chance to view the originals.

A SENSE OF PLACE : THE LANDSCAPE

'Nature is not on the surface, but in the depth.'
Cézanne

Ireland is a beautiful island, and Ulster a beautiful part of it. Visitors and natives alike comment on the feeling of space still to be enjoyed in Ireland, for it is an underpopulated country. Perhaps like the Highlands of Scotland the reasons for its underpopulation are far from beautiful, and every hillock and tree, every stream and field bear mute witness to years of constantly unremitting labour as well as to sporadic outbursts of tragedy and violence. The mythologies of this land are ancient and numerous while new myths and martyrs are created daily: and there is no-one more myth conscious than the emigré. In him and through him the homeland takes on a mystical significance that modern tourism seeks to define, encapsulate and dispense *ad libidum*. The ould sow may still eat her farrow, but the modern world wants to see it done and recorded with the regularity of feeding time at the zoo.

The eighteenth century created tourism, with young milords and their tutors crossing Europe in search of the *genius locus*, that spirit of place which held the key to the art and knowledge of the ancients. The motives for undertaking such educational and uplifting pilgrimages may have been rigorous, pure and Neo-Classical but the methods and effects were Romantic. While Edinburgh and Dublin were trying to recreate ancient Greece and Rome at home, the alternative mythology of their own Celtic countries was attracting artists and writers who sought the primitive thrill that they felt they could detect in the (faked) poems of Ossian and in the wild landscapes of Northern Europe. It was this same thrill that prompted Mendelssohn to experience the power of nature which had created Fingal's Cave on Staffa (the same geological phenomenon which here rises from the sea as the Giant's Causeway), and it was that self same thrill seeking, albeit at a lower aesthetic level, which caused the eponymous heroine of Mme de Stael's novel *Corinne* (1842) to find herself in the mysterious and barbarous Celtic wilds of Scotland, swooning in ecstasy at the sight of forests, hills and lochs.

The particular essence of Romanticism becomes too easily the general conventions of romanticism, and from there it is but one step to cliché. I mention this historical note because the Celtic landscape has evoked so many clichés in song, poem and picture; and the tourist, rushing from place to place *wants* the instant satisfaction of the cliché. Heaven knows he has enough to choose from, especially in the field of landscapes, for what the critic Brian Fallon has called 'the Bord Failte School of Painting' has many exponents in the six as well as the twenty-six counties. But that is a surface thing, sometimes with quite pleasant surfaces to enjoy. Beneath lies a landscape which attracts most Ulster artists at one time or another. I have shaped this book around thematic sections, for a straight chronology is pointless when such a short time-scale is involved. Obviously many artists will qualify for inclusion in more than one section, but nearly all the painters qualify for a section on landscape. Even today, when so much of the subject matter that attracted artists half a century ago is derided, when fashions in style and materials change frequently, the Ulster artist continues to have a landscape reference. Sometimes the landscape is the exclusive area of enquiry for a painter; sometimes it forms a symbolic sign system; sometimes it is an old friend or enemy to come back to for fresh stimulus, and sometimes it lurks there unbidden, refusing to be thrown out of the subject of a painting. Whatever his motivation, and whether consciously or not, the Ulster artist continues to derive much of his inspiration from the interplay of earth, air and water. The result of combining these elements *can* be air-filled mud, but it can at times coalesce to produce the fourth element, fire.

Within the umbrella title 'Ulster Landscape' specific tendencies can be determined. There is the Romantic (or romantic) landscape in which an intuitive feel for the medium of paint is made to serve an intuitive feel for the elemental mysteries of land and light. Then there is the Analytical landscape where structures are demythologised, where patterns in nature are subjected to a geometrical, reductive evaluation and where the numbered parts are then re-assembled and expanded into newly articulated spatial and colour dimensions. The end result can be as atmospheric and as aware of the sublime as the mimetic Romantic landscape and as such it is futile to over-classify and say that Basil Blackshaw is 'only' a Romantic landscapist and Derrick Hawker 'only' an Analytical landscapist.

In recent times a new awareness of the land and its ecology has led to a use of the land as an object and medium, not simply as a subject. One of the sub-categories by which this is known is Land Art, such as Christo's wrapped up landscapes, and it has its exponents as well as its critics here. These are treated within this chapter and also within the chapter on sculpture, for the inclusion of the very three dimensionality of the land itself, a tradition in Ireland from prehistoric times, extends the terms of reference beyond painting. Some sculptures intrude into the landscape, but others re-define it and become one with it. Last of the perceived landscapes, as against the landscapes of the mind, there is the urban landscape. The rural landscape painter may include a figure, a house, even a hamlet and still be in thrall to the land beneath, the sky above. The urban landscapist, however, has a horizon which is far more enclosed and enclosing. True, Belfast, like Edinburgh, has a Romantic landscape which surrounds the city and sometimes sweeps into it, but the view at the end of the street that gives you Black Mountain or Cavehill, Goliath and Sampson the cranes at Harland and Wolff, or even the white stillness of Stormont is subordinate to the landscape at ground level. Here the painter or sculptor must contend with what men are and what they do with and to each other. This *can* involve exterior scenes, but the shift may also be to interiors and this becomes the concern of the chapter on figurative art. Sadly, it also becomes the concern of the chapter which has forced its way into the narrative of this survey, that is to say the art that has emerged from our civil strife.

In 1957 Russia extended man's view of the world when the first Sputnik was launched. The earlier high altitude photographs of the curvature of the Earth, taken from American converted V2 rockets had mapped out whole areas but only from a single point. Sputnik and its many successors both Soviet and American allowed us for the first time to comprehend as a totality the land masses and the seas, the clouds and the shadows. The effect of seeing the macrocosm was suitably exciting and humbling to many; the sheer artificiality of those divisions on our school maps was finally made clear and we were given a vision of the world that could not be erased. This new vision inspired the monumental scale of much Land Art.

Also in 1957, at a local level, the Belfast Museum and Art Gallery mounted a large retrospective exhibition of the work of Paul Henry (1876-1958) the Ulster born artist whose direct and indirect influence on Irish landscape painting is still acknowledged. In a taped interview with Belfast art students in April 1971, and reiterated again in The Saturday Interview in *The Irish Times* on 14 August 1976, T P Flanagan spoke of the definitive vision that an artist can give to a place:

> 'Everything that I have enjoyed, say in the way of landscape in Ireland, I have enjoyed initially because I saw it with the sanction of a particular painter who took it and made something out of it. For instance, I can't go to Connemara without seeing the Twelve Pins the way Paul Henry saw them. That's why I never paint the Twelve Pins: Paul Henry has seen them and he's given me a vision of them which helps me to enjoy them, and as a painter he has performed a *necessary* function.'

That statement might equally apply to Terence Flanagan himself, for through him, cumulative series of paintings of place add up to highly personal but accessible definitions of the Lough Erne basin, Lissadell, and the boglands of Donegal. Born in Enniskillen, Co Fermanagh in 1929 he was brought up by two aunts with a house near Lissadell, Co. Sligo, the home of the Gore-Booths. The great Georgian house of

Lissadell has links with Irish nationalism and literature through Constance Markievicz (née Gore-Booth) and the poet W B Yeats who wrote evocatively of the house and its grounds. The literary connotations of the house are not lost on Flanagan who is an articulate and sensitive writer in addition to his skills as a painter. He counts several of Ireland's well known literary figures as his friends and in *The Irish Times* interview already alluded to he said, 'What Irish artists have to realise, as F E McWilliam the sculptor once said to me is that they are literary minded like the rest of their countrymen and that they should paint figuratively even if to do so is not fashionable elsewhere.'[1]

Terence Flanagan's artistic mentor was Kathleen Bridle, a Fermanagh art teacher with a love of modern art and a sensitivity for watercolour. After his time as an art student at the City of Belfast College of Art he went into teaching, and evidence of his strong compositional skill and his ability to work with a restricted palette was affirmed by a series of paintings of Dominican nuns in the convent school where he was teaching. He is particularly keen on serial production as offering alternative experimental solutions to a specific thematic problem. One of these early works, *On The Terrace* (1962), illustrated in both editions of Bruce Arnold's *Concise History of Irish Art* (Thames and Hudson 1969 and 1977) shows itself to be more than an exercise in simplification of colour and form, it is an evocation of stillness and silence. The image becomes the metaphor for a pattern of behaviour and in his landscapes one can often sense ramifications of time and space that exist beyond the physical confines of the canvas. This was to be emphasised in the mid 1970s by a number of watercolours and drawings which incorporate the text of eighteenth and early nineteenth century emigrant letters written to relatives still in Ireland. The texts are integral to the image and speak, via their rustic descriptions, of a world and a life beyond the page, beyond the ken of the old folks back home. But this is to leapfrog in time and to generalise from two particular and somewhat atypical examples, so let us return to the fifties.

Flanagan's first one-man show in 1958 contained a number of still-lifes and flower paintings each of which 'had a distinctive poetry appropriate to its subject'[2] as Kenneth Jamison observed. These ranged from lush painterly pieces to works with simple, almost Japanese gestures delineating the particular plant or object. The figurative remained in his work until around 1962, for example in the studies of workmen set against the mud patterns caused by building work at St Mary's College. This produced a series entitled *Men in a Muddy Field* in which gradually the play of tones and textures in the earth and the highlights on puddles enmeshed to supply a broad landscape reference which scarcely needed the figures of the title. In 1962 he exhibited a work called *Flooded Field* in the Irish Exhibition of Living Art which took this interplay of reflected misty sky and water to greater lengths. The horizontality and flat planes are now established, as is the concern with light as the definer (and trickster) of our visual sense. The brooding quietude remains intact and is made more obsessive by the covering of water. We talk of a blanket of snow covering the earth, so why do we only talk of a sheet of water? The silence continues in one of the last works of this period to have a figurative element; the painting shown in the Open Painting Competition of 1962. Entitled *The Vow of Colmcille*, it showed St Columba sadly turning his back on Ireland before going into exile. Flanagan used the low islands of Lough Erne to symbolise Ireland, and in his own words, 'I lost interest in the figure and the islands over his shoulder began to interest me more,'[3] so that, as is appropriate, the homeland comes to dominate the exile.

Like those islands in Co Sligo inextricably linked with W B Yeats, the islands on Lough Erne are so close to water level that they merge with the water's mirrored view of the sky overhead; what Seamus Heaney called 'their mutual flirtation, their eternal triangle with a moody light'.[4] This evanescent sparseness which marks his point of reference for the paintings of Lough Erne and Lissadell can be seen in *Autumn Lough* (no

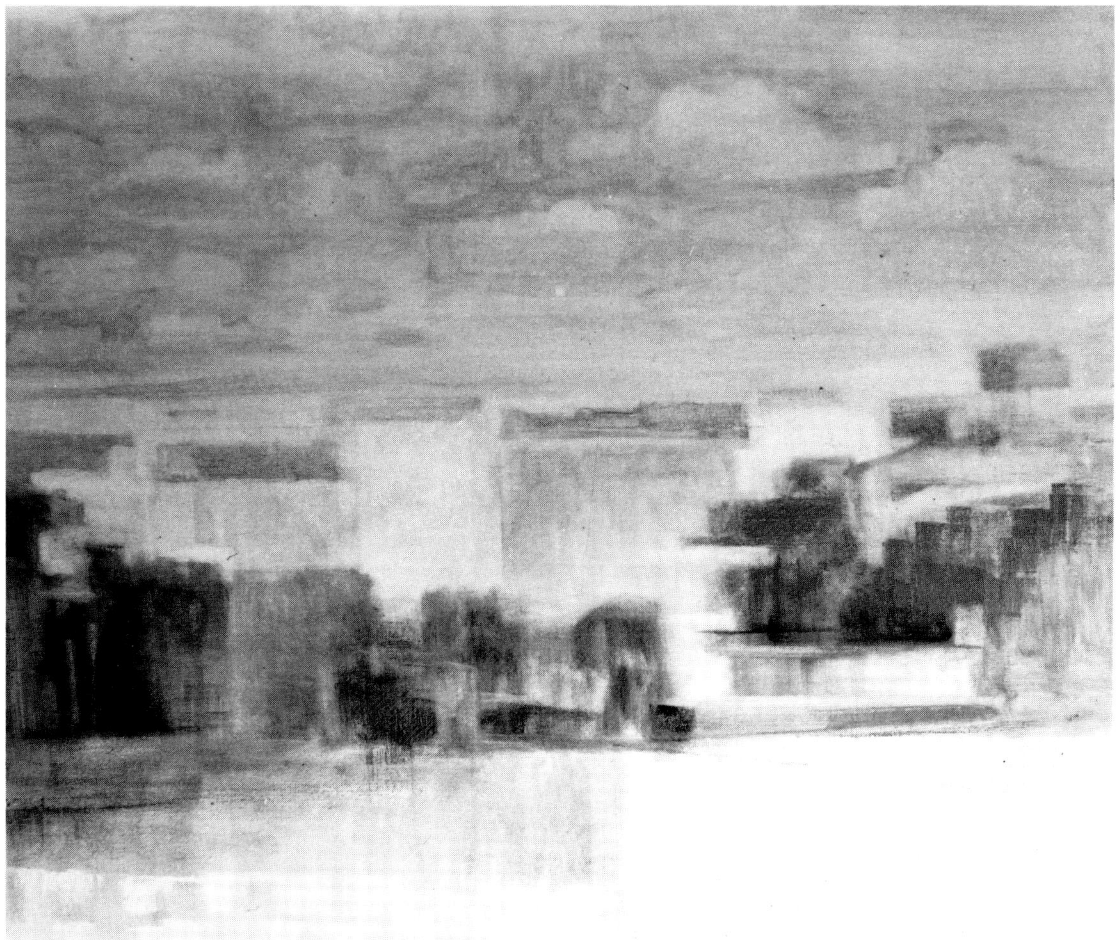

1 T P FLANAGAN
Autumn Lough
1961; oil; 53.9 x 76.2 cms; Arts Council of Northern Ireland collection

1) painted in 1961. This is restrained in mood yet assured in technique, the elemental subject and the pigment being shaped together into a personal kind of calligraphy. The essentially 'earthy' tones of the horizontal land masses weep into the pale colours of the water/sky and this diffusion serves to emphasise the veil that lies between the signifier and the signified.

During the period of these works, roughly between 1960 and 1966, the soft luminous washes approached but never became abstraction. Flanagan's working method of consecutive drawings before the final painting, and his preference for serial expressions of a theme led him not to abstraction but to what he termed 'a synthesis of all the aspects [of landscape]'.[5] The inherent danger is that such a synthesis, coupled with an excellent craftsmanlike handling of paint can lead to either preciousness or to formula. Terry Flanagan avoided this by the introduction of vertical elements to counterpoint the horizontality of the broad masses. These vertical accents can be seen in *Frozen Lake* of 1971 (cover plate) and in passing it is interesting to note that his earliest extant work is of skaters on a frozen lake. The reeds that rise out of *Frozen Lake* serve not only as themselves but also as units of measurement by which to comprehend the open space of the rest of the picture. This confident

2 TOM CARR
The Fence
1966; watercolour; 56 x 90 cms; private collection

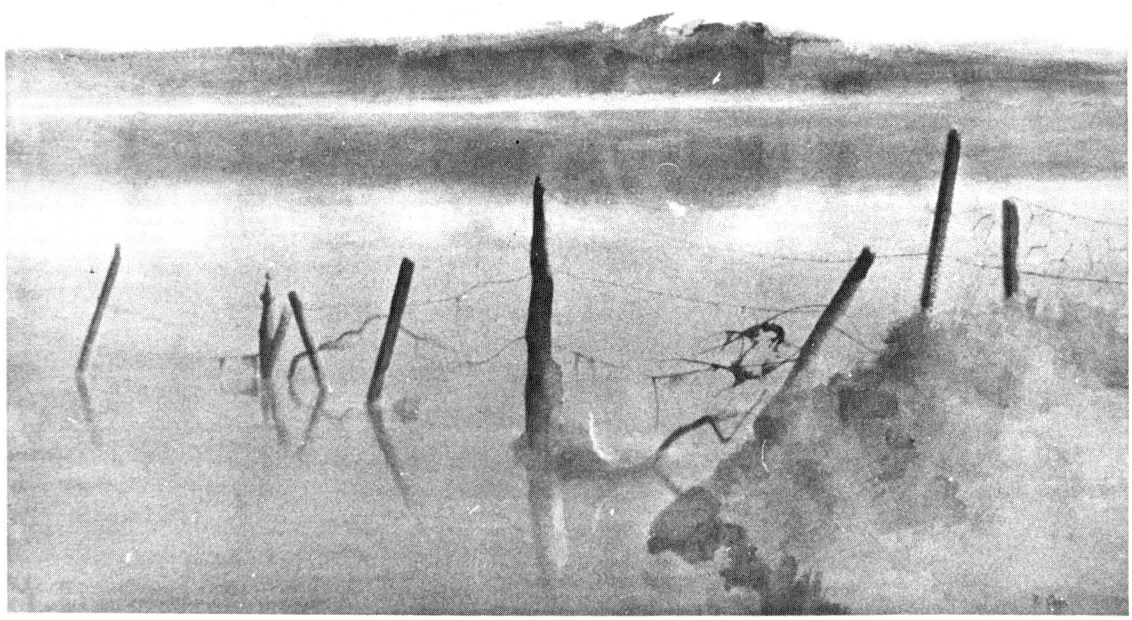

gesture making is, of course, a convention of style and method which the West absorbed from Japanese and Chinese art and it is to be found locally in the art of Tom Carr.

Carr, born in 1909, is of an older generation than Flanagan but the younger man acknowledges an affinity with both his compositions and his philosophy. While Carr is more fully covered in John Hewitt's book, it is relevant here to mention Carr's watercolours of landscape and flowers, especially as there exists a short but sensitive catalogue introduction written by none other than Terence Flanagan. In this Flanagan uses the word 'balance' several times and writes of the

> '... superb craftsmanship concealing the struggle with idea and idiom. In this sense his drawings have, as well as their obvious elegance, a marked phrasing; line emphasising mass, light and shadow complemented by colour, sometimes merely the colour of the chosen paper itself.'[6]

This may be seen in Carr's painting of tumbled fenceposts straggling into a lake (no 2) where the placement of the uprights with a 'just so' precision that looks accidental gives it an almost Zen assurance and silence. Tom Carr, who is a member of the Royal Society of Watercolour Painters, has had his work exhibited by that society in Japan itself. With T P Flanagan and Colin Middleton, Carr was chosen to represent Ulster art on a commemorative stamp for the Post Office in 1971, designed by Stuart Rose, FSIA.

Flanagan's punctuation marks acted as a system of balances in his work in the early to mid sixties and developed into a seductive search for line itself; a search which manifested itself in the sombre, dramatic and astonishingly rich series painted between 1966 and 1968. An Arts Council of Northern Ireland one-man show of March 1969 made public this series which is in fact five inter-related series: *Strule River*, *Boglands*, *In Summer*, *A Gortahork Sequence* and *A Stream Through Sand*. Not only does this represent a rediscovery of the virtues of black, as Kenneth Jamison put it, but also a development of the act of drawing; of the way in which line determines its own path and that of its attendant space. The *Stream Through Sand* series in particular is almost abstract, and at the same time an almost palpably real rendering of dunes, grasses and the meandering paths of small streams en route to the sea. These were done in oils, acrylic, conté crayon and watercolours, sometimes with more than one medium employed in a single work. Each medium acts and reacts in its own vital way. The dark swirling forms, co-existing with and balanced by the sinuous lines created pictures with a resonant emotional content reminiscent of the best of the internationally known Scottish artist William Johnstone. They had, too, some of the plastic monumentality of the work of Victor Pasmore.

These works are not derived from Sligo or Fermanagh but from the primitive landscapes of North Donegal, which until the mid sixties had been avoided by Flanagan because of that area's connotations with text-book and kitsch Irish landscape paintings. But now he reacted to the dark swirling skies, the wind blown land and the bogs of this county. Out of this emerged some of the most monumental of his works, and again

3 T P FLANAGAN
Gortahork [*2*]
c1968; oil and acrylic on canvas; 92.2 x 118.9 cms; Ulster Museum collection

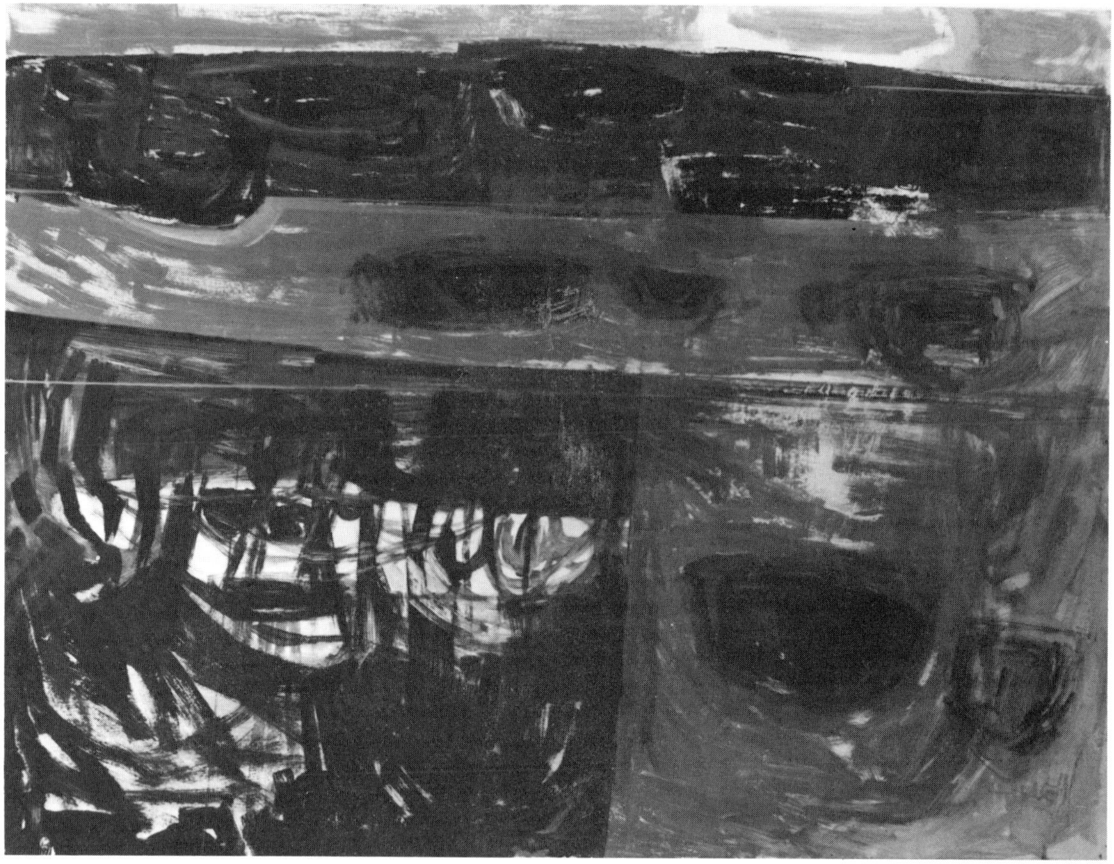

there is the interaction between the sky and the waterlogged land which has haunted his work throughout. The nearest Irish sculptural equivalent that I can think of which relies on the play of reflected light on masses is the late Gerda Fromel's stainless steel sail group which accentuates the horizontal of Ronald Tallon's cigarette factory for P J Carroll just outside Dundalk. This sculptural ensemble is 'read' in sections and this equally applies to the unifying divisions of the bogland paintings, of which *Gortahork 2* of 1967 (no 3) is one of the most striking. The artist himself sees it as 'a sort of collage of impressions unified in one space' 7 within a closely refined colour range. Flanagan has produced an image and a metaphor which is indelibly powerful and poignant too.

Inspired by the Bogland series, T P Flanagan's friend Seamus Heaney produced an evocation of the spirit of this painting in his poem *Bogland: For T P Flanagan*.

We have no prairies
To slice the big sun at evening —
Everywhere the eye concedes to
Encroaching horizon,

Is wooed into the cyclop's eye
Of a tarn. Our unfenced country
Is bog that keeps crusting
Between the sights of the sun.

They've taken the skeleton
Of the Great Irish Elk
Out of the peat, set it up
An astounding crate full of air.

Butter sunk under
More than a hundred years
Was recovered salty and white.
The ground itself is kind, black butter

Melting and opening underfoot,
Missing its last definition
By millions of years.
They'll never dig coal here,

Only the waterlogged trunks
Of great firs, soft as pulp.
Our pioneers keep striking
Inwards and downwards,

Every layer they strip
Seems camped on before.
The bogholes might be Atlantic seepage.
The wet centre is bottomless.[8]

To my mind this poem captures the essence of Flanagan's paintings perfectly: no words can better convey the melancholia of his pools than Heaney's 'The wet centre is bottomless.'

In the 1970s his palette lightens again and there is a move away from the Ivon Hitchens-like trailed brushstrokes and sombre tones towards a glowing colouration and a mature sense of pattern. The figurative reference returns and the jewel like coloured objects have a coherence which combines Japanese simplicity with the complexity of Celtic *entrelac* designs. Even something as simple as the string of onions behind the seated figure in his portrait of John D Stewart is a tour-de-force of pattern making. T P Flanagan's figurative work will be treated in the following chapter, but the consistency of his vision carries through and his landscape and object philosophy is clarified by one work exhibited in 1975. Entitled *A Study in Stillness*, it has words painted on to it, words that are integral to the mood of this work and to the experience of his whole output. The words read 'A Tree, A Bowl, A Shared Stillness'.

T P Flanagan's pictures are Romantic in feel and they produce a similar response in the viewer but they are arrived at by a method that is both an analysis and a synthesis. The art of Basil Blackshaw is more opulent, more highly keyed and with a richness which at times arrives at the same conclusions as that of Flanagan and at other times seeks another awareness of the elements of the landscape. Retrospective exhibitions can be two edged swords. They can show the development of an artist's style and philosophy and supply many answers to a critic's questions. But because they deal with the past (even recent works are consigned to the pigeon holes of history) they can have the effect of freezing the overview, especially when the retrospective exhibition comes at a time when the artist is still young. In 1974, at the age of forty-two, Basil Blackshaw was accorded the honour of a retrospective exhibition by the Arts Council of Northern Ireland. Before it opened some people I had talked to referred to Blackshaw in the past tense, as if his creative force had diminished; and certainly there had been a time in the 1970s when Blackshaw exhibited infrequently. Happily the 1974 show was, for this writer at least, a celebration of past riches and also a strong indication of a continuation of the maturity and simplification which had emerged in the late sixties.

Like so many of the artists in this province, Blackshaw is not solely involved with one genre; his portraits and figure paintings of animals and humans are as well known as his landscapes, but it is his response to the total environment which remains a paradigm of his art. Basil Blackshaw was born in 1932 and, as is well documented, his upbringing was centred on a country society of horses and hunting dogs raised by his family and their friends in the Boardmills, Co Down area. Such a childhood not only gives one a natural direct affinity with the life cycle and function of animal and mankind alike, it also provides an entry into a culture with a healthy bonhomie and an eye for excellence and beauty in the natural world. Blackshaw was one of the talented group of students to emerge from the Belfast College of Art in the years after the war; others included Cherith McKinstry (née Boyd), Terence Flanagan, Michael Baird and Robert Linton. His earliest excursions into the world of landscape have a curious contradiction between the physicality of the paint and the subject matter which was moodily restrained. Perhaps this is what John Hewitt meant when in November 1956 he wrote of Blackshaw's use of the word 'tension'. 'Tension is a particular form of relationship; it is a unity of opposites, of attraction and repulsion, of a drawing together and a pulling apart; without it there can be no equilibrium.'[9] Such tension still seems fundamental to an understanding of much of Blackshaw's production. Where T P Flanagan spoke of balances, that is, polarities reconciled to provide a stability, however nervous, Basil Blackshaw's tensions are opposites that constantly struggle. Thus even in the works of the early and mid fifties the dark skies of some of his paintings mark storms that are symbolic as well as real. No-one brought up as he was could remain unaware of the constant struggle in nature, and as one with what other writers have noted as a Romantic temperament, his response echoed the movements of nature. Sometimes the paint was thickly modelled, almost violently applied, perhaps consciously or unconsciously aware of the gestural nature of expressionism that was taking place at the same time in the School of Paris and across the Atlantic in the New York School. Certainly Mercy Hunter has noted that Mark Rothko is one of the painters whom he admires and the quiet notes of paint that Blackshaw contrasted with heavy pigmentation recall the combat that one finds in Rothko's large simple paintings where horizontal primal planes of colour advance and retreat before each other.

There is to be found in one of J. M. W. Turner's sketchbooks a swift watercolour sketch called *Pink Sky*: a horizontal sweep of pink is only separated from a blood red earth by a thin strip of watery yellow. It was done in the first quarter of the nineteenth century but in words as well as feeling it might almost describe a Rothko.

Nearly a century and a half divide them but the common link, as the American critic Robert Rosenblum perceptively pointed out, was a common Romantic affiliation for the Sublime, that ecstatic experience of the ineffable mysteries of Nature which afflicted poor Corinne, Henry Frankenstein and the Irish Romantic poet Thomas Moore who penned the following breathless letter to his mother on 24 July 1804 on first seeing Niagara Falls:

> 'Here all its awful subliminities rushed full upon me... My whole heart and soul ascended towards the Divinity in a swell of devout admiration, which I never before experienced. Oh! bring the atheist here, and he cannot return an atheist! I pity the man who can coldly sit down to write a description of those ineffable wonders: much more do I pity him who can submit them to the admeasurement of gallons and yards... We must have new combinations of language to describe the Fall of Niagra.'

Trying to find these new combinations of language without destroying the quintessential spirit of Nature became the Romantic goal. Even today the landscape painter is haunted by it when he confronts the paradoxes of natural phenomena. If this analogy with the Romantics is not exhausted, and I believe that the Scottish and Irish painters are still true heirs to that tradition, then I would say that where T P Flanagan has affinities with the cool spectral world of Caspar David Friedrich then Basil Blackshaw inclines to the sweeping dimensions of Turner or John Martin. This is not meant as a quantative comparison but as an expression of attitudes. Blackshaw's canvases of the fifties and early sixties do not have the bewildering size of many of the Martin and Turner canvases, nor is the movement of the forces of nature as apocalyptic but even on a modest scale he invested his forms with a restless energy. *Orchard* of 1956 (illustrated in the 1974 Retrospective Exhibition Catalogue) has hints of the flickering intensity that Van Gogh gave to his Provencal orchards in bloom. *Landscape* (no 4) is only 107 x 122 cms in size but it gives an impression of great depth and scale: the tumbled sky and the dragged and scumbled brushstrokes, while less heavily pigmented than earlier, betray an acute sensitivity to the physical act of painting. In 1977 he exhibited some tiny works, one as small as 12.5 cms square, yet these too were rich, immediate and intuitive in their handling of the few brushstrokes they contained.

People and animals have appeared in his landscapes, indeed in some the figurative element is absolutely integral to the mood as well as the composition of the picture. This is particularly true of those works which showed country people doing country things and becoming part of the landscape. From the labourers to the 'doggy-men', as John Hewitt accurately describes them, Blackshaw gives them a natural dignity which accords with the density of the land they inhabit. Gradually, as his range of experiences and references expanded he simplified his compositions, modulated his tones and his line and moved in one direction into the monumental horse paintings and disturbing figure studies discussed in the next chapter. At the same time his landscapes moved towards the structured calm of Cézanne. Parallel to this he developed a 'garden' theme in the late sixties; a theme or reference which was still being worked

4 BASIL BLACKSHAW
Landscape
c1960; oil on canvas; 106.6 x 121.9 cms; Arts Council of Northern Ireland collection

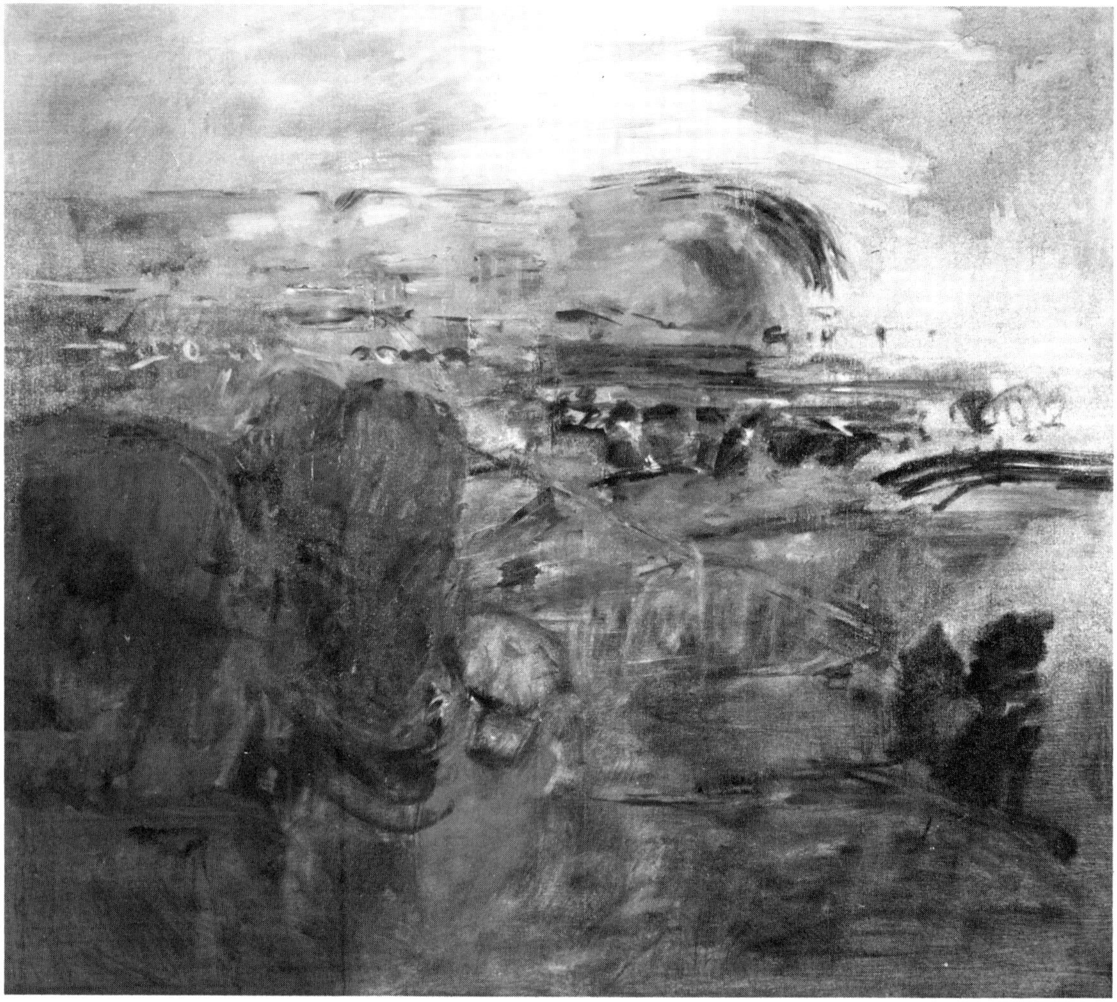

with profit in his one-man show at the Tom Caldwell Gallery in May 1977.

In mediaeval art, when the landscape 'out there' symbolised untamed barbarism, the 'hortus conclusus' or enclosed garden symbolised civilised order imposed on nature. Small and formal, such gardens appear in manuscript illustration and on tapestries as oases of calm and refinement. For Basil Blackshaw the garden was a small area (not necessarily a garden as such) which he knew intimately and with which he could develop a special empathy. 'Il faut cultiver notre jardin,' is how Votaire's *Candide* ends, a

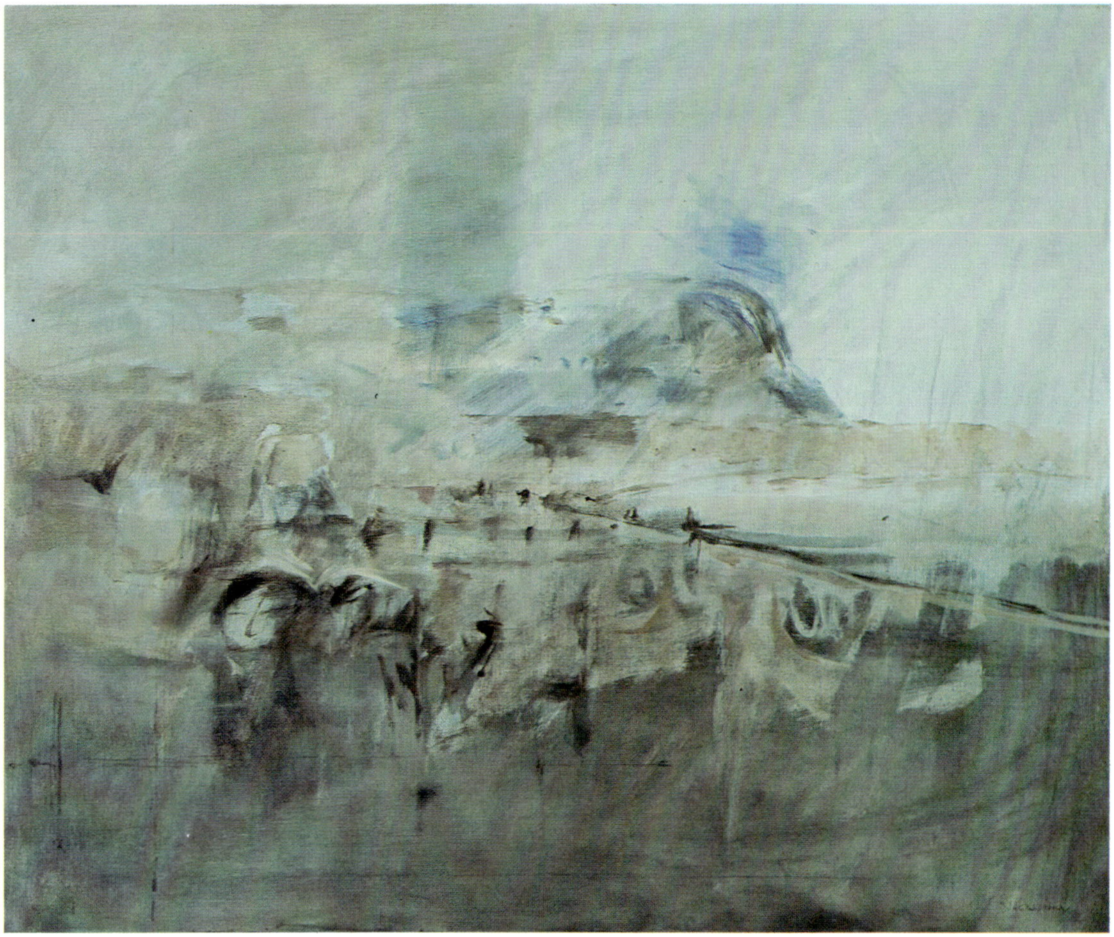

I BASIL BLACKSHAW
Landscape Towards Divis Mountains
c1967; oil; 63.5 x 76.2 cms; Arts Council of Northern Ireland collection

facing page 16

sensible plea for each to address himself to what and where he knows best. In Blackshaw's *Gardens* there is a more formal analysis of the elements and their actual and spatial relationships. Recently the continuation of this *leitmotif* has led to a restrained balancing, a pattern making almost, which is reminiscent of the gardens painted by Tony O'Malley.

For Basil Blackshaw the search for the underpinnings of landscape led him, as Kenneth Jamison has it, 'almost inevitably into a kind of conspiracy with Cézanne'.[10] Not a copying of Cézanne but an attempt to arrive at the same conclusions independently. This focussed on what constituted part of his territory or garden, and as he moved towards Cézanne, then inevitably writers could say that such and such a locality, in this case Colin Mountain, had become his Mont Sainte-Victoire. Like all pat comparisons it may be dismissed for its very facility but the truth remains that the area of the Lagan Valley and the escarpments that surround it *did* draw and hold Blackshaw. Out of this singular application, paralleled with his work in other fields, the horses and the Bacon-like, fraught portraits of his wife Anna Ritchie, grew a body of works which sometimes make direct reference to Cézanne's work, sometimes try to evoke his ghost by association and sometimes only hint tangentially at Cézanne's art. For Blackshaw this involved an organisational re-arrangement of the motifs of the composition and more importantly, it meant a redistribution of the planes of the picture space. The progression in space from the foreground to the background became flattened, and in some cases the actual foreground disappeared and the furthest distance became, by compensation of colour and form, predominant. In *Landscape Towards Divis Mountain* (no i, colour) the obvious precedent for this view is to be found in Cézanne's studies of pines in front of Mont Sainte-Victoire in which the vertical motifs help to parcel up the space and to draw the planes together. To illustrate how this involved a process of reduction, a getting back to basics, compare it with *Two Trees* of 1969 which like the aptly named *Cézanne Landscape* of 1970 is illustrated in the previously mentioned Arts Council of Northern Ireland Blackshaw Retrospective Exhibition Catalogue. *Two Trees* is as minimal a landscape as one could find; it has an economy which extends to the tonal range as well as to the lines which trace the form. The subtle modelling of the vertical emphases also draws attention to Basil Blackshaw's draughtsmanship which has the true function of a skeleton which is then fleshed out by the colours of paint.

The restraints and gradations which his palette achieved from 1967 onwards follows Cézanne's advice to Emile Bernard 'to begin lightly with almost neutral tones. Then one must proceed by steadily climbing the scale and tightening the chromatics.' If this analytical approach to purity and essence sounds like the antithesis of the Romantic and Expressionist approach of his earlier work, it must be noted that his admiration for artists like Kokoschka and Giacometti as well as his contact with the vigorous paintings of Anna Ritchie saw to it that sometimes strong colour accents counterpointed the Cézanne-like golden ochres and pale blue-greens.

Now, in the late seventies, the richly luminous earth colours of the fifties are again evident; but the lessons of over a decade of staining the canvas rather than covering it with thick impasto has given him a method for expressing atmospheric moods which was seen to advantage in the series *Journey to the Ponderosa* shown at the Caldwell Gallery. The effect is like the slightly blurred continuum of tones one gets while passing through a landscape in a car. The parallax effect of binocular vision means that the background is in 'focus', while the foreground is not. The Ponderosa of the title is a country pub, not a Western ranch; bonhomie in a Romantic setting is obviously still an important constituent in Basil Blackshaw's make-up.

I made reference above to certain similarities between Scottish and Irish painters with regard to the appellation 'Romantic' and there exists a further similarity in terms of the modelling of the plasticity of the paint. I have observed it too in landscapes emerging from Cornwall, before the tourists picked it clean (or dirty) but I would be loth to ascribe it solely to the Celtic psyche. However the very shapes of the land and coasts are so sculptural that it is hardly surprising that often the painted versions of the environment are built up so three dimensionally. There is no way that an eye nurtured on the lush greenery of Constable country can transcribe the brutal piling of shapes of Donegal, Connemara or parts of the Antrim coast without a mental shift and an attendant shift in paint manipulation. Encrustation is the word that springs to mind when thinking of a whole range of Irish landscape pictures and especially when thinking of many of the landscapes of George Campbell. Campbell was actually born in Co Wicklow in 1917 but he did live and work for many years in Belfast. But if it is difficult to actually claim him as an Ulster artist it is equally difficult to classify him as an Irish one since for many years he has divided his time and energies between Ireland and Spain. His work has continued to be seen here in the North on a regular basis and his treatment of primal energies in man, object and place has proved influential to many artists.

The Spanish writer and poet Lorca wrote once of the theory and function of the *duende* and ascribed to it much of that language of elemental mystery which the Romantics called the Sublime. Yet the *duende* is more primitive than that, and unlike the Sublime it is not so much a dark power 'out there' as one within the artist/performer. The *duende* is 'soul', it is the 'feel' that an artist may have at inspired or ecstatic moments and Lorca believed that it was best found in music, dance, song and live poetry: arts where the artist performs with and through his body. There is no formula for attaining *duende*, Lorca emphasised, it is a struggle which most artists lose; but those that achieve *duende*, like some gipsy or flamenco artists, find a communion with God through it and its emotional fusing of all the senses.

George Campbell would understand both Lorca's words and the Spanish context in which he placed his essay. Anyone who has heard Campbell on the radio will admire not only the way in which he talks so movingly about the arts and life, but also enjoy his mastery of guitar that has allowed him to become accepted as a player and interpreter of flamenco in Spain itself. Something of this power is to be found in the best of his paintings for he has searched for the vitality and primitive dignity that is found in people who live close to the rhythms of the land. There is still a lot of the pagan beneath the veneer of modern or historical civilisation and Campbell has a genuine talent for discovering it and holding it up to the viewer. It is easy enough to see connections between Ireland and Spain in their adherence to an uncompromising brand of religion (whether Catholic or Protestant), their sad histories of political violence, and in a tendency towards puritanism and pessimism in their national characters. George Campbell doesn't look at the two countries in such a mundane way; he looks sideways at the fringes and back in time to the Gothic. Gothic art and architecture has an emotional intensity and it also has a series of formal values which I find expressed in Campbell's work. In his studies of people and things he utilises a linear verticality which resembles the attentuated forms of Gothic sculpture; sometimes these stretched shapes are contained within a kind of mandorla, the almond shape which contains and defines the figure of Christ. Turn this sideways and you will find the formal device which predominates in many of his landscapes. An ellipse suggests movement around its length whereas a true circle is too perfectly balanced to suggest conflict or movement. The ellipse traces an orbit and the eye follows in much the same way that the eye moves along and through Celtic spirals. This restless energy was one of the elements from Celtic art assimilated by Art Nouveau artists and designers at the end of the last century and in particular they developed the 'whiplash' motif in which the lines snake around and around, and then the power is directed out through the tail of the line. This sense of power and movement can be seen in George Campbell's *Dun Aengus* (no 5). The subject matter speaks of Campbell's preoccupation with those places in the environment which still hold their magic even in ruin. Dun Aengus, on Inishmore on the Aran Islands, is a superb fort structure situated magnificently on the summit of a cliff high above the sea. Its lines of stone ramparts and the remarkable *chevaux-de-frise*, rings of stone defences, resemble huge sculptural land pieces which Richard Long or Robert Smithson would have been hard put to emulate. In a series of pictures on this subject, of which this is a representative example, Campbell traces the expressive line of the ramparts, the eye being directed in from the right of the picture, through the centre where it picks up the broad horizontal masses of the land and the lowering skies and is then directed round and out through the right again. The stones of the wall are built up by flickering strokes of paint and the composition is strengthened by the piled up verticals of the grasses and bracken on the left. This piling up, a modelling of strokes which gives height as well as depth, is a Campbell trademark and one which he uses to express the man-made edifices which grow out of the rocky landscapes of Andalusia as well as Connemara. The rich browns and greens, shot through with blacks and sudden vivid blues often glow with an intensity which is reminiscent of the brilliant facets of Gothic stained glass. Like stained glass, the flashes of colour provide a constant sense of movement while the dark line gives a coherent structure to the final image. George Campbell's landscapes are patternmaking of the highest order, intertwined sombre and bright passages have the tactile feel of some of the great woven tapestries.

Someone who has worked with both the late Gerard Dillon, who is discussed both in Volume 1 and in Chapter Two of this book, and George Campbell and who shares the latter's love of

5 GEORGE CAMPBELL
Dun Aengus, Inishmore
1970; oil on canvas; 91.4 x 129.5 cms; Arts Council of Northern Ireland

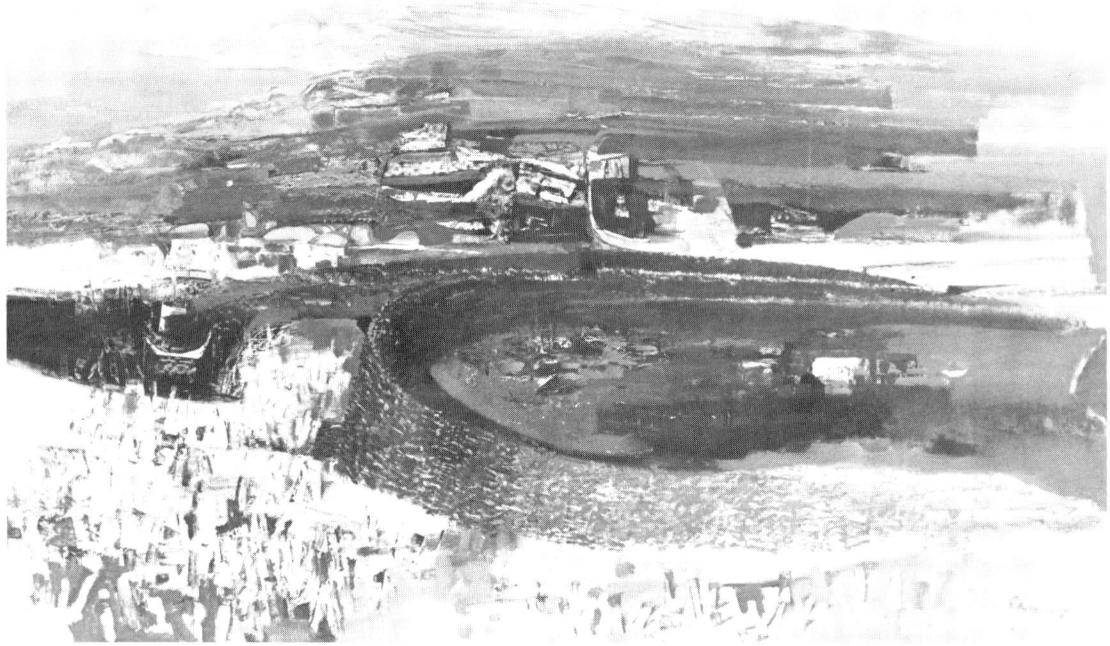

Spain is Arthur Armstrong. Born in Belfast in 1924 his working life has mainly been spent outside the province, with Dillon in London and with Campbell in Dublin and Spain but his work is shown and collected in the North and his art remains a response to the textures of landscape. It is impossible to describe Armstrong's work without recourse to the word 'texture'. Campbell's work is also textured but with Armstrong the sense of texture is broader, building up in large blocks which recall early cubism, and the brooding colour scheme, predominantly earthy, provides a slower sense of movement than is to be found in Campbell's work. Like so many Irish artists Armstrong goes West where the raw vitality of the landscape from Connemara to Donegal provides the artist with Lego bricks enough to play with. The shapes can be built and re-built with infinite variety and Armstrong has frequently interpreted the sense of structure very well. The massed shapes provide the bass notes and the eroded textures the melody. This involves a manipulatory skill in balancing the heavy brown tones with the scratched and modelled lines that rhythmically emerge from them in the form of individual rocks or walls. The stately mood of Armstrong's work requires first hand viewing

6 ARTHUR
ARMSTRONG
Field Patterns
c1971; etching; 33 x 25 cms

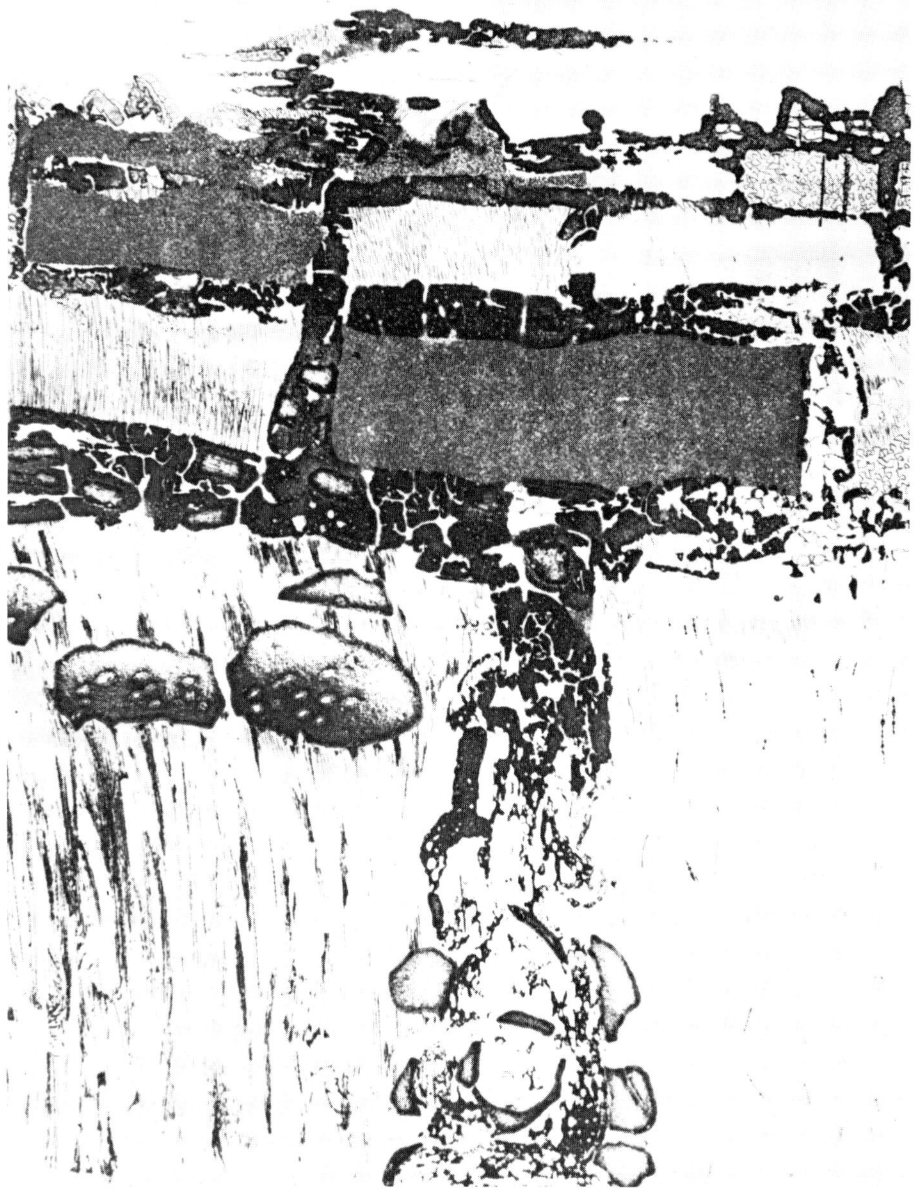

because in illustration the massiveness becomes a drab heaviness and the smaller elements which are meant to emerge as in a relief become flattened or even lost. For this reason I have chosen a print rather than an oil to illustrate this artist. *Field Patterns* (no 6) is an etching in which the subtle browns of the ink are able to suggest shades ranging from black through to a sunburned gold of dried grasses. Even in monochrome the essential elements of Armstrong remain, the off centre geometry, the revealed structure of walls, fields and furrows, the contrast of solid form with organic line. In recent years Armstrong's oils have become even browner and slower in feel until the encrusted sweep of the paint has become conventionalised and what was once earth has become treacle. They are still rich in a sombre kind of way but the glow now seems to be in the oil and varnish rather than in the image itself.

A much younger painter who at his best shares the Campbell/Armstrong knack of combining sensuous tone and texture with a feel for space is Malcolm Bennett. He was born in Derby in 1942 but has lived and worked in Ulster since about 1950 and now lives on the Ards Peninsula, a part of the province which has proved a stimulating environment to several artists combining as it does the wavy land forms of Co Down's drumlins and the island-speckled stretches of Strangford Lough on one side and the Scottish bounded North Channel on the other.

Malcolm Bennett's attitude to the landscape has been a changing one ranging from three dimensional pieces, through mysteriously romantic canvases to works which are deliberately ambiguous in conception and interpretation. He was one of the founding members of Group 63, which was always a loose confederation of artists and attitudes rather than a cohesive and polemic unity. Bennett's approach suggested a concern for simultaneity and parallel evocations of place rather than the impressionist's desire to define one moment and one space. In the 1960s his work showed several lines of thought operating at one time, rather than the chronological progression of 'periods' through which the public believes an artist must pass. Like Derrick Hawker, Bennett produced some wall mounted three dimensional pieces in which the constituent elements of the landscape were analysed, deliberately conventionalised and re-formed as large Jigsaw Landscapes. The fact that some of these pieces done around 1967/8 allowed for interchangeability of the component units highlighted the way in which the artist and the viewer both 'make' pictures by 'reading' or interpreting the same denotative elements in individual connotative ways. This was still true for him in 1971 when, as one of the four artists commissioned by the Arts Council of Northern Ireland to explore the theme *Ulster Places*, he explained in the catalogue:

> 'My paintings present a series of multiple, sometimes superimposed, images of *pieces of the area* [my italics] which record the changing landscape over a period of time... I feel that a still photograph or representational painting can only record a split second in time, or a relatively small area. One has no idea of what the landscape would look like under different conditions, or what is behind the viewer.'

The paintings which constitute his contribution to *Ulster Places*, and those in his Arts Council of

7 MALCOLM BENNETT
Shore Line
c1967; oil and acrylic; 61 x 91.4 cms; collection the artist

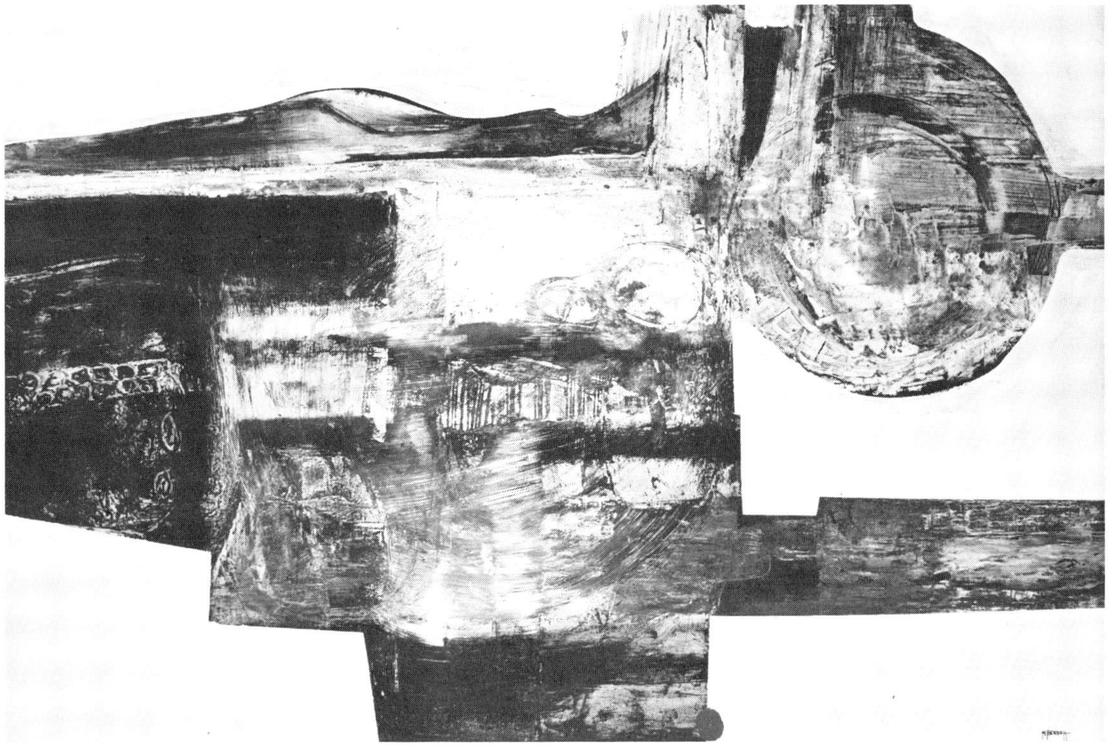

Northern Ireland one-man show of three months earlier showed this ethos in action. Whether landscape or seascape they conveyed an amalgam of moods by means of dramatic forms and restricted tonal range enlivened by a kind of etched texture. The work illustrated, *Shore Line*, actually dates from 1968 but it is useful as a compendium of Bennett's images, forms and methods (no 7). From a sensuous undulating curve at the top of the picture balanced by a very freely painted sky above, the viewer's eye moves through a range of geometricised shapes and attendant sensations. There are abrupt, shorn-off straight lines, suggesting missing pieces of the landscape, while within the framework of the pieces that do exist the paint itself is handled in three distinct ways. On the left are little shapes that are worked out of the underpainting, while other parts are modelled up. In parts the paint drips tantalisingly while elsewhere it is applied in dry, still strokes. Each method of application complements a shape and makes sure that, synthesised as it is, it never loses sight of the representational landscape reference. His work is sometimes reminiscent of the pale, washed colours and forms of some Blackshaw, Flanagan and Croft, and sometimes it is darker and almost lava-like, similar to the mysterious paintings of

Neil Dallas Brown who won First Prize in the 1970 Arts Council of Northern Ireland Open Painting Competition. And like this latter artist, Bennett's recent work, as shown in a one-man exhibition in 1976, reveals a move towards relating landscape to figures or objects which either extend from the land or melt into it. The sense of solitude and displacement remains, though not always successfully expressed, and his contribution to the Penta group show (Octagon Gallery, 1977) revealed that the ambiguity of images still preoccupies him.

A curiously recurrent feature of much of Ulster landscape art is a symbolic, romantic melancholia, articulated by means of conventions such

8 LOUIS REED
Moonrise
n d; watercolour, ink and charcoal; 39.3 x 44.5 cms; private collection

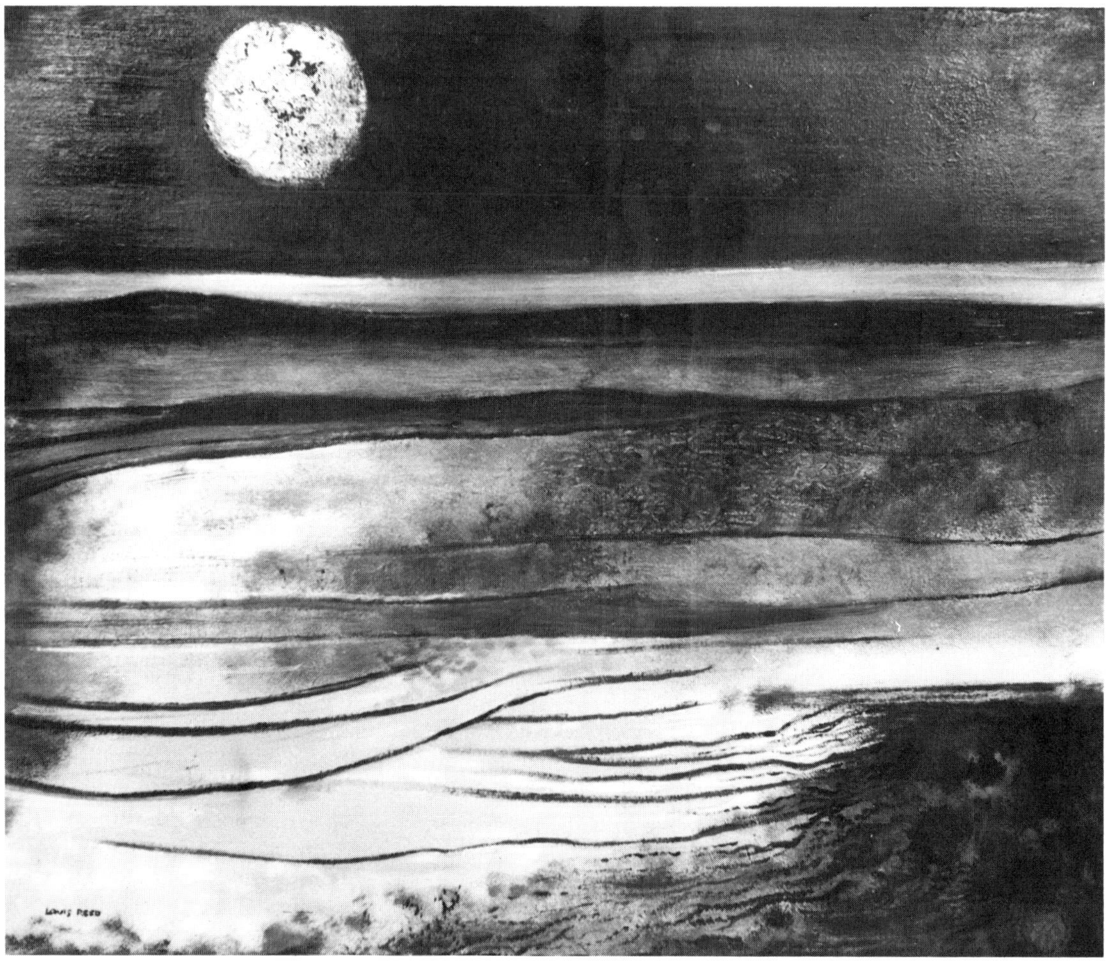

as the moon; water and its reflections; solitary objects or empty vistas. Of course, it is true that such conventions are also part and parcel of stock images for landscapists the world over, and the random use of such imagery can produce hack, would-be Romantic landscapes of mind-numbing banality. It is equally true that even the most over-worked stereotype can be revitalised if handled with genuine feeling; and again it has to be said that the Celtic fringes cling to this particular landscape 'humour' with tenacity. It might be because the land is so full of potent, pregnant culture memories, as suggested at the beginning of this chapter, or it might be because of the dour pessimism inculcated in the people by religion in both its forms in Ireland. It might have something to do with the weather: a wet Wednesday in Conlig would hardly inspire one to Claudian landscapes of noble peasants in the Elysian fields. Whatever it is, it echoes the achingly beautiful but sad tones of some Irish traditional music, even though that too can be butchered beyond recognition by interpreters who lack, dare I say it, *duende*. Whether it is sentiment or just sentimentality, most Ulster artists who adopt a landscape idiom are struck by the sense of mystery and melancholy in it. There are so many examples that I will choose only three before turning to Colin Middleton, in whom *all* the modes and moods meet.

Ignoring my own terms of reference for the moment, let me cite the work of Louis Reed who died in 1977 at the age of 91. An eclectic in many ways, Reed evolved a style which incorporated sources as diverse as Cézanne, Oriental Art and Max Ernst into landscape fantasies (his word) which often had Irish titles and presumably Irish subjects. If so this was an Ireland only he had seen, an Ireland of pale pinks and blues, dream palaces and full of Eastern promise. The romantic surrealism which suffuses his work really owes much in terms of colour and disquiet to Paul Nash. This may be observed in *Moonrise* (no 8) where the pale moon illuminates and throws into relief an empty landscape which combines the simplicity of Chinese art with the otherworldliness of Henri Rousseau. Reed's nearest equivalent, and a vastly more controlled talent at that, is Tom Carr.

Very much younger is Lawson Burch, born in 1937 and his works, more obviously local in derivation of subject, are often small in scale. Where Reed goes off into a fantasyscape of ruined pavilions and misty waterfalls, Burch presents a darker, starker use of romantic imagery in which the very ordinary elements of man and nature are re-aligned by means of light effects into rather fraught, sadly mysterious compositions. Sometimes the handling of the conventionalised forms; moonlight, reflections or dark skies, is painterly, and at other times it is more linear, verging sometimes on a kind of rhythmic cubism. Even if his works don't always coalesce then at least, as in this work (no 9) they represent a landscape sensibility which is primarily concerned with metaphor.

David Crone was born in Belfast in 1937 and his response to landscape was more violent, more expressionist than that of many other Ulster artists. But the expressionism was controlled within architectonic 'walls' that had the effect of bouncing the colour back and forth to produce a vibrating vortex. Between the time of the *Aspects of Ulster Landscape* exhibition of 1965

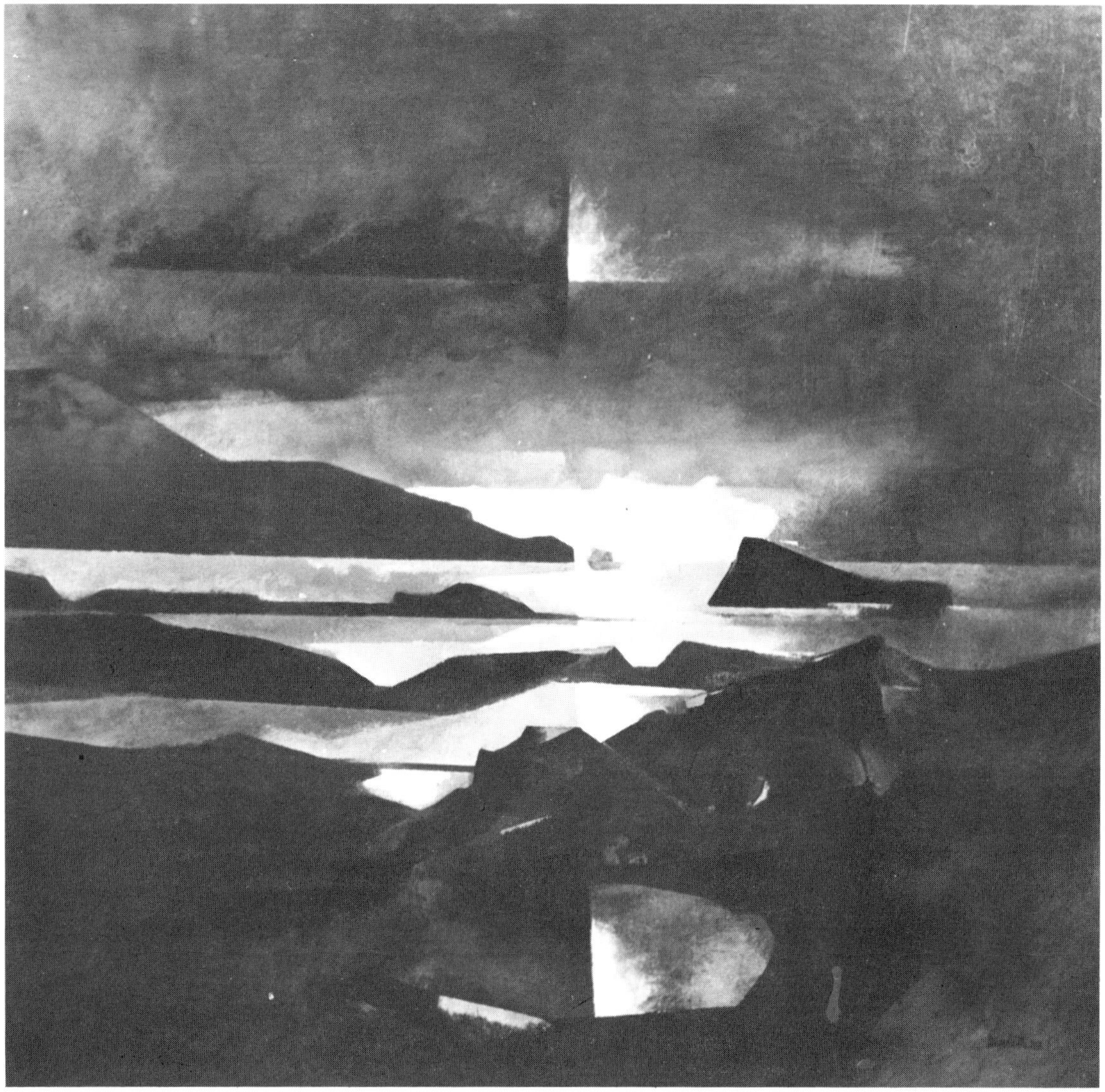

9 LAWSON BURCH
Estuary Light — Donegal
1975; acrylic on canvas; 61 x 61 cms; Keith and Jo Baker collection

and his one-man show in 1968, Crone's works have landscape titles but they look more like details of earth formations rather than the whole vista. It is their sense of containment which attracts; that and the lack of perspectival reference which landscapes normally offer. When one loses some references to sky, sea, recognisable human elements and even to the scale of the area being examined then the spectator has to concentrate the more on the interplay of colours and fragments in what is given. Compositionally these works resembled early cubism, even to the brown/green colour range. A little later Crone's work opened out towards a horzontality which, however, rarely inclined to the CinemaScope format beloved of many landscapists. The horizontals were sliced by verticals as if in weaving. It became difficult to determine if there was a logical, 'natural' sequence to the painted planes. What *might* be clouds or mists puffed past and through what *might* be hills or rocks. This rhythmic shift, complemented by a predilection for the plasticity of the paint itself, sets up contrasts that mix the monumental solidity of William Gear's stripey columns with the nervous visceral strokes of Francis Bacon. Again this is purely a descriptive comparison.

Figurative elements had never really been absent from Crone's work and they remained as clues to the drama within the picture space, that is to say man and his constructions acting on and being acted upon by the environment. In 1970 David Crone was one of two Northern Irish artists, the other being Denis McBride, who were included in the Irish contribution to the travelling exhibition *Celtic Triangle* organised by the Arts Councils of Wales, Northern Ireland, Scotland and the Republic of Ireland. Writing then of his work Crone noted in the catalogue to that show that

> '... shafts of stone, or stone crosses, themselves like figures with figurative elements within their forms were my main concern. Gradually the rigid structure of those artefacts dominated the canvas and they became like quarry sufaces with cracks and fissures, or buildings with windows into which one might penetrate to perceive again a figurative element. Recent work has dwelt upon figures held in an artificial framework within the landscape, like a train containing commuters.'

That was seven years ago, but even now the landscape reference still crops up in his work although the over-all feeling is now of stasis with more restrained colour variegations, as can be seen in *Park* (no 10) which should be compared with an earlier work such as *Church Road* of 1972 (no 11). He seems to have returned to the detail rather than the whole, but still, even in those paintings of heads and other dis-located objects he retains a sense of mystery. The enclosed, almost trapped sense of locale which he developed in his landscapes hint, but never fully speak of a surreal country where all the elements can take turns at being dominant.

That brings me to Colin Middleton. He is the artist to disprove the validity of writing thematic art surveys, because every theme and genre, every style and method finds expression in his oeuvre... what is more they can all appear in one work. Rightly recognised as the major creative talent of the past twenty years here in the North, his very diversity and facility has earned him indignant criticism from those who fear that such a range of works implies an imp rather than a daemon at work. There is no need to offer here a chronology of his life and work for that is covered in the catalogue of the major retrospective exhibition of 1976 and in the monograph published at the same time. This contains a biography and a critique by John Hewitt, and needless to say he is again well

10 DAVID CRONE
Park
1976; acrylic on canvas; 75 x 100 cms; Arts Council of Northern Ireland collection

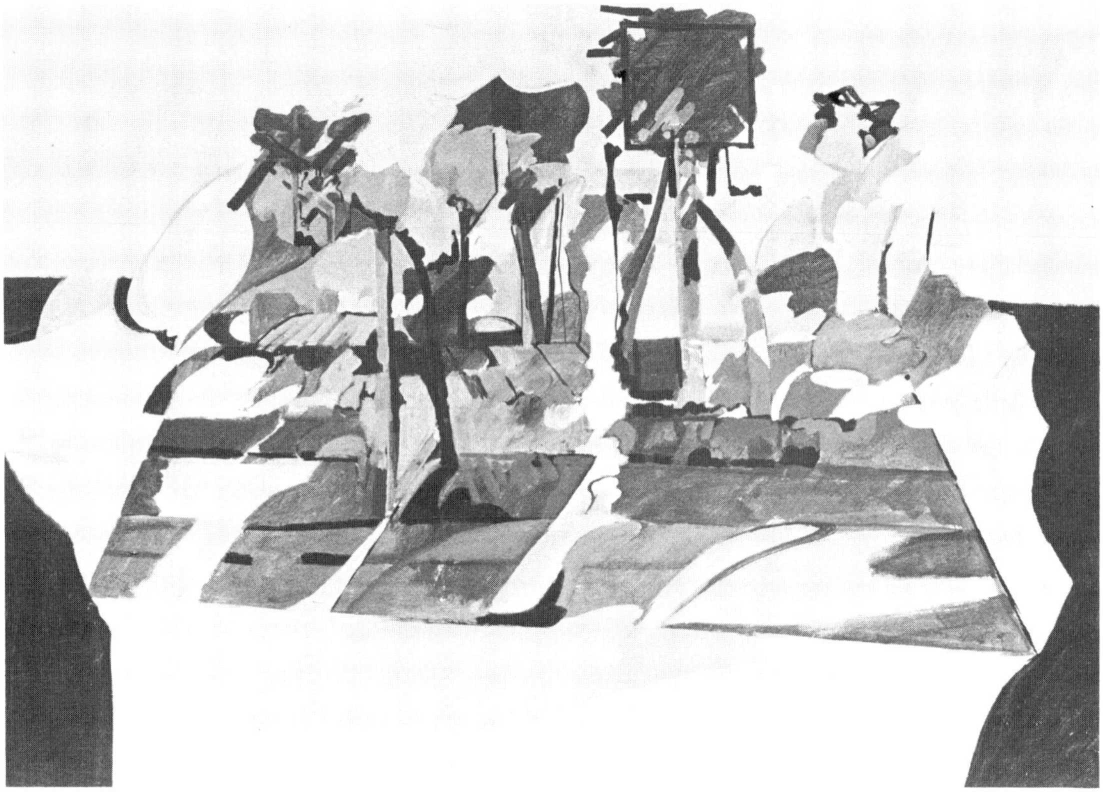

served by Hewitt in the companion volume to this, for Middleton was a major Irish artist well before 1957, the starting point of this book. In this and the following chapter my aim is to show not only the themes and stances he adopted in the past two decades but also to describe the formal elements and devices of his work and show which of these have been absorbed into the work and viewpoint of many younger artists. There is absolutely no doubt that, admit it or not, a great number of the artists working in this province have seen the land, the human figure and the power of myth through the eyes of Colin Middleton. Those eyes and the brain behind them produce an agility in jumping from reference to reference which makes one think of a true jazz musician — indeed jazz references appear in many of his titles. The jazz man can follow a line like the rest of them, then like Paul Klee he can take that line for a walk, leaping ahead and out into a solo which is the essence of all his experiences. He can insert quotations from other works so quickly that he has gone on to something else by the time the audience realises it. He can be as full of wit as he is of invention, and that is guaranteed to rile people who like

II COLIN MIDDLETON
Swan River Sunset II
1972; gouache; 20 x 20 cms;
Ulster Museum collection

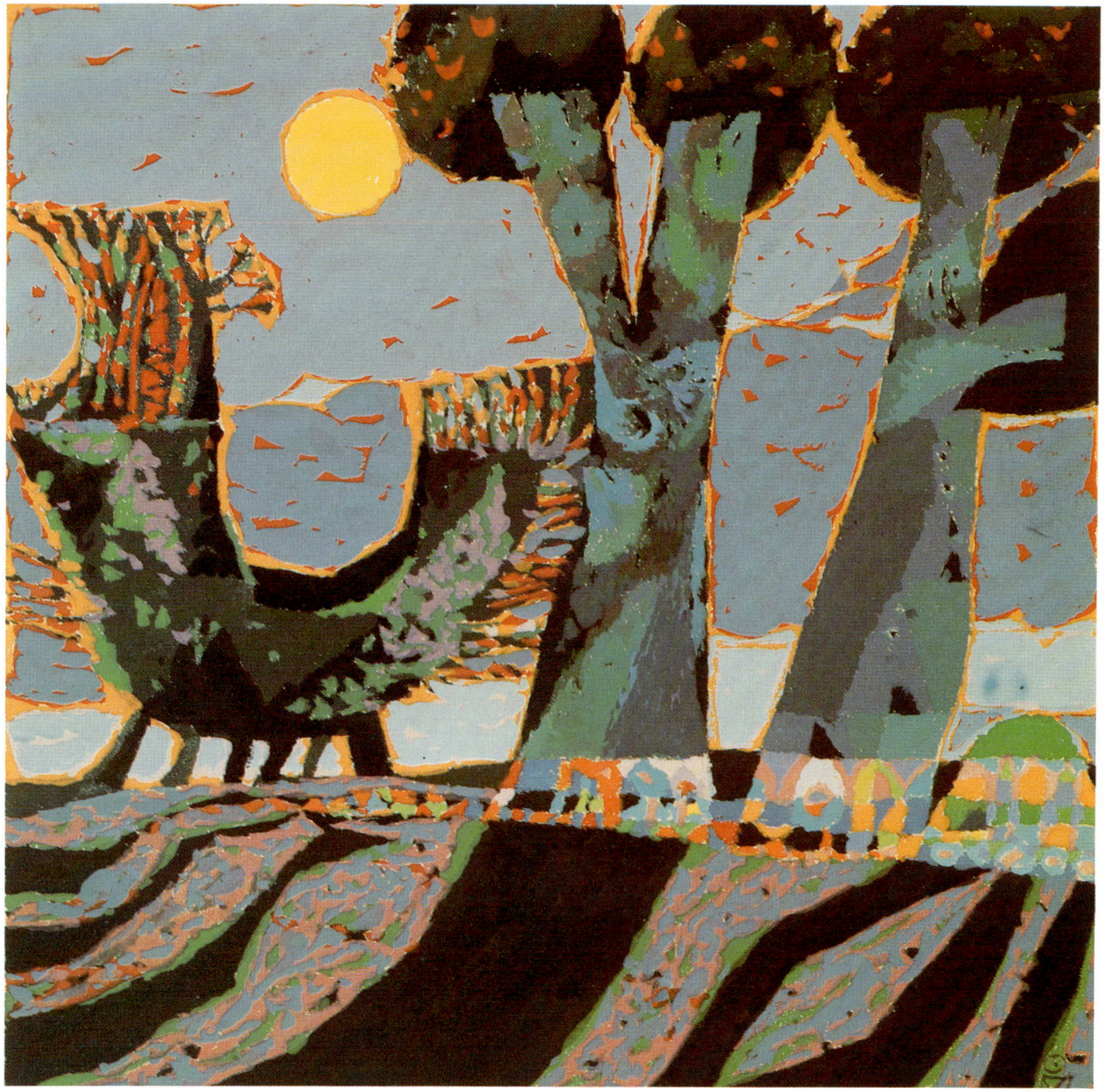

facing page 28

11 DAVID CRONE
Church Road
1972; oil on canvas; 91.4 x 127 cms; Arts Council of Northern Ireland collection

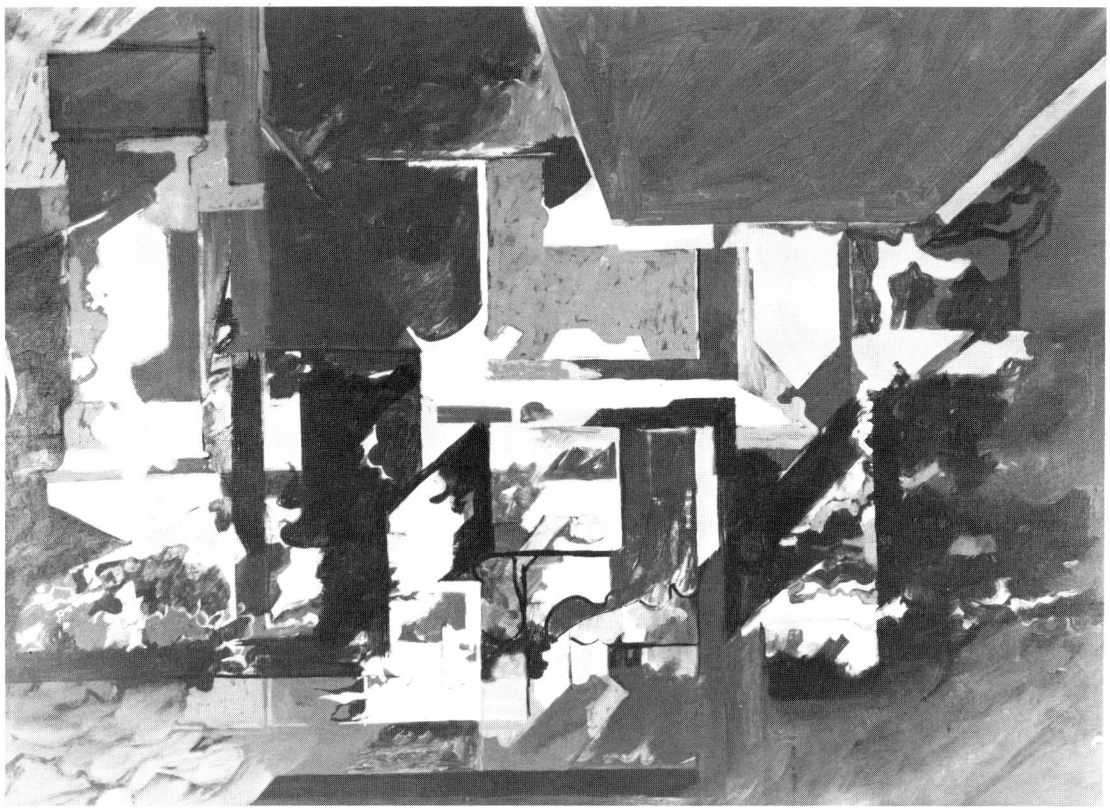

'real' artistry to be serious. Colin Middleton is all this and more, evolving in a straight line and then feinting and going off at a tangent as a thought or shape or texture takes him. He may go back through time and his own consciousness and re-discover a previous line of enquiry, bringing it out with flair and the accrued riches of his years. He may quote from himself or from anyone he considers worthy of quotation but he remains remarkably consistent in his final development.

In 1967 Michael Longley interviewed Colin Middleton for *The Irish Times*. Even after a decade the much-quoted words of that interview have an edge of intensity, they remain a credo that is worth quoting. After Middleton re-affirmed his concern with place, Longley said

> 'But not in the same way. You couldn't say that a painting like for instance *Woman with Owls* is concerned with place.'

> Middleton: 'That came right out of the Mournes, from Newcastle and the woods. Place is everything. Place is terribly important.

Places, places, places. I just can't go out for a day's sketching — that's meaningless, utterly horrible, terrifying. You've got to go to a place until it does something to you. Or, rather, you gravitate — when you get there you know you belong — it gets at you, it eats you. It's as though you've been there and always been there. When I go to a place there's got to be something in the bloodstream to belong to and the 'qualities' are there to get the old machine ticking... There's got to be some sort of place, particular places, holy places. Once you get there you know you're kith and kin. The stones start to talk.'[11]

This pantheistic belief in the spirit of place extends, rightly, to the dignity and respect that Middleton accords every component part of the scene. He recognises and knows how to use the inherent and particular qualities of the materials he uses as well as the objects he paints. They say you have to be very, very close to a cat before she'll tell you her *real* name; Middleton probably knows the real name of every rock and twig in the old, unspoken language. In this respect, in spite of, or because of his assimilation of the elemental traits in past and present artists whom he admires, Middleton remains, for me, the painter most uniquely capable of expressing the animus/anima of the Irish landscape. The stones *do* start to talk. He is no lover of the Renaissance, which he sees as a logical, 'civilising' force that destroyed or at least forced underground the old spirituality of things, his beloved archetypes. Even so, whether he acknowledges it or not, he shares with Michaelangelo the mystical Neoplatonic belief that the true subject of the work is contained within the material, waiting only to be liberated by an artist who is more midwife than creator. [12]

There exists a trap for the unwary critic who seeks to classify Middleton's work into categories such as 'landscape', 'fantasy figures' and the like because the interconnecting links are so strong that the one initial impetus may blossom into several related, but superficially different pictures. And since his understanding of both the shapes and the familiars of the land may be expressed in symbolic terms, in the same way as the ancients gave form to their river spirits as reclining figures surrounded by their attributes, Middleton's landscapes may cradle the form of his figurative archetypes. In 1967 the artist defined the archetype as a symbol which in turn was a 'communicating vessel'.[13] The female archetype figuratively or as the metaphor for the changing yet eternal landscape remains the thread of continuity in his work.

An analysis of the formal schema of the landscapes reveals some of the structures and devices which abound throughout his pictures. As has been noted by others,[14] the move to Coleraine in 1955 after the years of the so-called 'Ardglass Period' resulted in a series of landscapes which sought to reflect the more geometric shapes and light effects of that northerly region. Some of these settled for a format consisting of a horizon some two thirds up the paper or canvas: above this might be a projecting rock promontory or solid trains of cloud. Beneath the line of the horizon would be horizontal bands delineating the furrowing or folding of the land. These would be bisected by vertical or diagonally vertical lines to produce a slightly chequered effect which might be filled in with broad strokes of colour, as in *Sundown Canalridge II*

(1960) illustrated in colour in the Middleton monograph. Or then again the blocks might be handled monochromatically so as to expose the spare light around piled turf stacks in the sombre boglands. The precedent for the precise division of picture space exists in some of his landscape sketches of the late 1940s and also in Middleton's usage of the standard language of international surrealism. The Surrealists often presented their figures on a vast stage, whose scale was revealed by the simple device of painting stage(y) planks, lines which converged at the horizon. This became a cliché when taken up by the graphic designers of the thirties and forties who would place their objects, usually with elongated horzontal shadows, on such a sharply perspectival stage.

A glance at an early Middleton excursion into the Daliesque such as *The Toy Box* (1948) shows a fascination with stage sight lines which re-emerges in the delightfully inventive surreal works of the early 1970s, for example *Metro: St George's Day, Barcelona* or *The Wilderness of Fiorenza Cossotto: Tierra del Fuego*. In his landscapes, the verticals, however chequered, assume a dramatic monumentality that echoes the strength of the fantastic rock formations of the Giant's Causeway. The personal relevance of strong verticals may be understood by looking at the re-touched photograph of a weathered breakwater (crowned with egg-like stones) which graces the covers of both the Middleton monograph and the retrospective exhibition catalogue.

There is a danger that in codifying the units of Colin Middleton's language the vigour, the beauty and the mystery may be lost. Let no-one forget that the use of a repertoire of shapes and symbols is not a constricting experience for Colin Middleton. Out of this stratiform sign system he can produce landscapes of expressionist energy and concern; of calm simple delicacy; or of precise geological clarity. The diversity of his responses drawn from nature is best illustrated yet again by a poet, Seamus Heaney, with his dedication *In Small Townlands: for Colin Middleton*.

In small townlands his hogshair wedge
Will split the granite from the clay
Till crystal in the rock is bared:
Loaded brushes hone an edge
On mountain blue and heather grey.
Outcrops of stone contract, outstared.

The spectrum bursts, a bright grenade,
When he unlocks the safety catch
On morning dew, on clouds, on rain.
The splintered lights slice like a spade
That strips the land of fuzz and blotch,
Pares clean as bone, cruel as the pain
The strikes in a wild heart attack.
His eyes, thick greedy lenses, fire
This bare bald earth with white and red,
Incinerate it until it's black
And brilliant as a funeral pyre;
A new world cools in his head.[15]

Others have latched on to Middleton's striated forms and his textures with differing degrees of success. An Arts Council poster by Cathal Caulfield has the formal fluted shapes of a Middleton landscape. His bandings that become chevrons echo distantly in some of the works of artists like Brian Ferran and Joe McWilliams, while his weathered surfaces and geometricised space, themselves derived from the same impetus as Pasmore and Nicholson, surface in the jigsaws and later Connemara pictures of Derrick Hawker.

The relatively small output of the period 1957-61 with what John Hewitt called their 'tweedy textures' led on to the works of the 1960s, with their large simple areas in which cubism and constructivism meet in landscapes and figure works whose polished and eroded surfaces resembled close-ups of sculpture by Henry Moore. These works, two dimensional passing sometimes into three dimensions, have a pared down dramatic quality as in *Anvil Rock I* (1965) or *Granite Mountain Spelga* (1968/70). Then, after working his way through the ranges of brown, grey and black, the little red accents that found their way into many of these works begin to grow larger and to flower brilliantly in the vividly coloured reds, purples and oranges of the paintings which derived from his visit to Australia in 1972. I have chosen one of these small, tremendously powerful paintings as a perfect example of the Middleton landscape. *Swan River: Sunset II* of 1972 (no ii, colour) shows an other world landscape with tree forms silhouetted against a livid sunset. The mood is more baleful than in, say, the watercoloured patterning of the previous year's *Winter Sun: For Louis Armstrong*. In the Swan River painting the anthropomorphic tree forms, especially the scorpion-like one, seem to walk on legs of deep shadow. This is landscape come alive, threateningly palpable as a dream or a vision.

Middleton's personal kind of surrealism is based on a programme of objects and vistas which have passed through the artist's own filtration system, but another kind of surrealism is possible, based on absolutely ordinary places and things seen out of context. Although not primarily a landscapist as such, Charles Oakley, who taught at the Art College in Belfast for twelve years from 1962 to 1974, did make use of the decayed and derelict in the landscape for surrealist ends. Ruins have always fascinated the romantic artist, embodying as they do the repossession of man's artifacts by nature. Indeed, along with follies, Temples of Love and other constructed views they are an important part of the eighteenth century's concept of the picturesque. But ruins are also the repository of old memories and close to the highly charged feelings of the Gothick. A ruined castle may evoke a frisson in the viewer but so too can a ruined cottage set up thoughts of the 'short and simple annals of the poor'. Charles Oakley's extremely representational studies of tumbled down Irish cottages overgrown with briars are oddly disturbing *because* they are so ordinary and underplayed.

Another English artist who worked here for several influential years is Derrick Hawker (born 1936), and indeed the West of Ireland is still both his spritual home and the focus for his art. His early abstracted (but not abstract) works just about hold a recognisable reference but there is little doubt that his contact with Colin Middleton, the art and the man, produced a considerable tightening up of his images, colours and shapes. The *Belfast Lough* series of 1967-70 illustrated a concern for lines of movement in land, air and sea with images intruding through the lines and in and out of the edges of the picture space. The swirling shapes formed very carefully choreographed discrete units with the figurative information reduced to its essence.

12 DERRICK HAWKER
Jigsaw No 4
c1969; mixed media; 91.4 x 81.3 cms; collection the artist

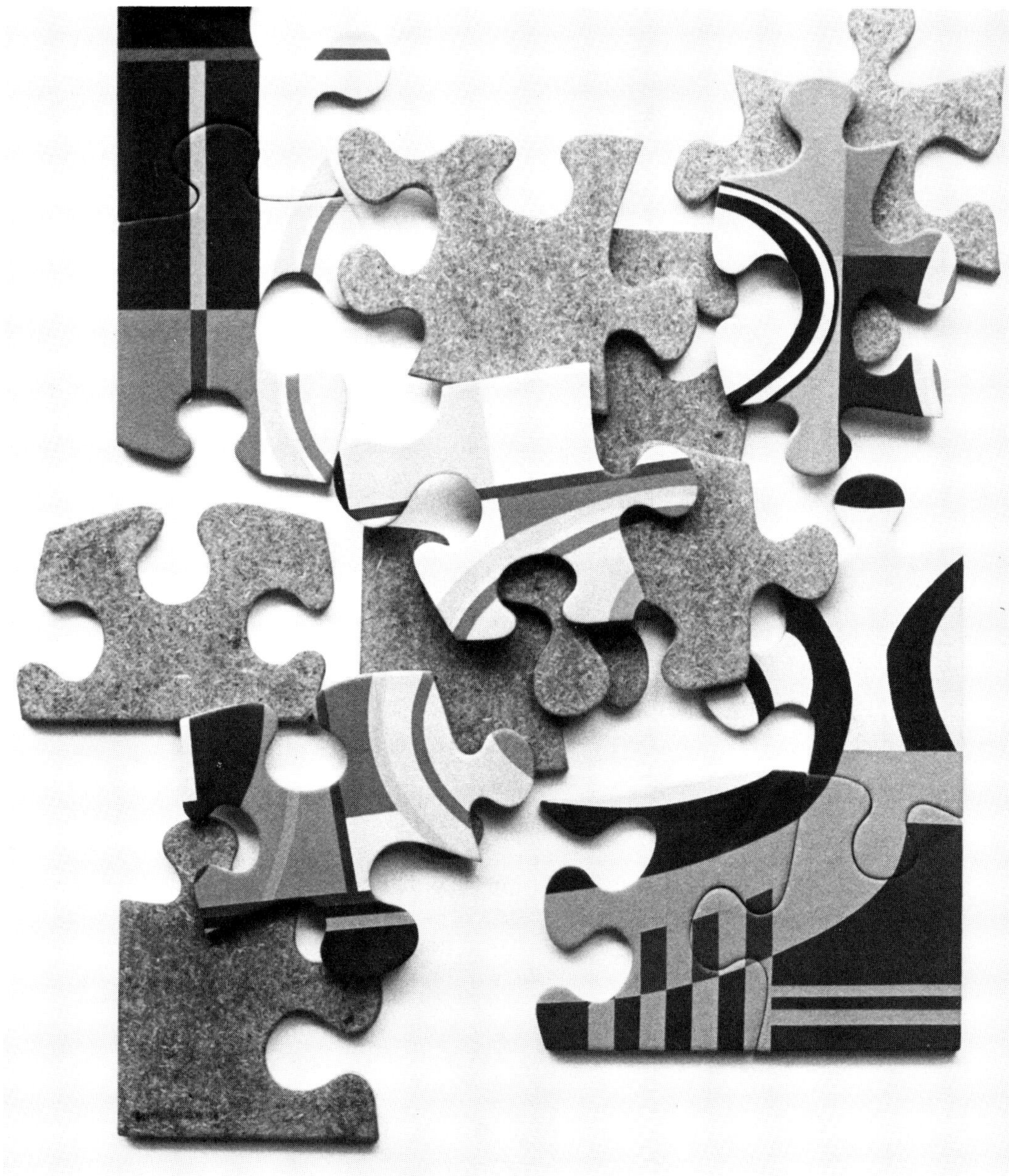

13 DERRICK HAWKER
Connemara AM/PM
1976; photo-lithograph; 30 x 35.5 cms

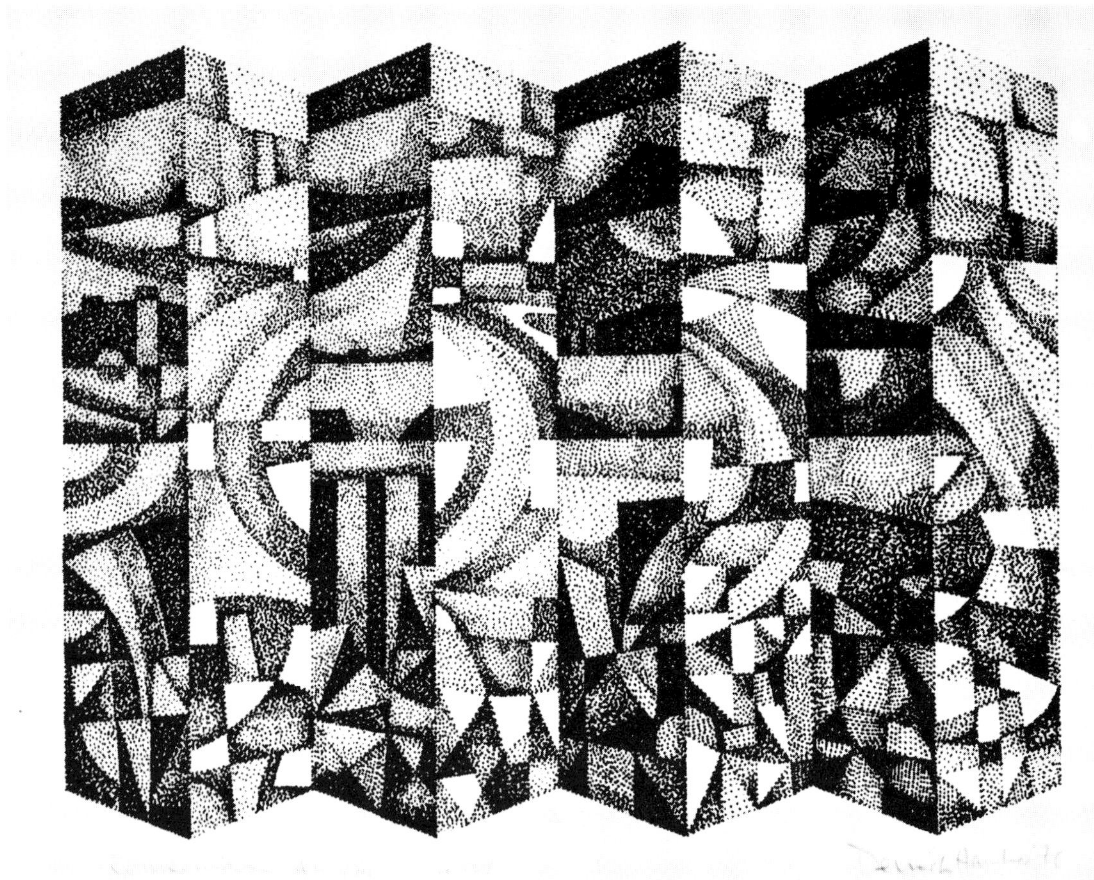

The handling of the pigment resembled Middleton in stippled effects, dry brush strokes and the feel for the understructures. It was no real surprise when this was extended to real rather than implied planar structuring. The architectonic units became three dimensional and independently of Malcolm Bennett, Hawker developed a Jigsaw series. The jigsaw is a code, normally capable of having only one solution but that would be too dry, too analytical for an artist so Hawker's jigsaws seem to imply that there is an open ended, interpretative possibility open to artist and viewer alike.

The example illustrated is *Jigsaw Number Four* of 1970 (no 12) and there is a contrast between the grainy plain units and those more highly coloured units which provide extra, sometimes contradictory information. There is even something of Pop Art in this in the same way as Roy

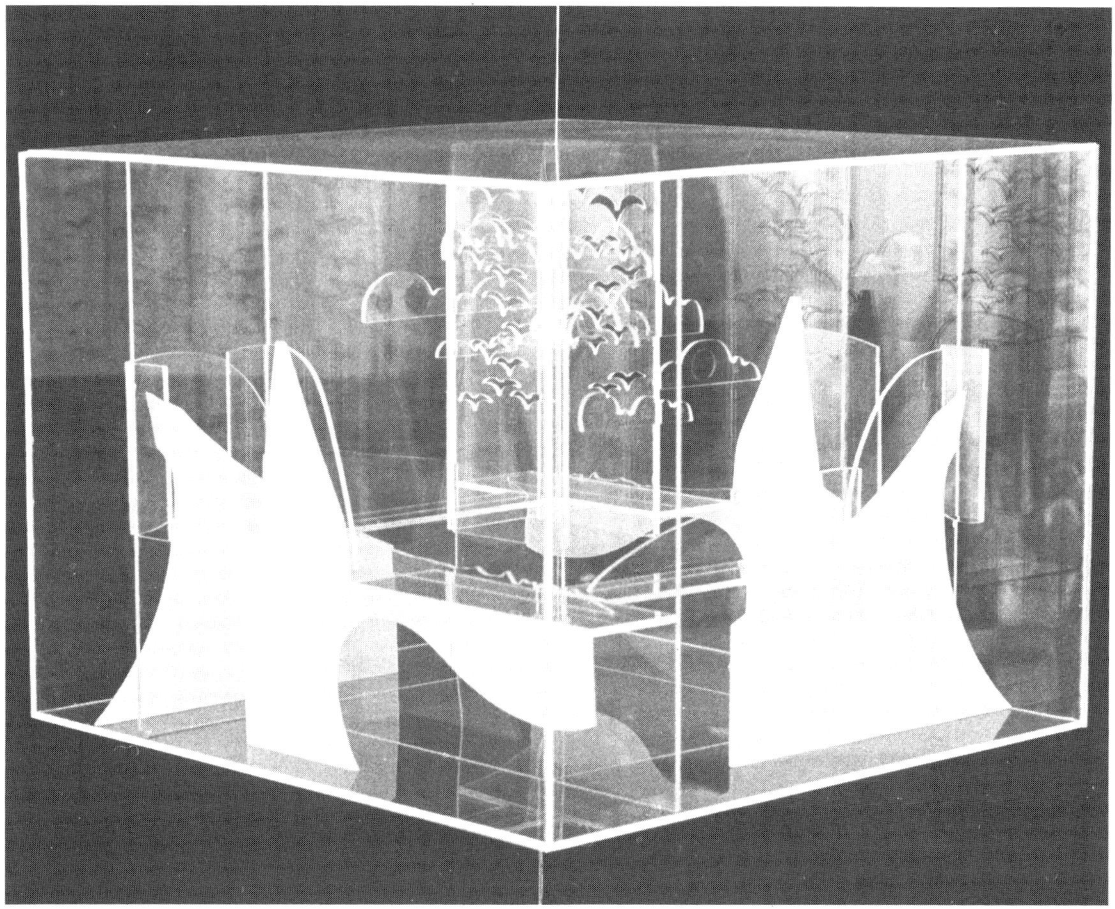

14 R J CROFT
White Park Bay Box
1970-71; perspex; 76.2 x 101.6 x 101.6 cms; collection the artist

Lichtenstein's reduction of images to the conventions of the comic strip forced our attention back to the original as mediated by the method of production. The popular format of the jigsaw used to explore the landscape is both a clever metaphor and a very romantic response to its changing moods.

More recently the grainy wood/paint surfaces have evolved into rather pointillist works. The technique of building up area by varying the compression of the dots is the basis of half-tone printing. Thus it suits mechanical fine printing methods too, but the way Derrick Hawker has used it, in *Connemara AM/PM* (no 13) for example, the pointillism is not there as a short cut for the printmaker. Photolithography copes happily with tones so the dot technique is Hawker's way of showing the passage of light over the dense tarn-speckled Connemara landscape. The folding of the view, creating an effect like a Chinese screen produces an analogy for a time shift as well as a light shift.

Like Derrick Hawker and Malcolm Bennett, Richard Croft once employed three dimensional forms in his search to establish an alternative language by which landscape could be described. Croft was born in London in 1935 and has been working in Belfast since 1959. In the sixties he was associated with Group 63 and his work was expressed in two apparently antithetical forms: landscape painting and optical or kinetic works. Of course there is no reason why they cannot be compatible, since real, as against implied, movement in art can also suggest the perpetual changes of light. In 1971 he exhibited a perspex construction called *White Park Bay Box* (no 14). The banded, overlapping layers of translucent and opaque perspex set up configurations of light and tones as the viewer moved around it. Distortions and resonances created by the reflective/refractive nature of the material were complemented by small wave like forms to produce an effect that approached the glittering facets of light that the Irish film maker Patrick Carey has captured in his *Oisin* and *Waves* films. There also existed a strong formal link between this perspex box and the flat planes of Croft's better known paintings. Although the shapes which appeared in his early painting were more solid he soon developed a repertoire based on a few simple forms bordered and thus defined by streaked and swirling dark lines. His tonal range became simpler too, concentrating on pale earth colours, ochres, light greens and lemons. These are delicate colours which reflect much of the light that falls on them so there again a link exists between the easel paintings and the perspex pieces. A typical Croft landscape would consist of a high horizontal form which would sweep down lines that curve to right or left dividing the space into segments like those of an orange. Usually there is a busy area of small details just near the point at which the curve meets the 'horizon' and this eye-catching complex acts as a foil to the broad empty areas loosely described by the low key colours. These contrasts of busy/quiet and tight/loose are found just as frequently in his paintings of still lifes and in the recurrent theme of pale fishing floats beside new or decayed fishing boats.

In 1976 he exhibited a series of works based on the landscape seen through and mediated by the ornate Victorian cut glass of a bar door. The *McCrory's Bar Door* series of which this is an example (no 15) reaffirms his vocabulary of devices and colours, a vocabulary which can be rather conventionally articulated, and also harks back to the fresnel effect inherent in the kinetic pieces.

Lack of space means that I cannot do justice to the landscape elements that form a vibrant thread running through the work of Gerard Dillon and Daniel O'Neill, two Ulster artists of considerable stature who are sadly no longer alive. However the landscape as such was not their primary concern and the environment forms a symbolic backdrop to the lives, actions and dreams of the figures who inhabit it. Therefore these artists will be discussed in the next chapter as well as in John Hewitt's volume. A survey such as this also means that I cannot devote much space to the more academic land-scapists. I do not use the word academic in a pejorative sense but even so there exists a closed

15 R J CROFT
McCrory's Bar Door [2]
1975; acrylic; 45.7 x 40.6 cms; private collection

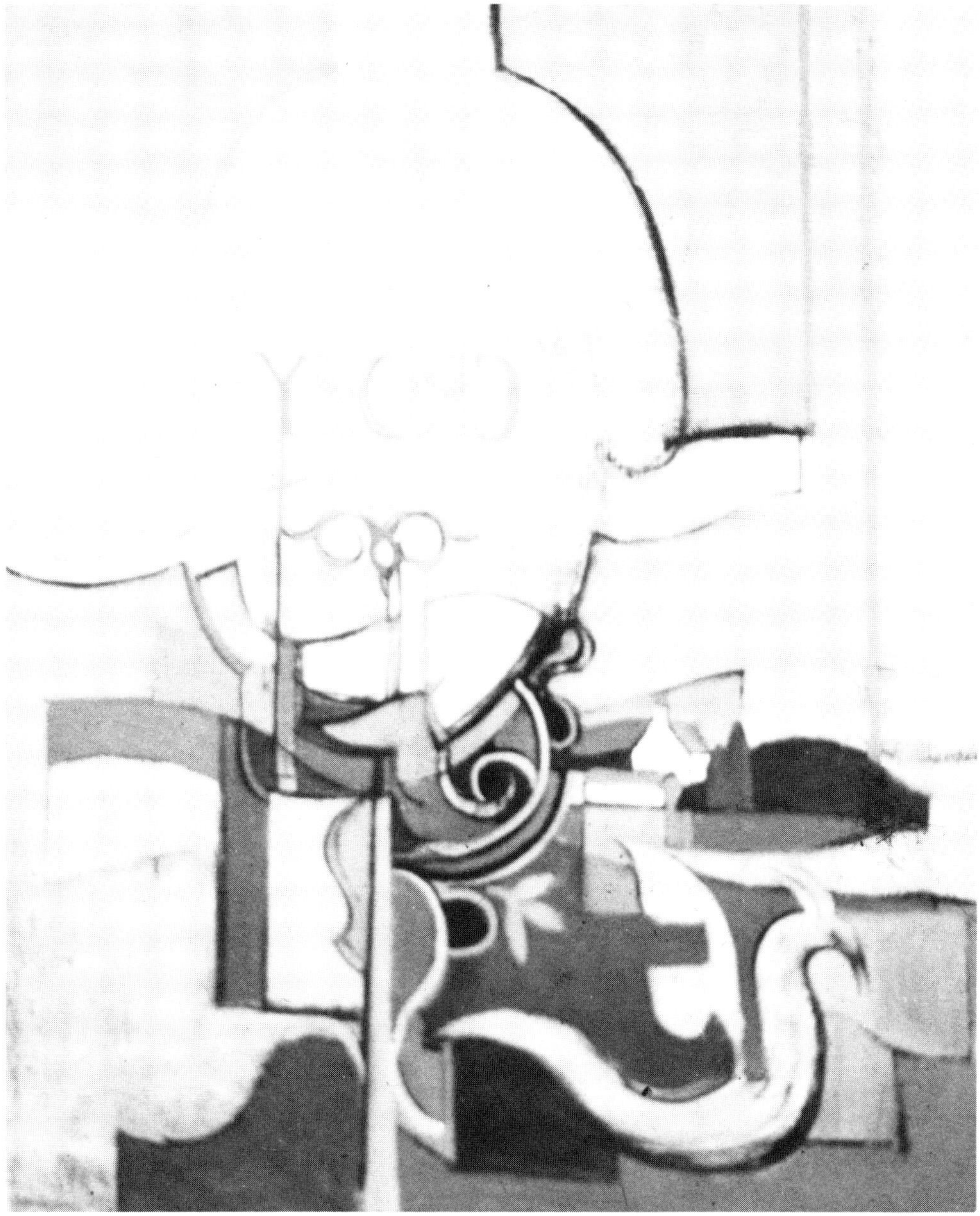

door feeling to much of the landscape work which still forms a large part of the work exhibited in the Royal Ulster Academy and by those who are associated with it. Frequently the compositions are sound, the handling of paint is meticulous but there often exists a lack of progression or rapport with the subject which provokes no sense of extended experience in the viewer. They are just simply there. This reduces painting to the level of decoration and it is significant that along with the tearful waifs, elephants on the veldt and buxom senoritas, landscapes are perpetual examples of popular art. Impressionist works and scenes of Spanish villages are successful in print (that is to say reproduction) form, but many chain stores and supermarkets sell landscape originals. These are often hack works reduced to a few pot-boiled forms which can be painted quickly ad infinitum. Generally wide-screen in format and expressionist in the technique and primary colours employed these pictures are mere formulae: a cottage on the left is balanced by a tree on the right (or vice versa), the hill is reflected in the lake and sheep are optional. As conveyor belt products of a supermarket society their aesthetic level is as low as their price, but these identi-scape originals are also found 'up market' in galleries throughout this island, sometimes with fairly hefty price tags attached. Certainly the standard is higher than those turned out by the Belgian painting factories, but in the final analysis the Irish exponents of this very free, sketchy landscape idiom (such as Kenneth Webb and Maurice Wilks) have allowed their very facility in painting to sap their ability to probe and experiment.

An inevitable reaction to the number of two-dimensional stereotypes that are produced world-wide is found in the work of artists who have eschewed the traditional media and who have developed lines of thought and expression based on their bodies and the actual physical constituents of landscape. Divergence from the inherited precepts of 'what' and 'how' will seem heretical to many artists and art lovers; it will seem stupid and incomprehensible to others and to others yet again it will, quite simply, not be Art. The disengagement from the past is seen by many young artists as a return to first principles — not an attack on art but on its icons. It is also an attack on the idea that art is put in a frame, hung on a wall and sold in a gallery. Among other things this led to a utilisation of standardised, non-arty documentation products such as maps, photographs, graphs and the like.

Sometimes this can involve the actual marking of the landscape as in the work of Walter de Maria, Christo or the late Robert Smithson whose *Spiral Jetty of the Sun* in the Great Salt Lake, Utah, is not only a work of great scale like the dolmen and tumuli of old, it is also a response to the eternal mythologies of place. Sometimes the piece is experimental with the artist moving through and re-discovering the landscape as he goes. Some of Joseph Beuys' works have taken him to physical environments where he has encountered the terrain on a one-to-one basis; wading in bogs, covering himself with mud, etc. The young English artist Richard Long was represented in the *Arte Inglese Oggi* Exhibition in Milan in 1976 by documentation of his walks through those landscapes which possess the most primitive resonances. In 1971 and 1974 this brought him, inevitably, to Ireland where he produced *A Walk of 164 Miles: A Line of 164*

16 PHILIP ROYCROFT
Page from log of a journey
1975; photocopy, map, ink, photographs; 20 x 28 cms; private collection

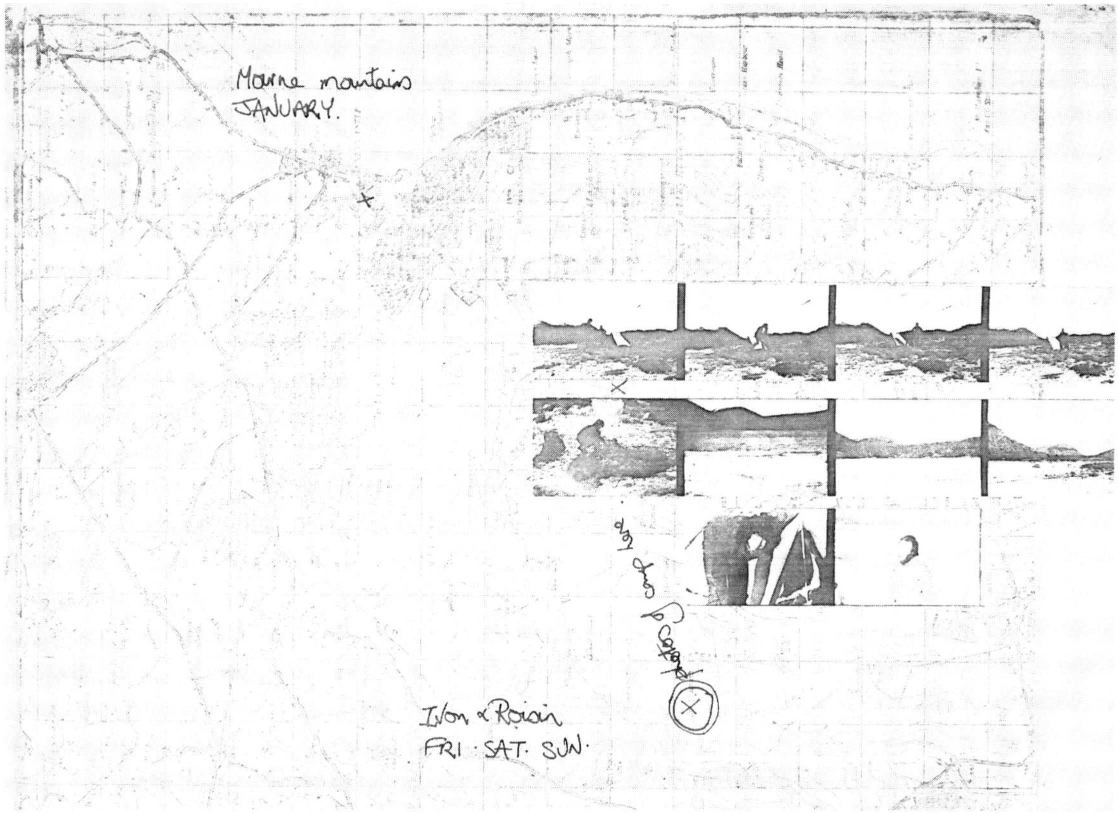

Stones; Stones in Clare and *Half-Tide*. The philosopher A N Whitehead said that we experience more than we analyse, and such forays back to the land are proto-analytical, sometimes mystical re-shapings of the eighteenth century Romantics' excursions to grapple with the Sublime. One young Ulster artist who developed an experience/analysis situation in his attempts to understand the phenomena of nature is Philip Roycroft. In a walk, or true pilgrimage, Roycroft journeyed 430 miles through Ireland, sending back post cards as 'fixes' to the Art and Design Centre in Belfast. These not only plotted his course but acted as notes for consideration by the non-participants. Roycroft, born in 1952, did this piece while still an art student, and perhaps motivated by the same tendencies that made Henry Thoreau try and find himself at Walden Pond, he also undertook periods of isolation in nature, attempting to live off, with and in some wild and inhospitable stretches of countryside. Illustration no 16 is an extract from a log kept on one such trip. Extreme yes; silly, no, for what

Roycroft was doing was producing a personal reassemblage of experienced phenomena; gathered and determined by a number of personal and cultural criteria and expressed in such a way that the denotative primacy of his sojourn can be understood on several connotative levels by others, including the artist himself. I have only used Roycroft as an example; others are doing things similar to him. Still others are experiencing different sensations while working with the land, and indeed the back-to-the-earth-with-eyes-and-minds-open movement makes artists of everyone from Sunday trippers to Mourne Wall Walkers.

NOTES

1. T P Flanagan interviewed by Caroline Walsh, *The Irish Times*, 14 August 1976.
2. Kenneth Jamison, 'Painting and Sculpture', *Causeway: The Arts in Ulster*, Belfast, 1971, p 54.
3. Taped interview by students of the Ulster College of Art and Design, 4 April 1971.
4. Seamus Heaney, 'Appreciation of T P Flanagan', *The Irish Imagination*, ROSC, Dublin, 1971.
5. Taped interview, op cit.
6. *Tom Carr and George Campbell* Exhibition Catalogue, Arts Council of Northern Ireland, n d.
7. Letter by the artist quoted in entry for *Gortahork 2, Irish Art from the Ulster Museum*, catalogue raisonné, Belfast, 1978, quoted here by courtesy of the Ulster Museum.
8. Seamus Heaney, *Door into the Dark*, 1969, reprinted by courtesy of Faber and Faber.
9. Reprinted in full in the catalogue to the Blackshaw Retrospective Exhibition, Arts Council of Northern Ireland, Belfast, 1974.
10. Kenneth Jamison, op cit, p 53.
11. Colin Middleton interviewed by Michael Longley, *The Irish Times*, Dublin, 7 April 1967.
12. Statement printed in the exhibition catalogue *Colin Middleton Paintings 1960-1970*, Arts Council of Northern Ireland, 1971.
13. Longley and Middleton interview, op cit.
14. *Inter alia*, Kenneth Jamison, op cit, p 50
15. Seamus Heaney, *Death of a Naturalist*, 1966, reprinted by courtesy of Faber and Faber.

FIGURATIVE AND NON-FIGURATIVE ART

'The language, be it verbal or visual, that of artist or author, is a living phenomenon, continuously in a state of metamorphosis; it increases in sophistication as the ideas it expresses increase in complexity or obscurity. As each artist discovers new terms, so they add to the ever-expanding language available to all artists.' [1]

It was once considered that language had a finite grammatical and syntactical construction, that there was a correct way of expressing ideas and an equally correct way of analysing that expression. Just as language as a system of communication is now seen to be open-ended, so too are other communication systems seen to offer boundless opportunities in terms of subject, method and medium. The art of this century mirrors the expansion of knowledge and techniques which so dominates the non-art world. Allied to this is the rejection of previous theories, which in the case of art has meant a reaction against the rules and ideologies of classical Greece and Rome, the Renaissance, the academics and last year's style. There have been attacks by artists on Art itself and there have been fashions and 'isms' which have been taken up and dropped with the same swiftness, some say fickleness, as is to be found in the record industry and in the rag trade. The general public is to be forgiven for feeling bewildered, for it is difficult for any outsider not only to appreciate novel ideas and forms but also to be able to relate these apparently arbitrary manifestations to a continuous and evolutionary quest after artistic truths. Embracing other styles is an essential step in an artist's path towards self expression and in this province the spectator can, as elsewhere, find examples of any movement, from Hard

Edge to Conceptual. Whether or not such examples and excursions remain durable once the context and contemporary aesthetic has moved on is one test of the coherence and integrity of a work. Looking, albeit with hindsight, at works done twenty or more years ago by then up and coming young artists it is not difficult to see the influences and cross references. Nor is it difficult to see which works have stood the test of time now that the shock of novelty has worn off.

Happily, Ulster and other Irish artists are less inclined than many to stampede after new forms of expression. Their tread is more measured and sometimes appears conservative by comparison with international art centres. Even this apparent conservatism represents a modernity which many members of the general public find incomprehensible. The artists discussed in this book, and in particular in this chapter, constitute, for better or for worse, Ulster's avant-garde. However, it would be inaccurate to describe contemporary Ulster art as conservative, but one can sense in 1977 the same introspection which the selectors of *Art Spectrum Ulster* noted in 1971, and which is hinted at in the various contributions to another survey of the local scene in 1951. By introspection I mean a state of mind in which the artist is prepared to assimilate international influences but at the same time rightly allocates such influences a subordinate position in his hierarchy of priorities. While this does not mean that Ulster subject matter is the automatic focus of attention for the Ulster painter (see Chapter 4) at the same time there is something which produces work which is distinctively located in this environment.

The works mentioned in the following pages range from traditional portraiture to computer generated shapes; from accessible subject matter to symbolism that holds as personal a relevance as Rosebud did for Charles Foster Kane in Orson Welles' film. Let us begin with the human figure which for so long formed the basis of the study of structure and proportion for every apprentice painter. Inevitably there was a global reaction against what mistakenly appeared to be an exclusive concern of academicism and in 1958 when a contemporary reviewer came to examine the works in the Pittsburg International Exhibition of modern art (Ireland being represented by Gerard Dillon and F E McWilliam, among others) there was a note of astonishment that, in the midst of the welter of huge Abstract Expressionist canvases some painters clung to subjects like landscapes and figure painting. Such a viewpoint was not only biased, it was inaccurate. The study of human anatomy and physiognomy was still vitally important to artists, and representational figure painting, albeit executed as part of a non-academic philosophy, constituted an important facet of modern movements such as Pop and Hyper-Realism. Even the portrait, which has unfortunate connotations of board rooms and bourgeoisie, is a vehicle for many stylistic variations. The Arts Council of Northern Ireland exhibitions *Ulster Faces I* and *II* and *Women of Ulster* showed that the human head could be treated with traditional conventions, as in the portraits of *Billy Blease* and *Elizabeth Begley* by John Turner and in the study of *Doreen Hepburn* by Pat Coogan. These shows also allowed the public to see portraits by artists such as John Middleton, who are not usually associated with portraiture, and also to examine the way in which the banal pin-up could be used as the starting point for Pop-influenced portraiture which not only captured likenesses but also analysed the myth of personalities. This was seen in works such as Peter Hardie's *George Best* (he later produced a poster of the footballer for the Arts Council of Northern Ireland), Graham Gingles *Dana* and Colin Harrison's witty and inventive pop icon, *Ruby Murray*. These exhibitions served also to remind us of the excellent figure paintings that have emanated from the brushes of Terry Flanagan and Basil Blackshaw. Mention has been made already of the former's *Portrait of John D Stewart* in which the writer sits four square to the viewer, hands on knees, staring out with the painted lack of compromise that can be seen in the Ulster Museum's *Portrait of Seamus Heaney* by Edward Maguire. Blackshaw's portraits and figure paintings seem more obsessive. Like Louis Le Brocquy he has been drawn to the pale, intense face of James Joyce, producing several sketchy, painted, expressive studies. Basil Blackshaw has had the single honour of having one of these hung in Joyce's Martello Tower. His portraits, from the controlled energy of *Laughing Girl* (1956) to the apparent simplicity of the series on *Jennifer Johnston* (mid 1970s), show a highly charged draughtsmanship and handling of paint. These are extremely emotional portraits and they convey feelings of vibrancy and movement, feelings which can also be said of his figure paintings except that these latter further convey an anxiousness and hermeticism. From Giacometti he learned a precision in locating figures in space and from that artist he also added elements to his existing inclination towards elongation of figures and flickering brush strokes. A work like *Anna on a Sofa* (1972) in which horizontals and verticals meet at the hunched, withdrawn figure sitting at the end of a sofa recall not only the enclosed universe of Francis Bacon but also a long line of Northern European painters of tense, linear suffering such as Matthias Grunewald. Significantly, Blackshaw has created religious paintings too; not cosy gentle-Jesus-meek-and-mild pictures but visceral, stark themes like *The Crucifixion*, aptly described by Kenneth Jamison as being 'taut as high tension wires in a summer landscape'. That word tension again: and it is descriptive also of his well known paintings of race horses. Not the colourful impressionism of the race meetings of Dégas nor the anatomical exactness of Stubbs, but a quieter, more monumental solidity surrounds these Giacometti-like works. In the last two or three years the static sculptural composition of these works has been replaced not simply by horses in movement but by tense, almost cruelly observed 'shots' of the exact moment when horse and rider fall. The series entitled *The Fall* has the distancing effect of Eadweard Muybridge's action photographs and the immediate impact of Expressionism.

The nudes of Basil Blackshaw have a certain air of detachment about them; those of Neil Shawcross are sometimes delicately withdrawn, and sometimes they have an irrepressible gusto about them. Shawcross (born 1940 in Lancashire) is one of our finest colour essayists and figure painters. His paintings in the 1960s were of delightful child-like figures spread across the flat picture space, and his colour scheme was fairly restrained. At times he gives the impression of being a naïf, not only in the simplicity and innocent vision he possesses in his work but also in his collection of genuinely primitive painters and of ephemera and bric á brac. He derives a tremendous satisfaction and stimulus from objects as diverse as old advertising, Victorian photographs and other mementoes of popular art and sentiment. From these twin loves of innocent art and popular imagery he evolved not simply a series of paintings which deftly captured their simplicity of subject and composition, but he was also able to adapt that simplicity to his nudes and portraiture. The obvious precedent for his oil paintings of nudes is to be found in Bonnard's works of his wife standing in front of curtains or wall paper, submerged in the bath and so on. Like Blackshaw, Shawcross places his nudes very close to the background 'wall' but the effect is very different. The latter's figures are softly flowing and the background pattern is often more boldly accentuated so that the human figure merges into the overall colour pattern. They are sketchy in the sense of having a spontaneity and delicacy about them, and this sketchiness is extended further in his water-colours. In these the opulence of the oils is replaced by a concentration on bold, firm brush strokes which complement the elegant simplicity of line. The colour is as bold as the brush strokes but the colours — greens, purples and pinks — achieve a remarkable fusion of softness as well as of brightness because Shawcross allows the areas of paint to run into each other. *Cat in a Window* of 1976 (no iii, colour) is a delightful example of this. The economy of line and the glow of colour recall both Matisse and Braque, artists whom the painter admires; while the humour of the simple doll-like cat is a Shawcross trademark. Simple as the end result may seem, it is the result both of excellent control of the medium and of an element of chance. Many artists in this century have allowed chance to determine certain factors in their works, and Neil Shawcross likes the random way in which certain colours run together, just as he likes the structured effect created by seeing the pencil drawing through the water colour pigment.[3] Shawcross also designed the stained glass windows for the new extension to the Ulster Museum. While the colour is extremely powerful the effect is not totally satisfactory, possibly because, as the artist himself admits, there is less personal control over the medium than with paint and also because the individual pieces of glass are so separate. Just as Shawcross is able to reduce forms to their essence in his drawings and paintings of objects he is able to do the same with his portraits without losing the character of the sitter. In fact, the very 'shorthand' that he employs catches the important features much in the same way as a cartoonist reduces lines to an essential few. But Neil Shawcross is not a caricaturist even though he is drawn to subjects with strong features as can be seen in the splendid 1968 full length portrait of Solly Lipsitz (no 17) in which no background is allowed to interfere with the directness of the sitter.

Nudes and portraiture also figure in the work of Colin Harrison (born 1939) who taught at the Ulster College of Art and Design from 1964 until 1972, and who still exhibits in Ireland. Like Shawcross the figures painted illustrate a very private world of symbols, but Harrison's technique is very different from that of Shawcross. Colin Harrison is a superb draughtsman and his extremely representational paintings often allow for the squaring up and preparatory drawing to exist as an integral part of the whole. His portrait of Ruby Murray already alluded to on page 43, was not *one* work but many; pin-ups that were images pinned down and analysed meticulously

17 NEIL SHAWCROSS
Portrait of Solly Lipsitz
1967; oil; 91.4 x 91.4 cms;
Arts Council of Northern Ireland collection

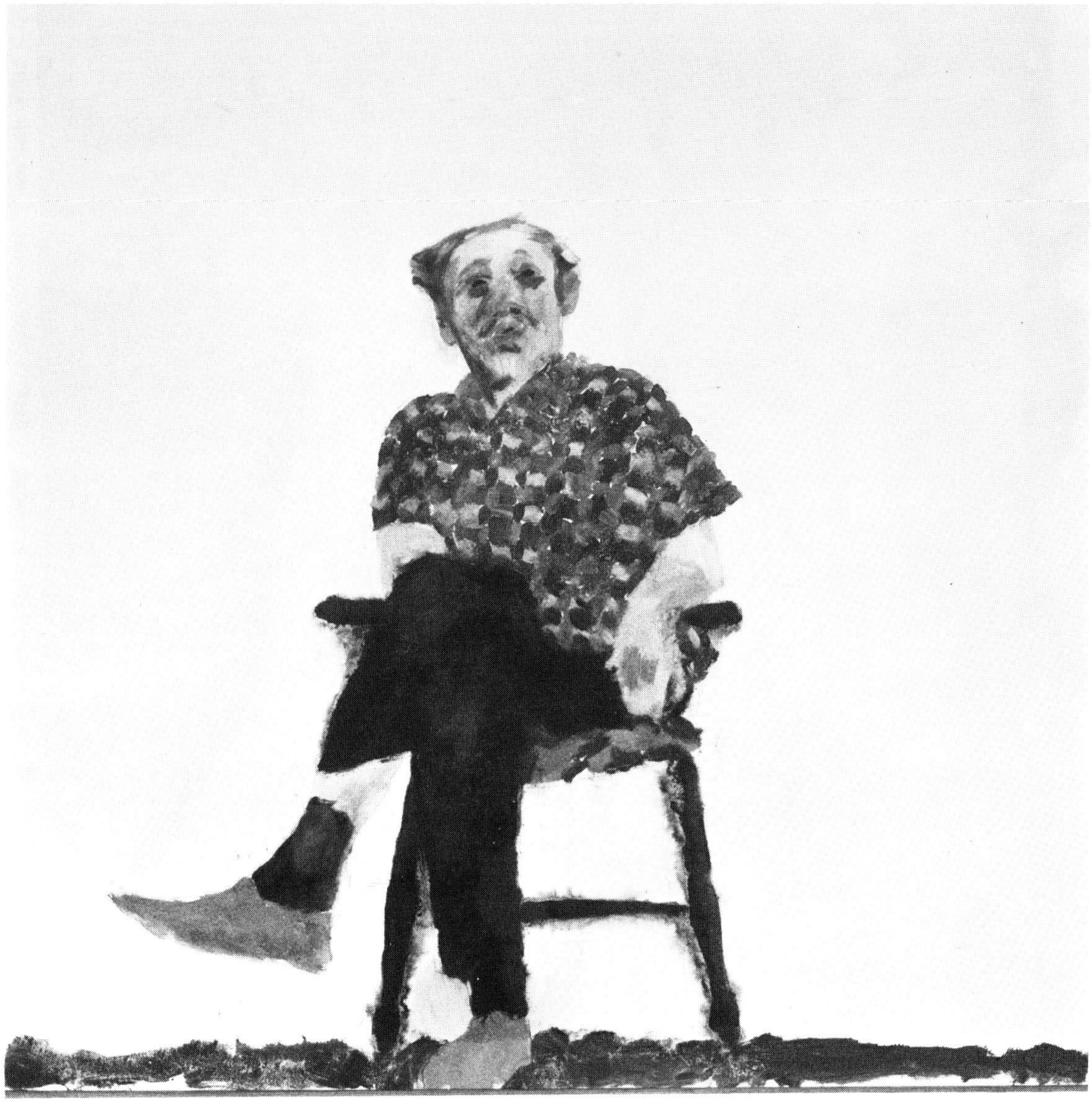

18 COLIN HARRISON
William Bogle with memento of Arnold
1975; oil and pencil, canvas on hardboard; 50.9 x 61 cms; Ulster Museum collection

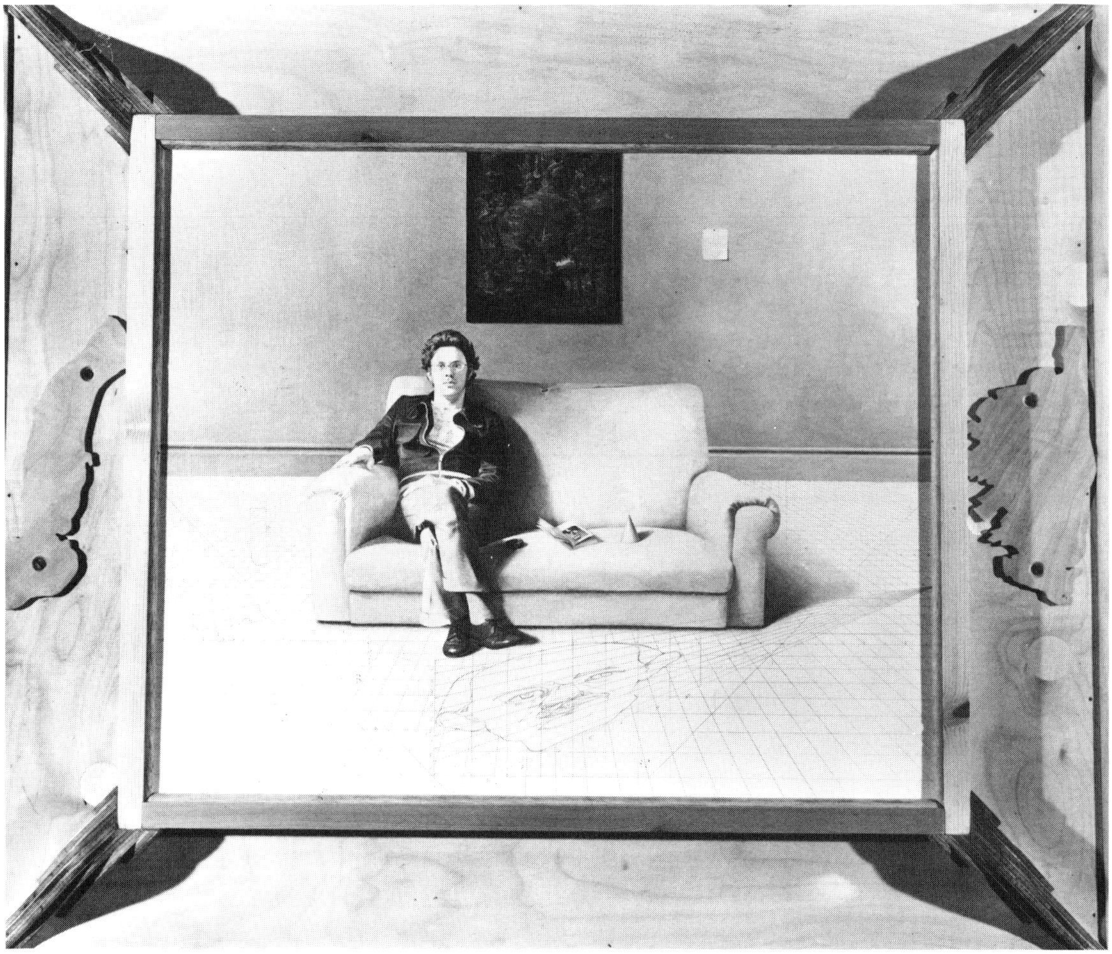

like a butterfly beneath a magnifying glass. Harrison took figures from popular culture like John Wayne, Fred Astaire and Ginger Rogers and evolved a complicated and highly original mythology around them. With the artist William Bogle he mounted an exhibition entitled *Corsica* for the Arts Council of Northern Ireland in 1971. This was no picture travelogue but a fascinating if often obscure symbolic journey through objects and images which had been collected and collated with logic and an extremely private key to the codes they contained. Corsica crops up again (along with the Mull of Kintyre) as one of the two plywood emblems which frame and add to the symbolism of Harrison's extremely detailed *William Bogle*

19 COLIN HARRISON
Anne and the dog
1974; cryla on canvas on hardboard; 56.9 x 46.8 cms; Ulster Museum collection

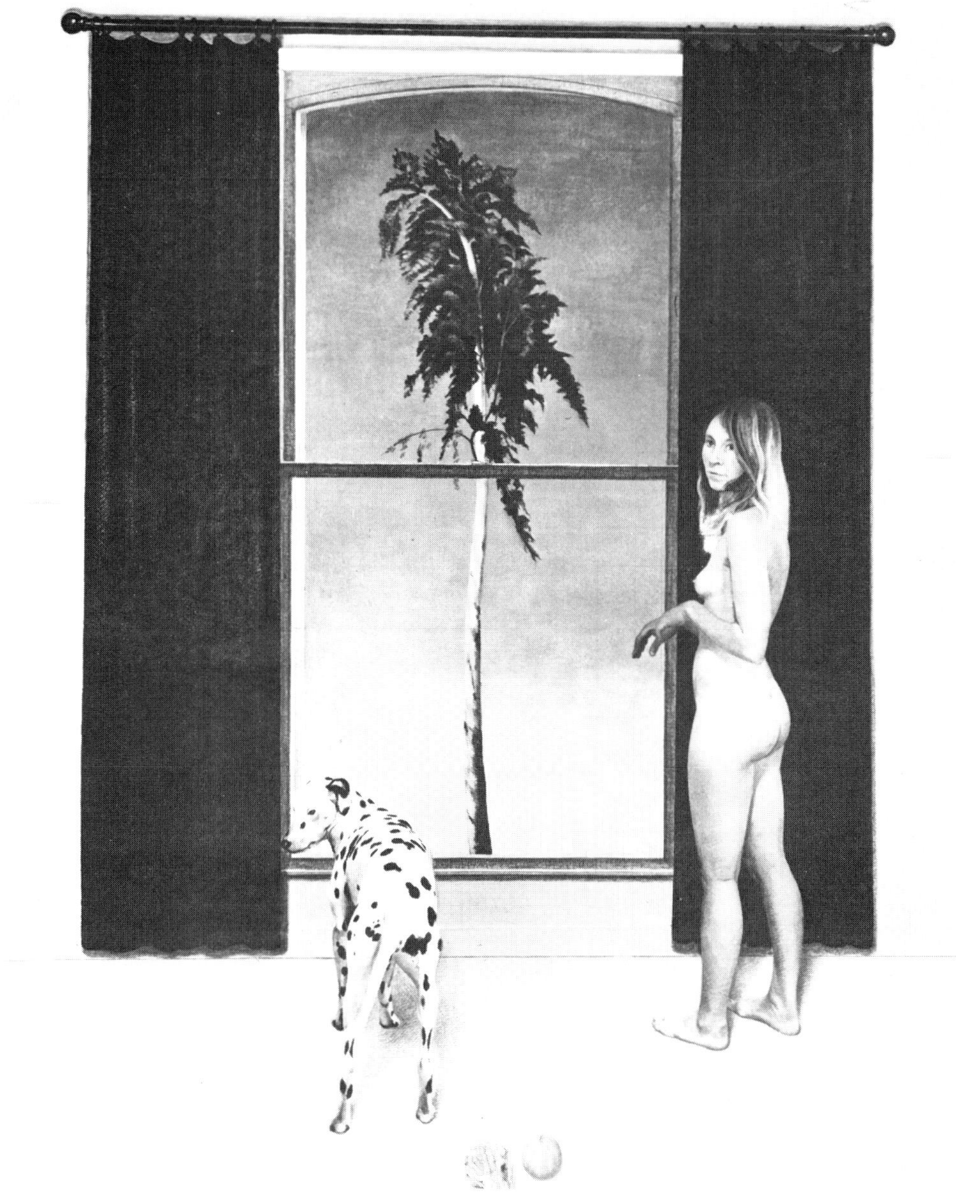

20 CLIFFORD RAINEY
Portrait of William Scott
1976; pencil on paper; 57 x 76 cms; Ulster Museum collection

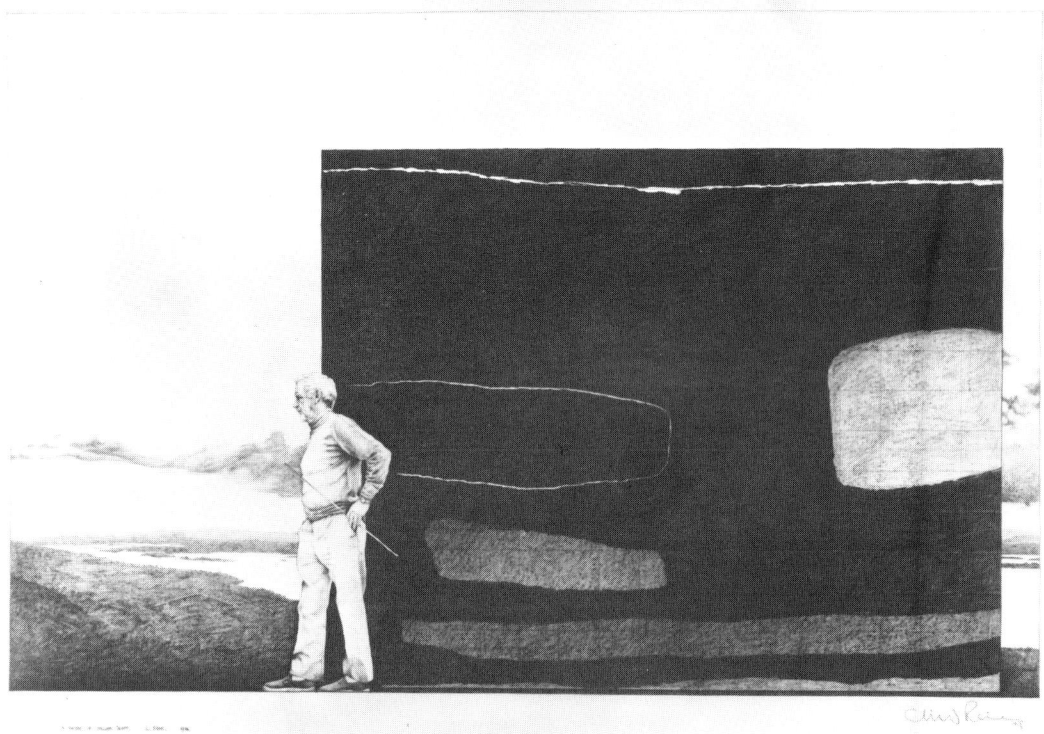

with memento of Arnold of 1974 (no 18). The anamorphic head of Arnold (Schoenberg) recalls the mysterious skull which occupies the same picture space in Holbein's *The Ambassadors* and the name of Holbein is appropriate to the unnerving clarity of technique and presentation. Equally disturbing is the painting *Anne and the dog* of 1974 (no 19) in which both the dog and the nude stare back out at the spectator, while the security of the interior is threatened by the dis-located tree outside. The tree, 'a silver birch in an oppressive blue sky is ... a reference to German Gothic painting ... [and] the fruit is a reference to similar, overblown, unhealthy fruit appearing in Carlo Crivelli's paintings, particularly *The Annunciation*'.[4] Something of the same unnatural naturalness may be sensed in the work of another excellent draughtsman, Clifford Rainey. Rainey (born in 1948), like Colin Middleton, trained as a damask designer, but then he moved on to a formal art education and working experience in glass works in Finland and Denmark. His work as a sculptor is discussed in Chapter 3 but his drawings echo the same precision and linearity which is to be found in his glass and metal sculpture. He frequently places his extremely representational figures on the bottom of the drawn line of the picture

21 BRIAN FERRAN
Pat
1971; mixed media; 71.1 x 50.8 cms; collection the artist

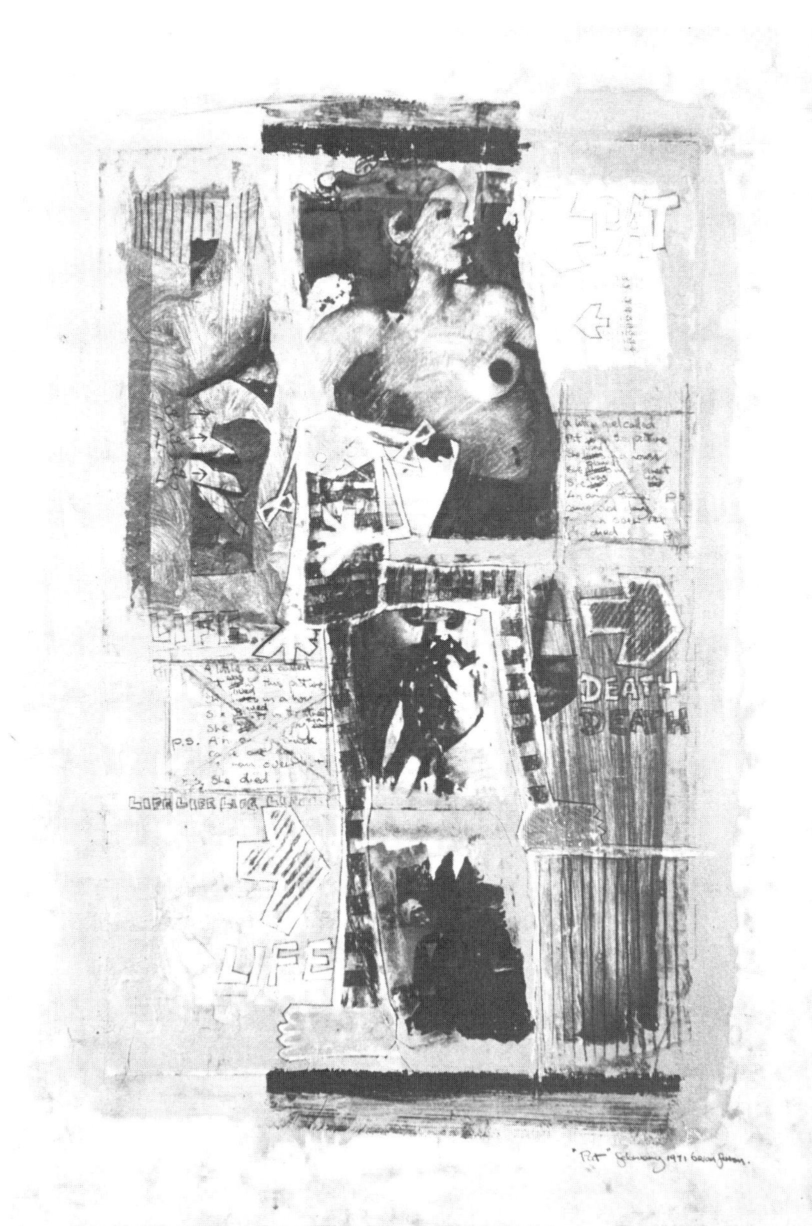

space, posed with the same stance and monumentality as the extremely hieratic figures of Egyptian art. This can be seen in *A Portrait of William Scott L. Erne* of 1976 (no 20), in which the distinguished artist is seen with a Rainey transcription of a Scott painting and both are set against a background of Fermanagh, where Scott was brought up. The carefully formalised composition with its Egyptian overtones is somewhat reminiscent of David Hockney's work and this is also hinted at in other portrait drawings such as those of F E McWilliam and Gordon Lambert.

All the figurative references so far have been particularised, but the human figure may be more generally used as a type which represents many individuals sharing the same cultural or symbolic identity. Until recently Elizabeth Taggart (born 1943) painted plump circus ladies and pinstriped gentlemen with patent leather hair. These beaming stereotypes were painted in a colourful, jolly, way which both resembled the naïveté of actual fair ground painting and at the same time symbolised the slightly vulgar humour and life of the circus, the fair, and the seaside postcard. The stereotypical figures of Brian Ferran's paintings are the produce of a more complex mythology and personal expression. Ferran (born 1940) has a vigorous technique in which figurative elements have increased or decreased over the years as he moves through successive evolutions of style. What appears to remain constant are free brushstrokes, a predilection for vertical emphases in his compositions, and a concern for emotions and motivations. To this end he likes to make use of formal shapes which have symbolic and emotional overtones. A rectangle divided vertically into three equal divisions, one red, one white and one blue, makes a simple formal pattern. But at the same time that pattern can be read symbolically as a flag, and not just any flag but that of a particular country. Change the colours; change the shapes to horizontal bands, or crosses, or stars and what you have are never neutral patterns but images capable of inspiring men to thoughts of patriotism or hate or love. Many American 'patriots' were insulted when Jasper Johns, the Pop artist, first used the Stars and Stripes as the subject of a painting, and in Ulster certain colour combinations can have an extraordinary effect on sections of the community. Brian Ferran not only recognises the emotive impact of symbols but also builds pictures around them. A work like *Pat* of 1971 (no 21) belongs to a tradition which begins with Cubist collage and is revitalised by the works of Robert Rauschenberg in the late 1950s. Rauschenberg, Richard Hamilton and other Pop painters incorporated photographs, magazine clippings and the like into their works, painted over and around them and produced works which have a narrative content. A 'reading' of *Pat* might begin at the top with the female nude torso, which has been personalised by the artist having added paint to the photograph. An arrow and a word tell us this is Pat. The figure and glimpses of anatomy on the left plus the repetition of a single word proclaim that this is Life. The graffiti-like quality is emphasised by the stylised childish drawing of the pigtailed schoolgirl who occupies the central space and by the starkness of the words. In the lower half the arrows point to the left, to Death, and the twice repeated story of Pat has all the verbs changed from present to past tense. The stories are themselves cancelled or crossed out (as in Hamilton's *My Marilyn* series) with crushing finality. This heavily marked picture, with the

22 BRIAN FERRAN
Táin Series
1975; acrylic and water-colour; 38 x 29 cms; collection the artist

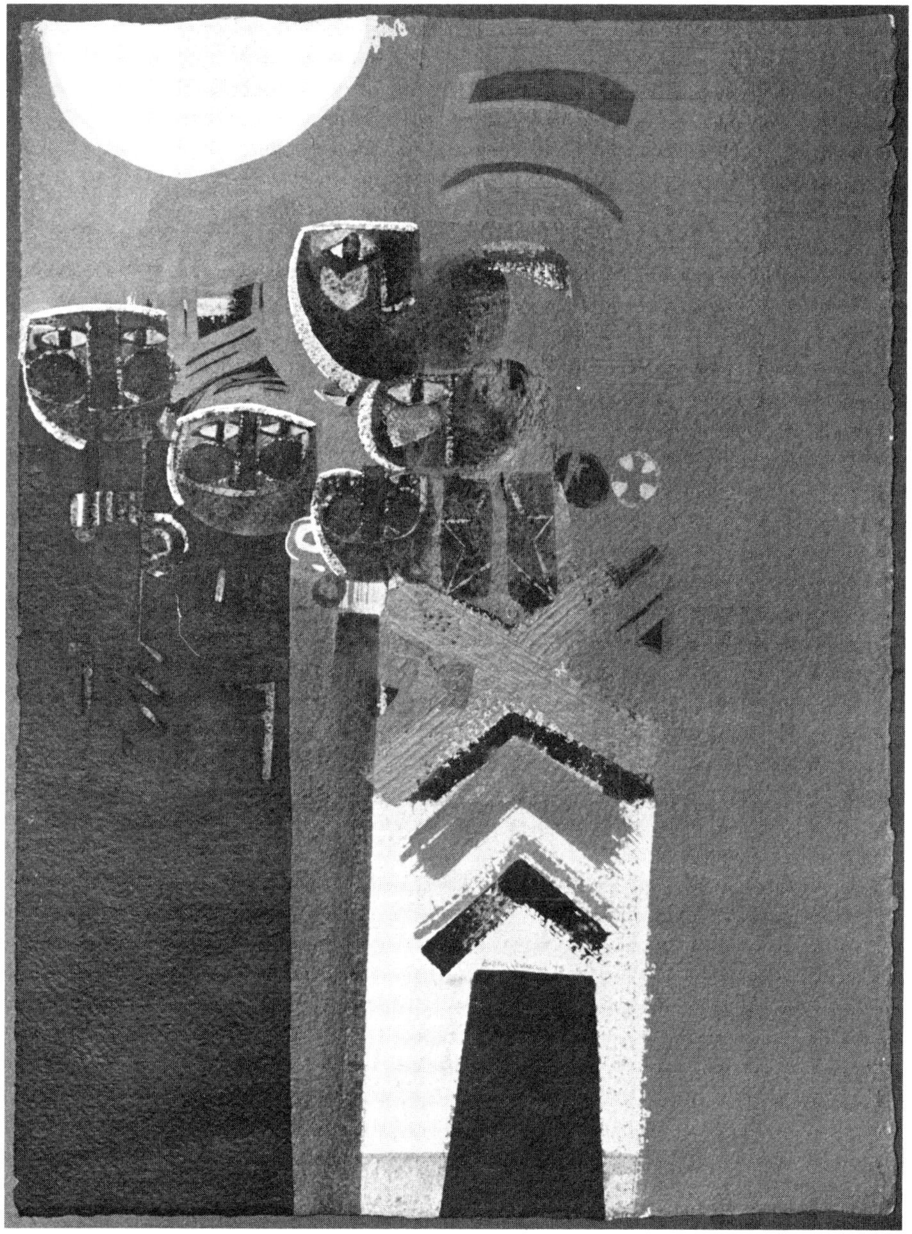

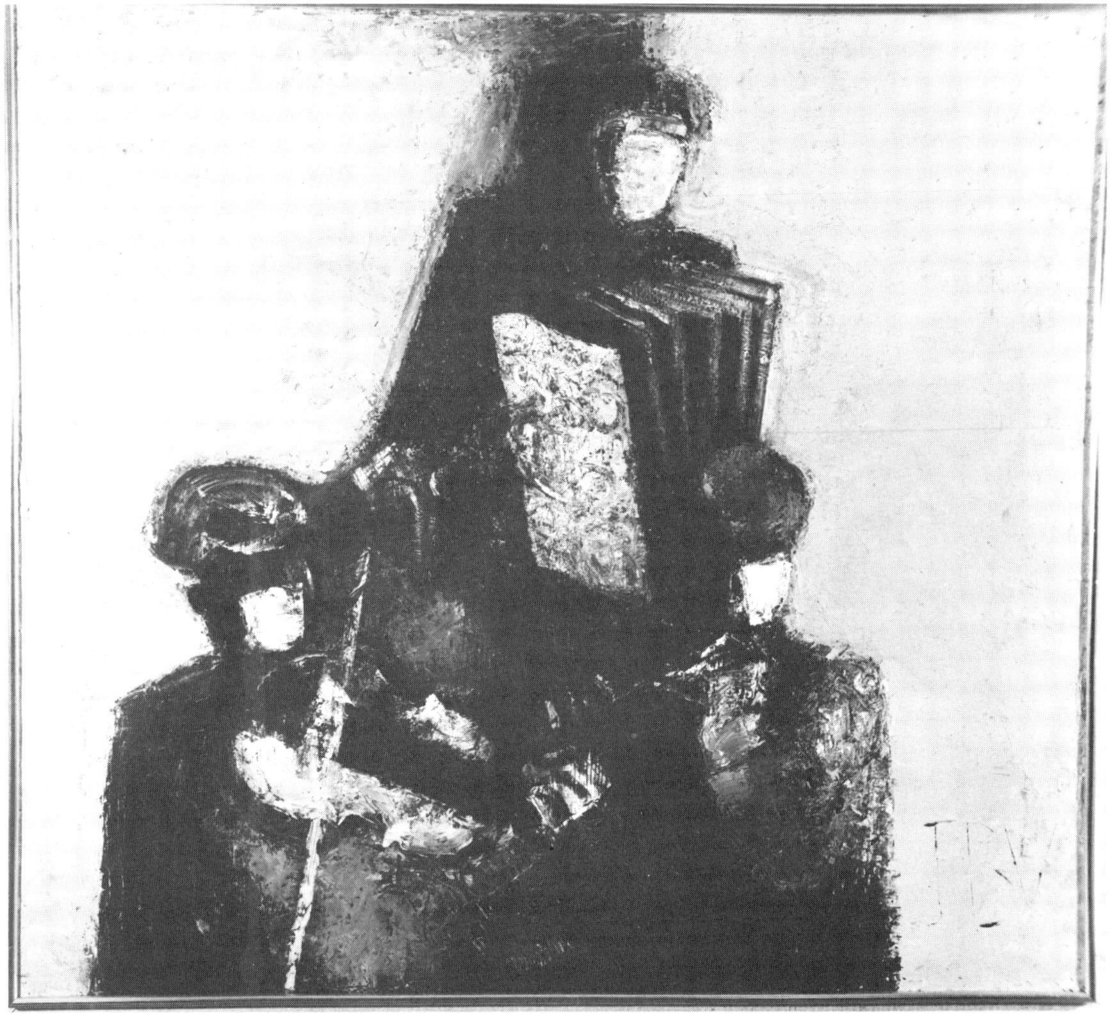

23 JOHN VALLELY
Trio
1973; oil on hardboard; 122 x 135 cms; Ulster Museum collection

crosses and chevrons which constantly appear throughout his work, has an irony built on the juxtaposition of the many types of visual communication. Such a painting is also full of cross references and in a series executed in 1975 Brian Ferran tackled a literary, and much illustrated theme, that of the Táin bó Cuailnge.

Heroes may be real, if larger than life, people or they may be projections of cultural aspirations and achievements. Men make myths, creating powerful images of heroes and gods. Lest they

III NEIL SHAWCROSS
Cat in Window
1976; watercolour and pencil; 34.5 x 30.5 cms (sight); collection the artist

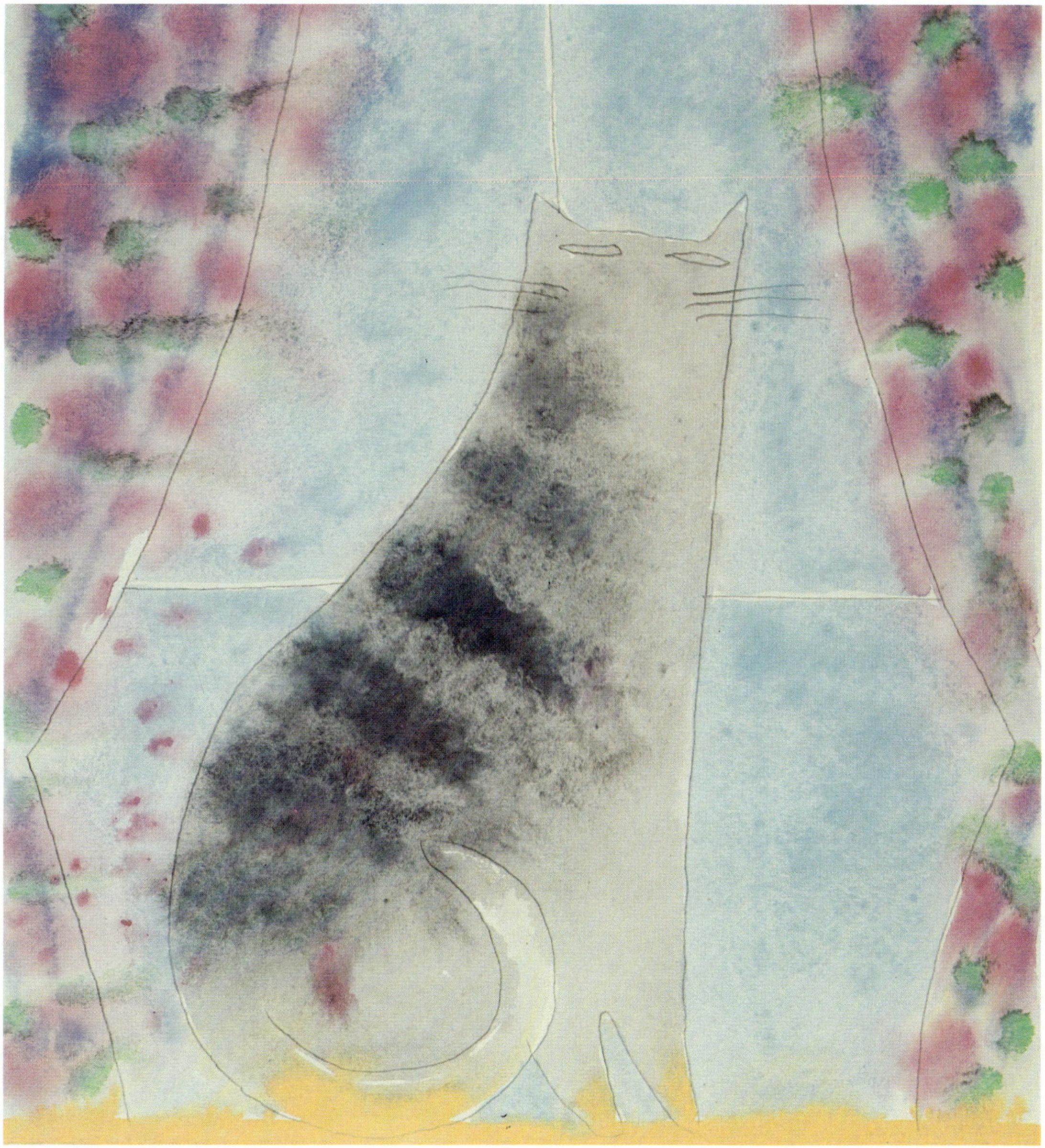

facing page 52

became more powerful, men also give them weaknesses; Achilles his heel, Superman his kryptonite. Brian Ferran has explored the vitality of ancient and modern (see Chapter 4) Irish mythology in a number of works from 1966 to the present day. These works, especially the *Táin* series of which illustration number 22 is a representative example, operate on several levels. Firstly they derive certain formal elements and colours from Celtic art; secondly they are committed works which admire the power of the old myths, epics and sagas, while, lastly, the artist is able to stand back far enough to be able to see the funny, even the ludicrous side of the myths. The wild exaggeration of the prose description of Cúchulainn, the Hound of Ulster and hero of the Táin may have been composed to strike fear into the heart of enemies centuries ago but it now has a funny side to it. The work reproduced shows the heroes (or heroines) of the Táin as simple puppet-like figures. Their very rigidity and colourful verticality reminds us that totems and totem poles are not peculiar to the culture of the North American Indian.

John Vallely's figures are also generalised and symbolic and aspire to a kind of universal monumentality. Vallely (born 1941) shares, with George Campbell, a feel for music and he has made this the major theme in his work. Like Campbell he recognises that folk traditions in Ireland have parallels in other times and cultures, so although his painted figures are often of musicians playing fiddles, accordions and Uilleann pipes they stand for musicians and the language of music everywhere. These are not paintings of violent emotion but of a solemn grandeur which is expressed by the composition and the technique. *Trio*, 1973, (no 23) is typical of his paintings throughout the last decade. The figures are blocked out in a highly sculptural way; in this case creating a pyramidal composition, while in other paintings a similar pyramid massiveness is achieved within the form of only one figure. Another compositional shape which has sculptural overtones is the placing of a group of musicians in the horizontal rhythms of a frieze. John Vallely's handling of paint inclines to a heavy impasto. This can be so heavily modelled that, like the nudes of Frank Auerbach, the effect is of a low relief rather than a painting. At other times Vallely applies the paint in a drier fashion which in colour and in handling resembles the massing of landscape of Arthur Armstrong. While Vallely does paint other subjects, such as markets, country games and hunts, they are executed in a manner similar to the musician paintings and drawings which so permeate his whole being. In a logical extension to playing music and painting music subjects, John Vallely, with his wife Ethne, has produced and illustrated a book called *Sing a Song and Play It*.

Just as figurative subjects need not be particular renderings of one individual, neither do they need to refer to one place either. Vallely's work is closely bound up with the idea of expressing and conserving traditional folk values (it also accounts for the restricted progression in his work) while that of Cherith McKinstry was for many years concerned with universal themes of compassion and man's inhumanity to man. Cherith Boyd (she later married the well known Ulster architect Robert McKinstry) was born in 1928 and attended the Belfast College of Art at the same time as Blackshaw and Flanagan and has executed sculptural pieces in addition to producing

24 CHERITH McKINSTRY
Mary at Bethlehem
1962; oil on canvas; 77.5 x 99.3 cms; Ulster Museum collection

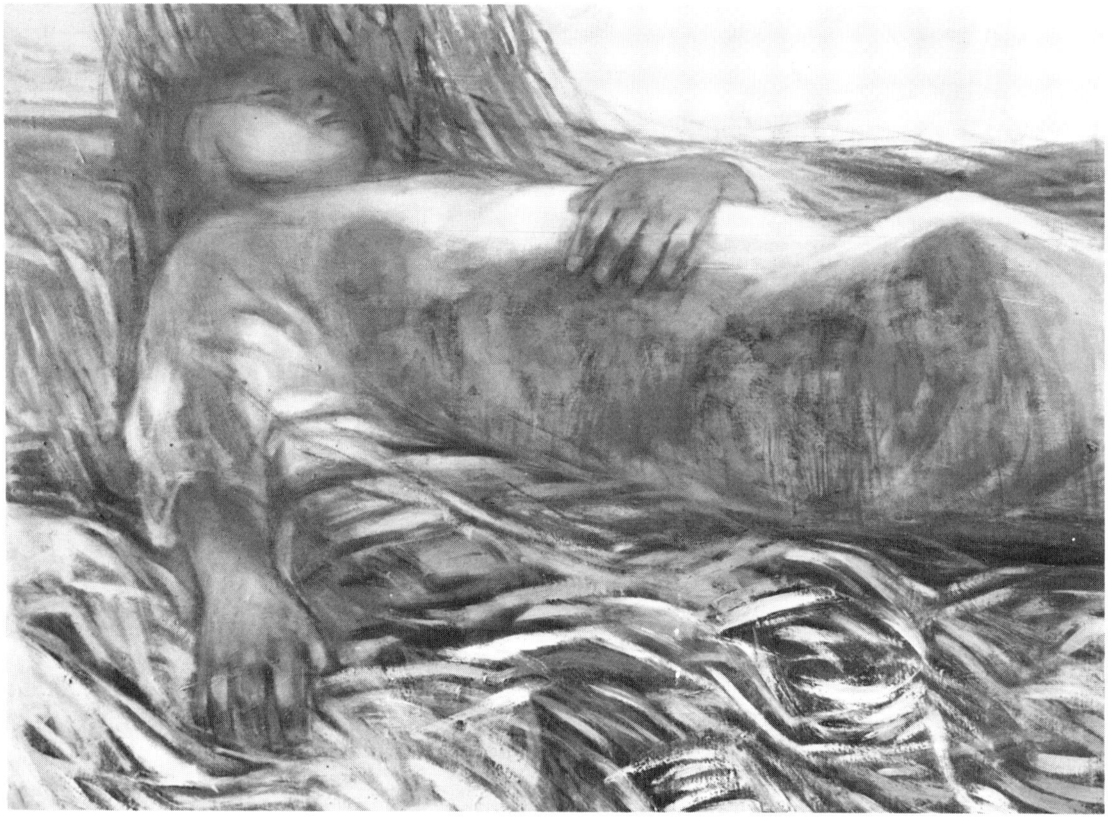

some memorable painted images. *Mary at Bethlehem* of 1962 is one of a number of paintings of this and related subjects, and as the reproduction (no 24) shows there are none of the usual trappings of a religious painting which would identify it as being uniquely religious in subject matter. Mary, on her rough, natural bed is a metaphor for the suffering mother everywhere. Another variant of this subject shows Mary, no longer asleep and composed but awake, crouching in bed, with a look of contemplation or even of concern for the future on her face. Well might she show concern, for millenia later humanity (sic) has merely refined its methods of cruelty. Cherith McKinstry's *They Don't Know What They're Doing* and *The Cover of 'Life' May 1968* show the common man being tortured, humiliated, but not totally destroyed by men in uniform. The latter work, derived from a Vietnam photograph used by *Life* magazine is more specific than most of her work. In addition to these themes Cherith McKinstry's paintings have explored more directly religious subjects to such as *Christ Crucified*, landscapes, and more recently a number of studies of single objects. In these, her large rounded forms have been replaced by a more compact unity (influenced by Charles Brady), yet her 'dry' brushstrokes remain.

A wide range of themes come and go in the paintings of George Campbell, but whether the paintings are of fishermen, musicians, exotic emblems or of his friends, the unifying threads are those of rhythmic time and vibrant colour (see pages 18 and 19). A painting like *African Objects* which won Campbell the first prize in the 1962 Open Painting Exhibition, has affinities with some aspects of cubism in the way in which the masks, drums, shields and spears form a flattened network of overlapping planes of paint. There is also a link in that Picasso, even before cubism, was drawn to the, until then, unappreciated savage beauty of non-Western forms. Campbell's work is also reminiscent of aspects of Braque and Matisse but not to the extent of their being direct influences: nor is his work as programmatic as some of the early masterpieces of modern art. In other paintings such as *Blind Flamenco Guitarist* there is an extremely forceful use of dark slashing stokes which contrasts with the almost dazzlingly bright highlights. Yet again, as in a number of street musician paintings, there is a solid austerity and massiveness which pre-dates and surpasses the handling of similar subject matter by John Vallely. Campbell's paintings exude a sense of vitality and sometimes of primitive energy. There is also that rare thing in art: a feeling of friendship is communicated to the viewer, as if Campbell is saying 'These are people, places, and things that make me feel excited, I want to share it.' And generally this comes across, even if some works are somewhat conventionalised. The exhibition of almost one hundred of his paintings of *Friends and Acquaintances 1944-74* in Belfast in 1975 revealed many stylistic facets in his work. Some of the gypsies and travelling men were dark brooding studies; predictably the dancers and some musicians were bright and multi-coloured. Indeed some of the latter were a little too close to the kind of Spanish scenes the tourists buy. A few, like the portrait of Paddy Maloney of the Chieftains, were remarkably economic in line and colour and throughout there was a keen feeling for people as public personalities. The very best, often the most symbolic, were of the private persons behind the public mask, for example in the portraits of French, Spanish and Hungarian clowns and the mime Marcel Marceau. It was no surprise that the show should also include portraits of his old friend, the painter Gerard Dillon, *Gerard Dillon, painter* (*1*) (no 25) is an extremely sensitive and compassionate tribute to the man whom James White once said was 'the clown in his own pictures'.

Dillon, who was born in 1916 and died in 1971 is also discussed in *Art in Ulster 1*, but as one of the major Irish artistic talents of the century some of his themes, styles and preoccupations must be outlined here. And outlined is all it can be, for in addition to his immensely prolific output, Dillon was a restless experimenter, often working on different works in various styles, techniques and media simultaneously. At the time when this book picks up the narrative of Ulster art in the late 1950s the artist was still resident in London, whence he had gone in 1945, and was producing work seemingly as traditional as *The Yellow Bungalow* (no 26) and abstract pieces composed of paint, sand, burnt string and any other material which offered an artistic

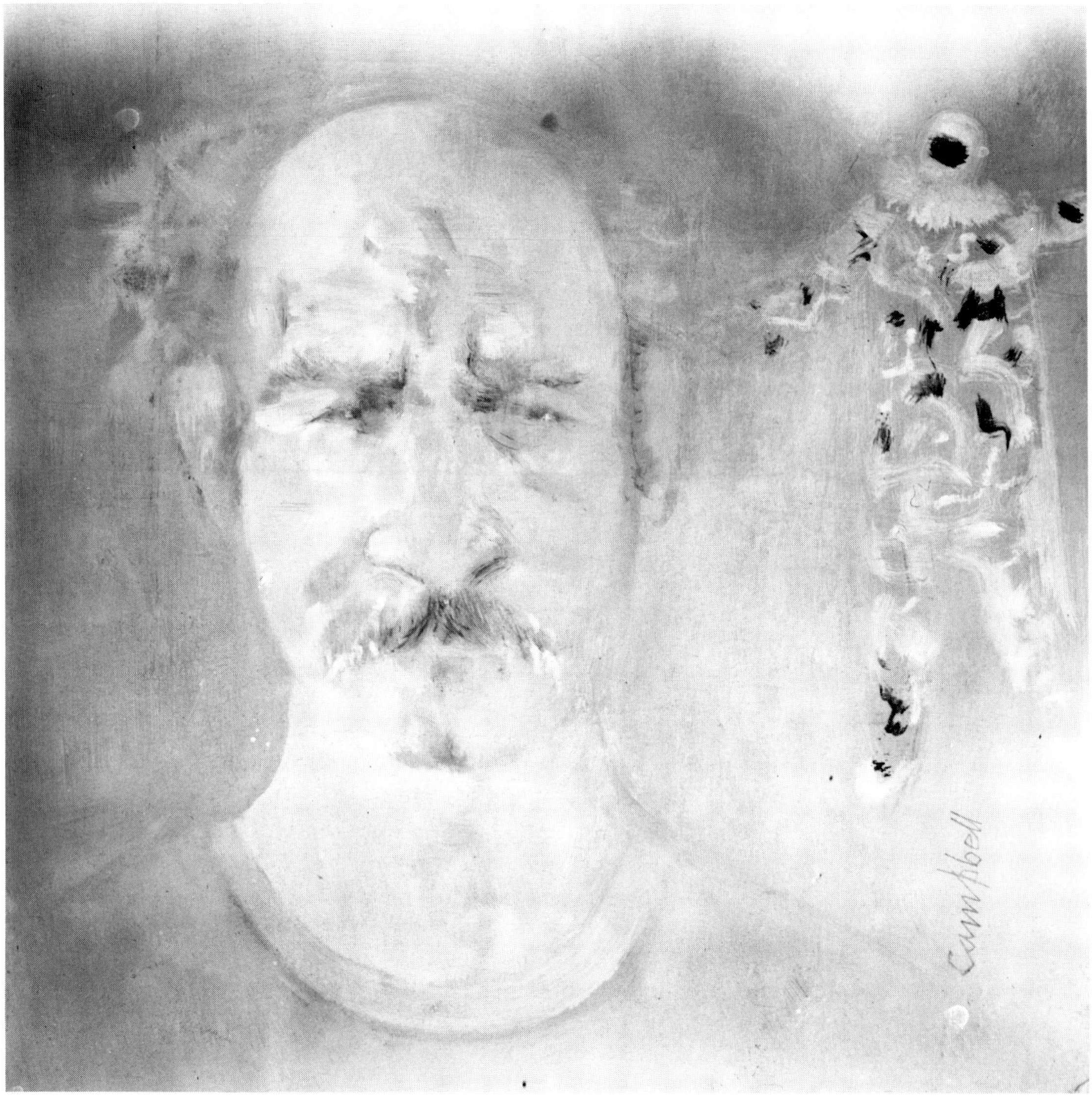

25 GEORGE CAMPBELL
Gerard Dillon, Painter [*1*]
c1971; oil on hardboard; 31.0 x 30.1 cms; Ulster Museum collection

26 GERARD DILLON
The Yellow Bungalow
c1954; oil on canvas; 76.8 x 81.2 cms; Ulster Museum collection

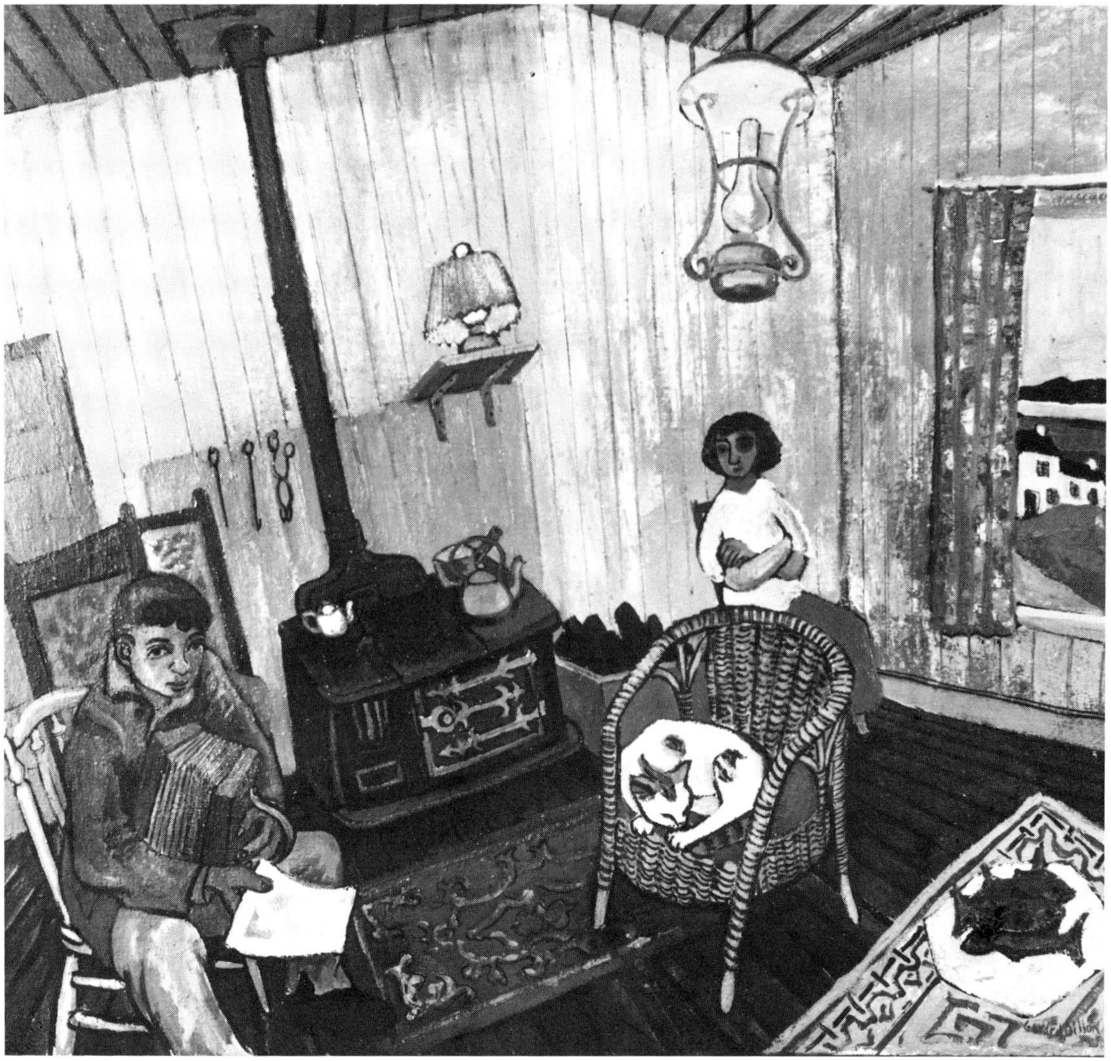

potential. This apparent contradiction was typical of the man. Many writers and friends of the artist have used the word 'innocent' when describing Gerard Dillon, but this does not imply that he was an untutored primitive. Rather his innocence was one of curiosity in exploring as many aspects of art and life as he could. To this end he happily boiled up old gloves and boots (the press had a field day) when he wanted to introduce leather into his works; he etched, he sewed and wove. He painted in a representational manner when that seemed appropriate and made abstract pieces when they served his purpose. And that purpose was often one of sheer exuberance, expressed not only at the level of technique but more so at the level of imagery. *The Yellow Bungalow* [5] refers back to the extremely strong figurative oils from the early 1940s onwards in which simply defined and seemingly trite subjects are raised to a kind of heroic stature. It can be seen in *The Fish Eaters* (1946), *The Cottage Gable* (*Two Youths*) *Connemara* (1956) and in interiors, sometimes complex, as in the multiple perspective of *Self Contained Flat* (1953); sometimes simple as in *Connelly's Bar Inishlaken* of 1956. The figures and objects in *The Yellow Bungalow* have a natural dignity and strength while the highly personalised rendering of the perspective conveys both a counterpoint of rhythm and also that sense of the imagination that Dillon held so dear.

Many of the figurative works also employ pictorial space in which components of the scene, fishermen, hookers and curraghs, horses and cottages are placed on top of each other rather than in receding planes of conventional linear perspective. These works have something in common with both the form and the spirit of the 'real' primitive painters such as the Tory Island artists or even George Campbell's mother, the remarkable nonagenarian artist Gretta Bowen. At the same time they owe a debt to the handling of space in Celtic Art with figures ranged in horizontal bands, and this serves to remind us that Dillon's work embodies a symbolic spirituality like that of Celtic Art where the mysteries of life, death and personal relations are openly expressed. [6] Some of the fantasy pictures such as *Glove Bird* and *Sea Beast* (both of 1962) or the collage, *A Bird's World* reveal a delight in 'creating' animals such as are found in mediaeval bestiaries. A curious feature of many of Gerard Dillon's pictures is that where two figures (either a man and woman, or more generally two men or youths) are shown, a space separates them even when they are supposedly together. This adds a note of detachment, almost of melancholy; it is the other side of the artist's mask.

One of his most celebrated themes concerns the clown, the pierrot, the harlequin. For centuries the clown has been recognised as a symbol of two quite different moods. Beneath the painted face or the smiling mask is supposed to lie a man of sorrows. Even a funny clown like Chaplin inspires a feeling of pathos in his audience, for comedy is never far from tragedy and it is said that clowns aspire to play Hamlet. When the master of horror Lon Chaney was asked what would frighten him, he replied, 'A clown at midnight.' During the last three centuries artists have recognised the ambiguities in the image of the clown and in this century Picasso's Harlequin family and Georges Rouault's tragic clowns have developed this theme. Gerard Dillon's pierrots and clowns often have dark natures at odds with their makeup, and most of the pierrots of the late 1960s have completely blank faces behind the masks. But the pierrots, like the artist himself, are capable of many moods and actions. Sometimes the pierrot is a detached viewer of events, at times the master of ceremonies or the chief protagonist of the action. Many are extremely funny, especially those with a large cheerful sun's face in them, for example *Everday Life* which has Pierrot contemplating a dog pretending to be dead while the sun dries his stylised washing. Others, such as *The Past Keeps Behind* which shows a tragic pierrot shunning a priest-like clown whose robe has grinning faces on it, have a grim poetry about them. Darkest of all is *The Brothers* (c1967) in which a pierrot slumps in grief onto the ground, beneath which are three layers of coffins each containing a grinning skeleton. This, like all his works, has strong links with the artist's personal life, a strange mixture of the hilarious and the tragic, recorded with honesty by Dillon. This contrast of gaiety, desolation and the macabre is a constant factor in most folk art, as well as in high art such as Beckett's plays.[7] Illustration number 27 shows two figures, together yet apart. The reds and greens of the sky and landscape are warm yet oppressive. The costumes and the spotted animal seem cheerful but the mood overall is one of contemplation and stillness. These late pierrots are executed in a flat cut-out fashion with the landscape structures created by dragging a comb through the broad areas of paint against which cavort the collage figures of the clowns and birds, nuns and animals. If there is fault to be

27 GERARD DILLON
Pierrots and Evening Sun
1967/8; watercolour and gouache; 32 x 57 cms; private collection

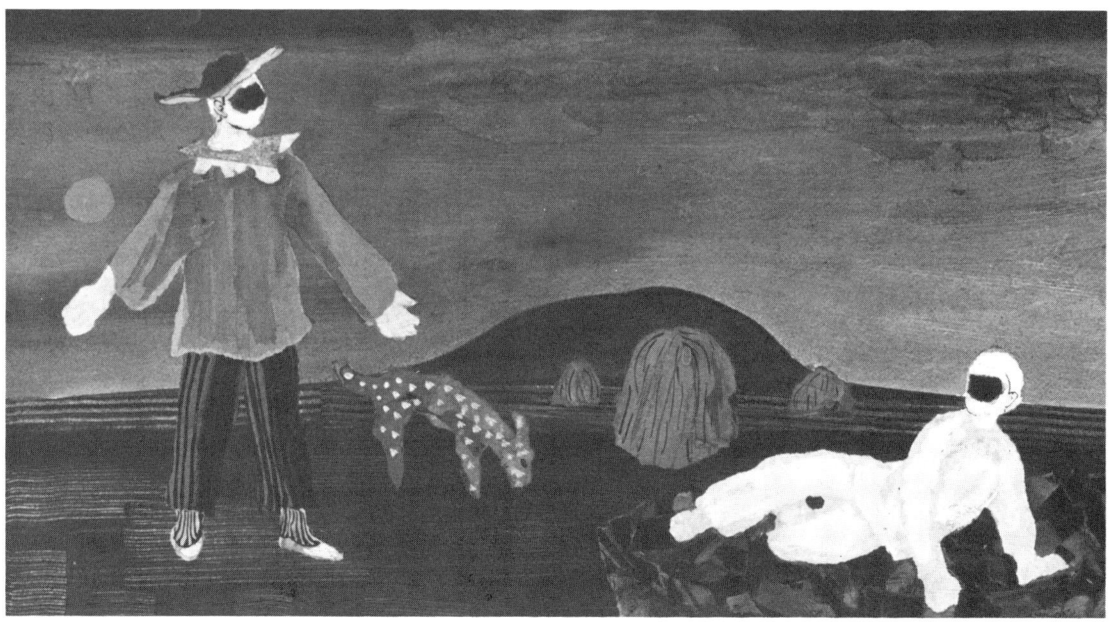

found in Dillon's vast output it is perhaps in his eclecticism. Sometimes he never worked through a theme (especially in the last twenty years of his life) preferring to move on to something different rather than towards an even more succinct distillation of what his talents could produce.

The name of Daniel O'Neill (1920-1974) is often linked with the other Ulster 'individualists' such as Dillon, Campbell and Middleton. This is partly due to his style and partly to his lack of formal art education. Unlike the others, however, his output was never as prolific and his reputation was made by works which more properly fall within the brief of the companion volume to this. In fact he left Ireland for London in 1958, returning only in 1971. Between 1952 and 1970 he did not exhibit in his native city of Belfast, but when his one man show at the McClelland Galleries opened in 1970 it was evident that the extraordinary luminance of his colour was still to the fore. Demure and elongated figures inhabited a warm, sunny landscape where once the environment had been harsher and viewed more oppressively. Dan O'Neill was certainly a Romantic artist; he cited Matisse, Vlaminck, Soutine and Rouault as influences, but the remarkable resonances of his colours, whether in 'dark' pictures or 'light' were evidence of an original talent.

The figurative motifs in the work of Colin Middleton are legion, and in the period from 1957 to the present day the spectator can see both the wide range of figurative elements he employs and also the consistency with which these elements, which often emerge initially in the 1930s and 1940s are given a context. As mentioned in Chapter 1, the landscape can be more than simply a terrain; for Colin Middleton it can be the repository of, and the vehicle for his archetype. 'What gives my work continuity is the constancy of the female archetype, no matter how many the disguises, the mother figure, the mother and child, the reclining figure, the single tree against the hill.' [8] And her disguises are many indeed. She may be a stately, sculptural form in sedate tones (for example *Ash* of 1967) she may be an Expressionist and voluptuous creature, as in *Hunter's Moon* (1951). Interestingly enough the full breasted female of this picture is atypical although her type appeared years before in *Fortune Teller* (1941) and *Columbus* (1947) for just as Middleton admires the Flemish primitives his female figures tend to have the small, high breasts associated with the work of Northern European painters or of the Minoan civilisation. Middleton's archetype may be cruelly mocking, like the Senorita with a gun in *Good Morning, Mr Goya* (1957) who has the assurance of an Ian Fleming heroine. Or she may be from the other side of the Mediterranean like the Eastern beauties of some of the untitled works of the 1970s. She will be from any place and she will be painted in many ways. *Black Madonna* (1963) (no 28) is one of her more abstracted manifestations. A dark female totem, she is surrounded by ribbons of colour, bands which are essentially Middleton and which can almost be read like music. Middleton also produced extremely linear figures which recall Klee; and the oriental figures mentioned above are the opposite, being built up out of overlapping folded layers of pigment. He also returned in the 1970s to an extremely representational form of surrealism where his women are small mannikins in chequered dresses dwarfed by their sur-

28 COLIN MIDDLETON
Black Madonna
1963; oil; 91.4 x 91.4 cms; Arts Council of Northern Ireland collection

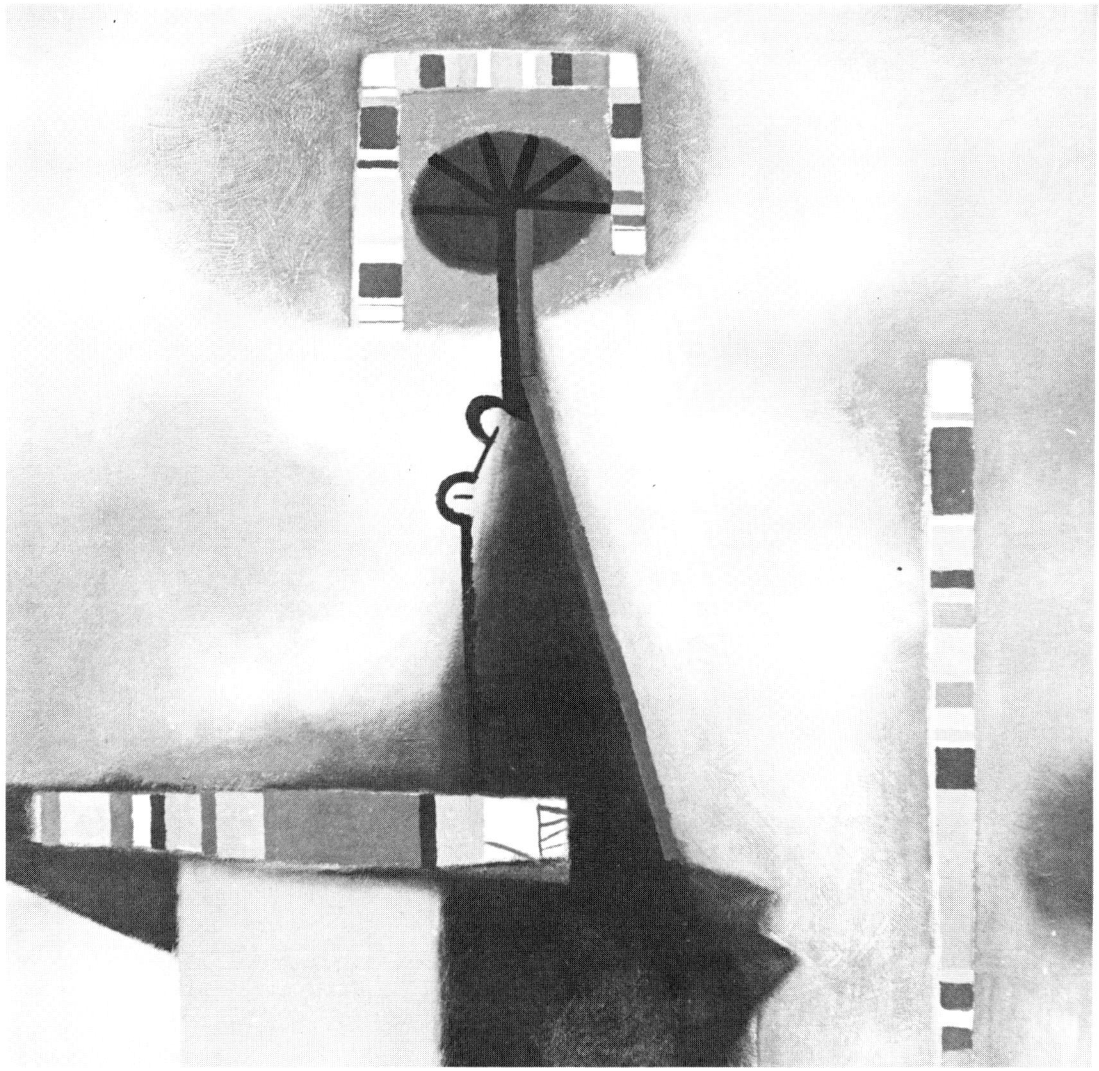

roundings. Like a witch with her familiars, the Middleton woman usually has something with her. It may be only a striped pole but more often it is a bird; sometimes an exotic bird like a cockatoo, more often a wide eyed owl, a seabird or a dark scavenger bird. 'The woman's a tree; the woman's a flower, the breast is an apple, the apple is an egg, the egg is a bird.' [9]

Female archetypes, and other symbols derived from the work of Jung are not unique to Middleton, and the work of James Millar, a young Belfast painter, is both dedicated to and derived from Carl Gustaf Jung's interpretation of the unconscious. The majority of the works he has exhibited since 1967 are monochromatic although more recently he has incorporated colour, somewhat uneasily, into his pictures. Many of his works are reversals of the traditional drawn image in that the lines are white against a black background. This graphic technique, more commonly associated with a technique like scraperboard, adds a surreal dimension to his tableaux of interiors with male and female figures. If Jung provides the subject inspiration then his time owes much to Picasso. In 1976 he

29 JAMES MILLAR
Illustration for 'Gulliver's Travels'
1976; photo-lithograph; 28.5 x 44 cms; reproduced by courtesy of Appletree Press

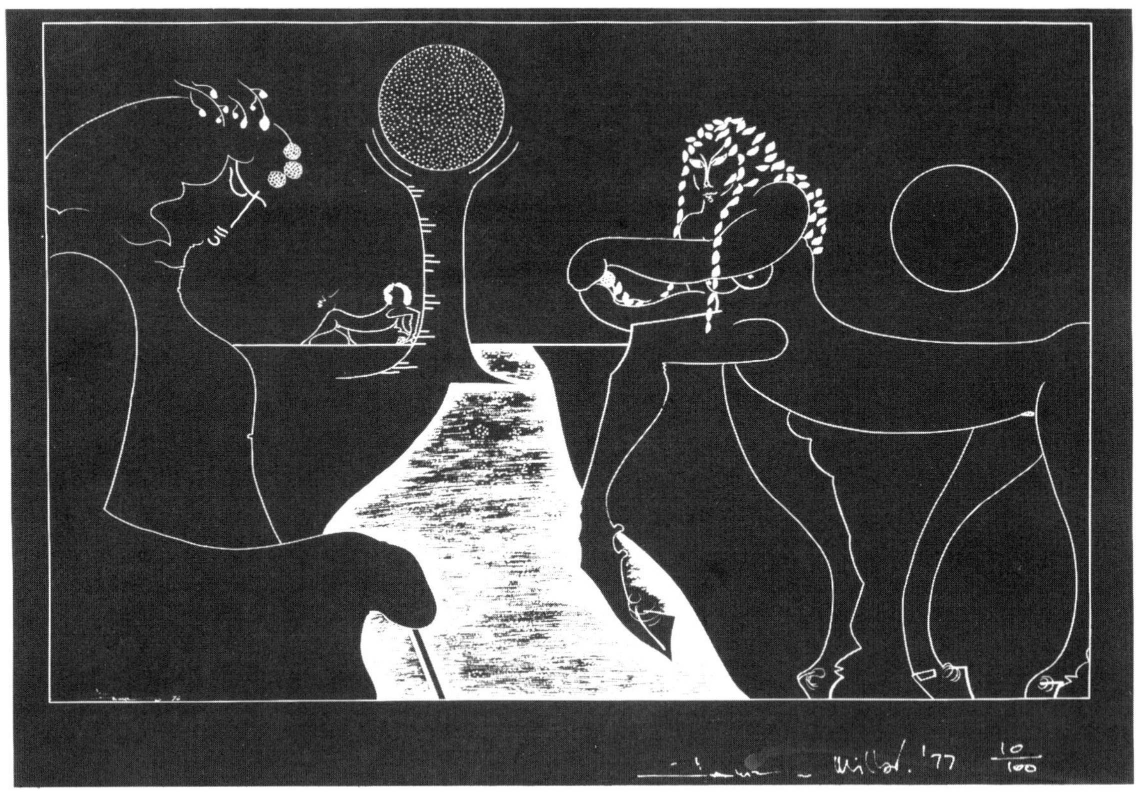

30 JACK PAKENHAM
Swanage Honeymoon
1974; ink drawing on paper; collection the artist

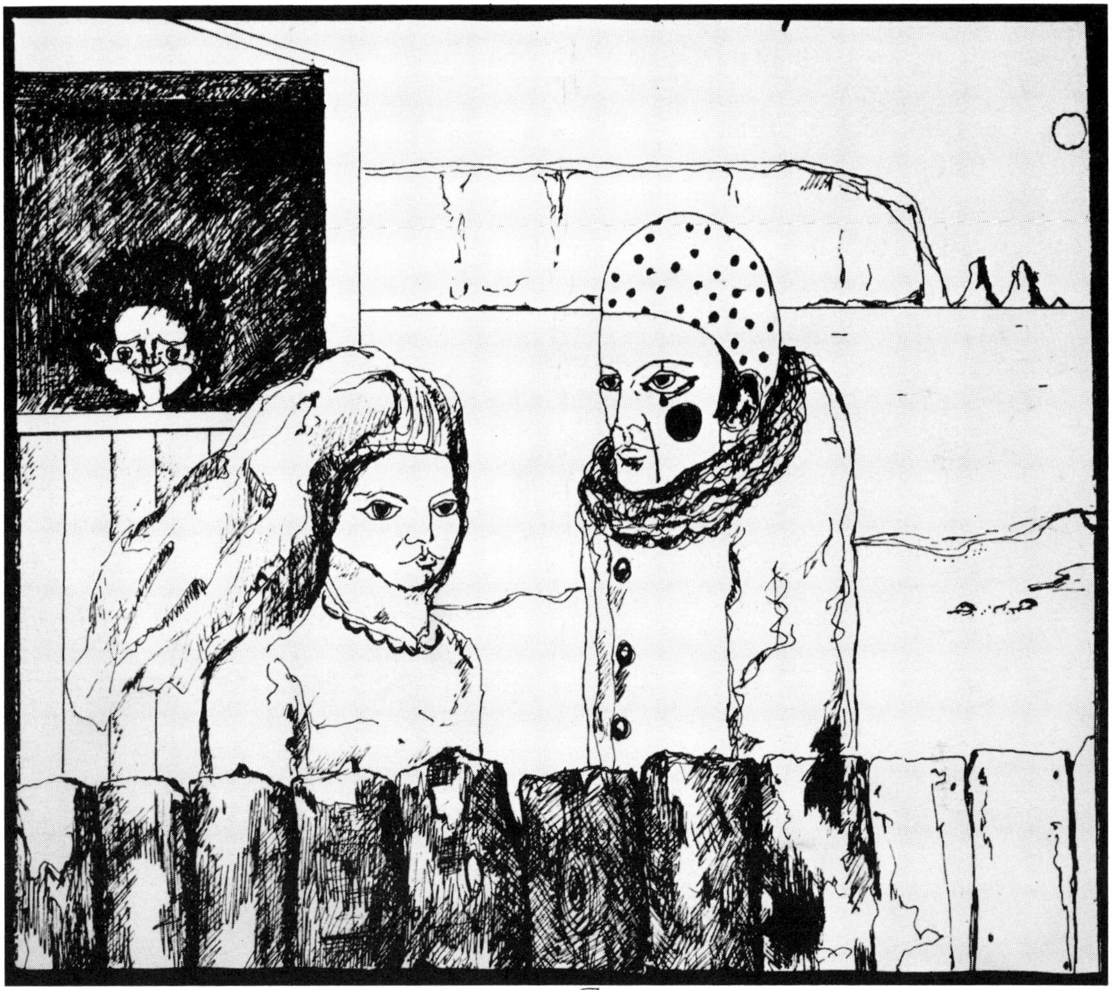

was commissioned to illustrate a locally published special edition of Swift's *Gulliver's Travels*,[10] from which this illustration is chosen (no 29). He has recently exhibited with Malcolm Bennett, Graham Gingles, Jack Pakenham and Paul Yates under the group name of Penta.

Like Group 63, to which Bennett, Gingles and Pakenham belonged at various times between 1963 and 1973, Penta is not a formal grouping of artists with a single manifesto. Indeed, although various loose formations of artists with similar aims or imagery (eg the Troubled Image

Group) have come and gone, no strongly didactic group of artists following a common aim or style has emerged in Northern Ireland during the last twenty years. Penta's statement of intentions argued 'that the particular kind of work which deliberately sets out to intrigue, disturb or even aggravate the viewer in an attempt to jog him out of his ordinary everyday perceptions and responses has been seriously neglected by the majority of Ulster painters'. The point is disputable, because the best work by major Ulster artists intrigues, disturbs and extends the viewer's experiences even if the subject matter is not overtly fantastic or symbolic. Admittedly, a lot of the paintings which originate here do extend a conventional cosiness, but that charge could not be levelled against the work of John Pakenham.

Artist/poet John (or Jack) Pakenham (born 1938) uses motifs and images which can, and do, have a double meaning. During the 1960s his figures were Expressionist and contradictory. Dark eyed androgynes stared moodily out of landscapes, interiors and environments which were altered by their presence. Who these watchers were remained an enigma but throughout all of Pakenham's work there exists a feeling both of suffering and of aggression. In the early 1970s he exhibited a series entitled *Clown and Bride*. Like Gerard Dillon, Pakenham understood the multiple metaphors that exist behind the clown's costume, the bride and the ventriloquist's doll. In a sense all are dolls or puppets who have a malevolent life of their own (see page 135). As can be seen from illustration number 30 these figures are heirs to a tradition which includes originators as different as Dillon and Federico Fellini. Pakenham has also published poetry and painted landscapes, the latter belonging to the Northern European Romantic tradition of landscapes made mysterious by winter or moon or early morning light. Some recent works are discussed on page 135.

One of the painters who has been associated with both Group 63 and Penta is Graham Gingles who was born in 1943. In the late 1960s his work showed a sensitivity for colour and form. Large, simple figurative shapes were defined by a loose but strong line, and the whole was held together by a vigorous range of colours applied with confidence. In the 1970s he has exhibited in many group shows showing that he had simplified his forms as he moved more into prints, assemblages and other three dimensional work (see Chapter 3). Another painter who has pursued a path towards a synthesis between colour and the figurative reference is Denis McBride (born 1939). It is no insult to say that many of McBride's works are excellent examples of pattern making because he has long demonstrated an ability to juxtapose formal shapes and colours to produce a satisfying two dimensional composition. Unlike simple design pattern making McBride's canvases have a deeply emotional content. The works are a complete visual impression, they show the painter's relationship with person, place and object. This involves a large measure of stylization with the subjects, for example trees, flowers and bedrooms, reduced to a series of simplified shapes. The very simplification adds a monumentality to the forms. McBride's trees resembled cut outs; recalling the shapes and techniques of late Matisse. One of Denis McBride's tree variations *Trees III* is here (no 31) seen *in situ* as one of a large scale billboard series of poster-prints

31 DENIS McBRIDE
Trees III
c1968; billboard poster *in situ*

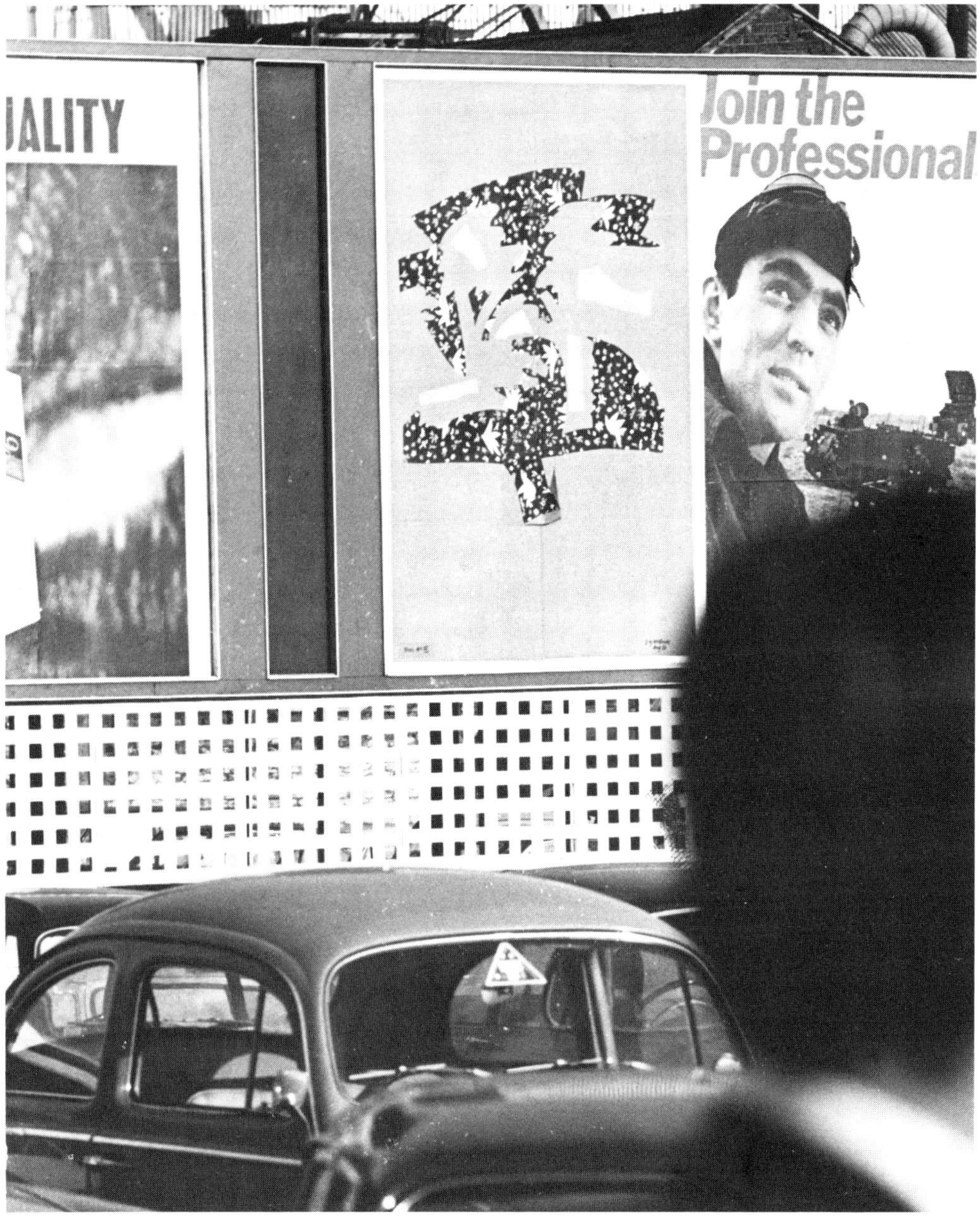

32 DENIS McBRIDE
Variation on Snowdrop IV
1967; acrylic on canvas; 121.7 x 137.6 cms; Ulster Museum collection

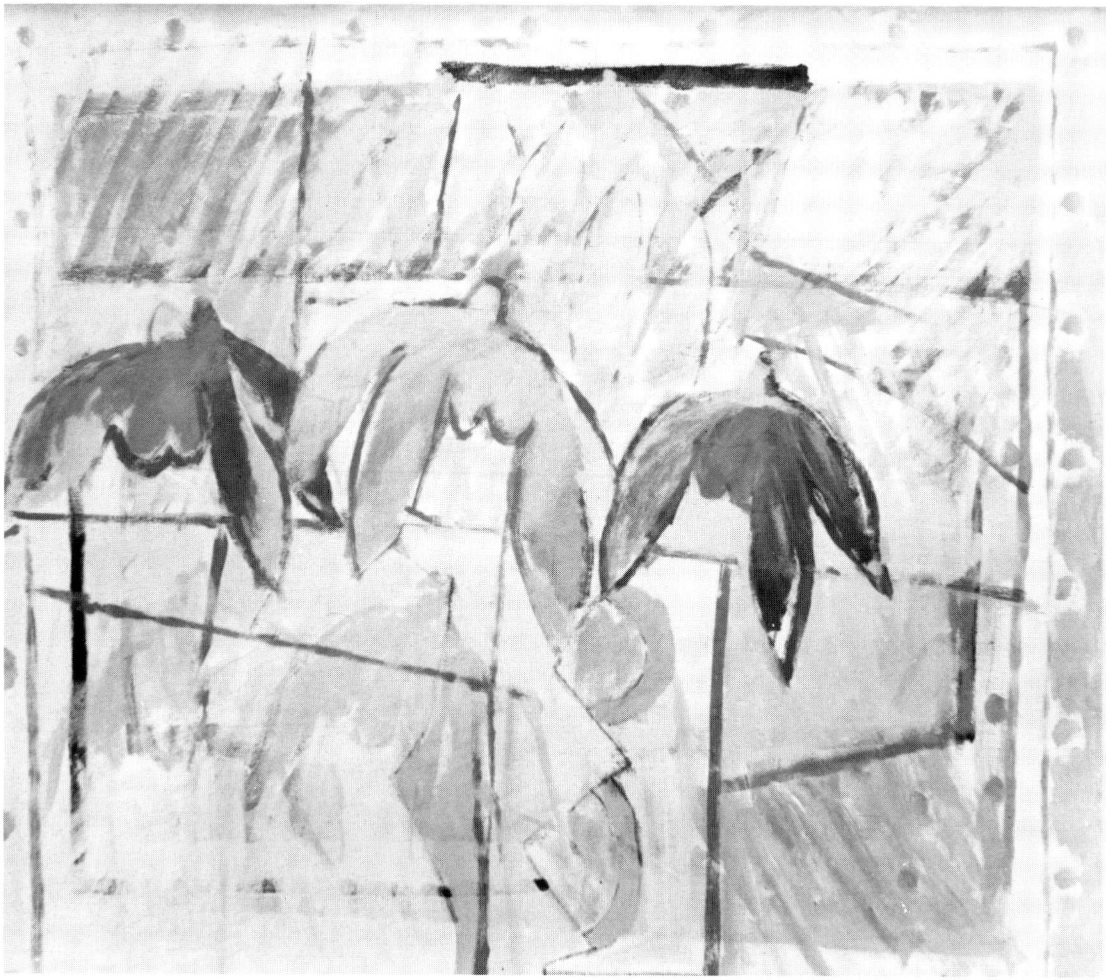

produced by the Arts Council of Northern Ireland in the *Celtic Triangle* travelling exhibition. Landscape is a fluid category and McBride has shown that it can include interiors such as the series *Landscape: Bed* where the patterns of bedclothes, quilts and wallpaper surround and enclose the stylised figures. These works reiterated the decorative flower/leaf motifs seen in his trees and in the often garish but successful colour contrasts. Flowers were a recurrent theme as may be seen in the *Variation on Snowdrops* theme of which illustration number 32 is an example. Simplified, open forms are located in expressively coloured areas producing a dramatic

33 WILLIAM SCOTT
Brown Still Life
1958; oil canvas; 89.5 x 99 cms; Ulster Museum collection

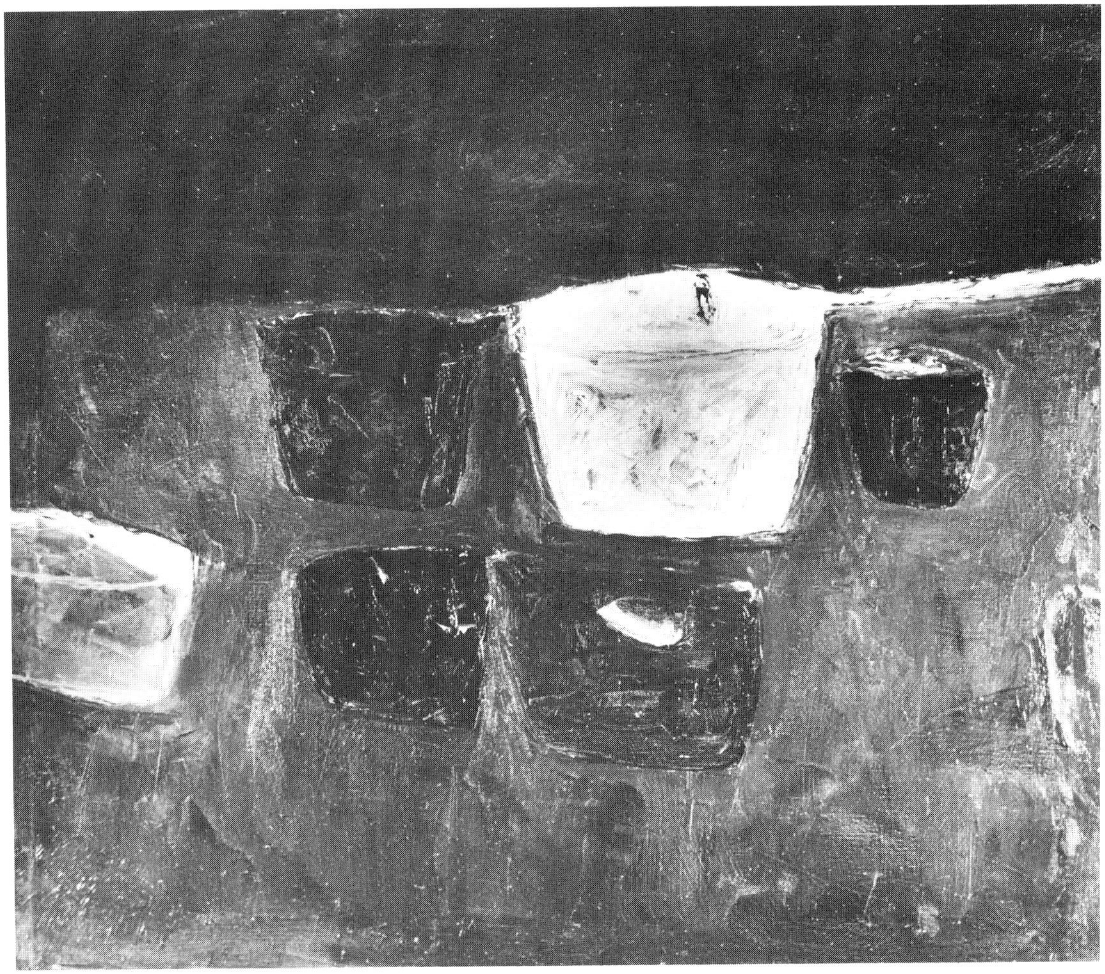

design. In recent years he has returned more to the human figure, and the impact of Synthetic Cubism has been replaced by a response to Expressionism as is evident from his recent De Kooning-like nudes and by the emotive shapes and subject matter of the work which is reproduced at the end of Chapter 4 on page 143.

The artists discussed up to this point have generally used the human figure as a starting point for their art, but there are others whose impetus is derived from a reaction to object and place rather than to man or animal. The senior figure in this group, and the Ulster painter with the biggest international reputation is William

34 WILLIAM SCOTT
Egypt Series No 3
1972; oil on canvas; 203.2 x 254 cms; Ulster Museum collection

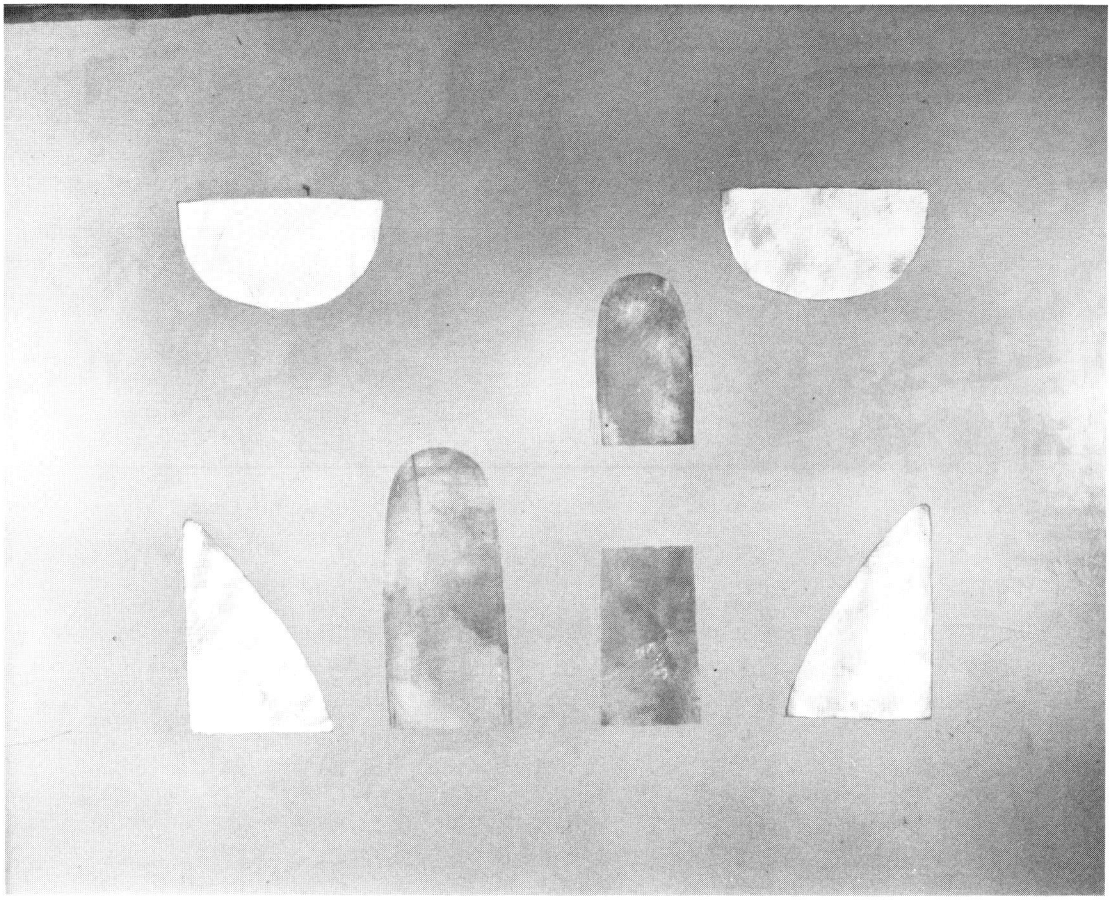

Scott. Because he was born in 1913, he is discussed in *Art in Ulster 1* and because he was born in Greenock in Scotland (but was brought up in Enniskillen, Co Fermanagh) Scotland rightly claims him for its own. Even so he has a right to be included in this volume because his work over the past two decades has achieved a stature and nobility that is unique. It also took until the late 1950s for his work to achieve public recognition in this province. With T P Flanagan, William Scott was fortunate in having Kathleen Bridle as art teacher and mentor when he was growing up in Fermanagh, and he acknowledges a debt to her having shown him Cézanne and later avant-gardists. Certainly his still lifes have that sense of monumentality and timelessness that one finds in Cézanne or Morandi. He can invest the most simple arrangement of objects like kitchen utensils or fruit with a sense of poetry. The heavy impasto of some of the works of the 1950s, for example *Brown Still Life* (*Pots and Pans*) of 1958 (no 33) has been superseded by a flat series of planes on which appear the simple outlines of the same few objects which continue to fascinate him. The pots and pans are amazingly concise statements, but lest their 'just so' precision of shape and colour seems restrictive it must be remembered that his art seems to grow richer the more minimal it becomes. As one critic summed it up,

> '... one feels at times as if Malevich or even Ben Nicholson had been radically revised by Rothko or even Whistler, for something akin to the hard-edge formalities of the first two has been beautifully transmuted by the tonal romanticism of the latter two.' [12]

In addition to the influence of individual artists such as Cézanne or Jean Dubuffet there are hints of the monumentality and sensuality which is to be found in the cultures of the ancient Celtic, archaic Greek and Egyptian past. From 1968 onwards he produced a number of works with titles and forms derived from his understanding of the essence of Egypt and Egyptian art. *Egypt Series No 3* of 1972 (no 34) is one such work, in which the immensely solid shapes are so well balanced that the rhythms they set up allow the forms, textures and colours to float serenely. His works have a heroic quality whether in a small still life or in the huge mural (2.74 x 14.02 metres) for Altnagelvin Hospital, Londonderry (begun 1959, installed 1961) which is, with F E McWilliam's *Princess Macha* sculpture for the same hospital, one of the major public works of this whole island.

In the past few years T P Flanagan has produced some interesting object paintings which are 'studies in stillness' (see page 13). The Arts Council of Northern Ireland has a superb pale watercolour of a window on whose sill sits a bowl and an old oil lamp, and recently he has executed some single flower studies including a few of a rose wrapped in transparent cellophane. These works have a symbolic value and are curiously disturbing, seeming to denote the past rather than the present.

'The past is a foreign country, they do things differently there' is L P Hartley's opening to *The Go Between*, and in many of the prints of Jim Allen we are shown a landscape of memory. Allen, born in 1941, is one of this province's best print makers and is at present in charge of the Endhouse Prints workshop established in the headquarters of the Arts Council of Northern Ireland. His paintings show the same draughtsmanship that is evident in his drawings and prints. Allen has worked in most techniques open to the printmaker including experimental techniques such as photo-colour etching (in which he executed an intricate, detailed and delicate print of the rooftops of Belfast), but the methods he prefers are etchings and aquatints. In the 1960s his works were influenced by Pop art, producing multiple images on the one plate or disjointed close-ups of objects. By 1970 his subject matter had become apparently more conventional with strongly representational images of landscapes, rooms and objects. Pop still had an influence in that several of the works were derived from old photographs. *Figures in a Landscape No 2* (no 35) combines a clarity of technique with a bleached or faded look to the figures who stand in the awkward posed way that

35 JAMES ALLEN
Figures in a Landscape II
1972; aquatint; 27.8 x 38.1 cms

one sees in old snapshots. The bleaching out of tone can also be seen in prints of the Middle East like *Dome of the Rock*, so that some areas are highly lighted, others silhouetted and precise details are made more intricate by having light, empty areas around them. The play of light and shade is very evident in the landscapes and prints of buildings in landscapes and the very choice of images is highly Romantic with clouds or moonlight sometimes apparent. Pop art gave the everyday object a new significance. Jim Allen often concentrates on objects or effects which he explores in paint, pencil and print. The aquatint *Sea Pebbles* is both precise and mysterious, qualities which can be seen in a screenprint version of *Room with Chair* (no 36) where the broad areas of colour add to, rather than detract from its other-worldliness. Another notable image has been a wave seen at the instant of its breaking.

As has been already mentioned, Charles Oakley (born 1925) has long been concerned with the

36 JAMES ALLEN
Room with Chair
1976; screenprint on paper;
42 x 60 cms

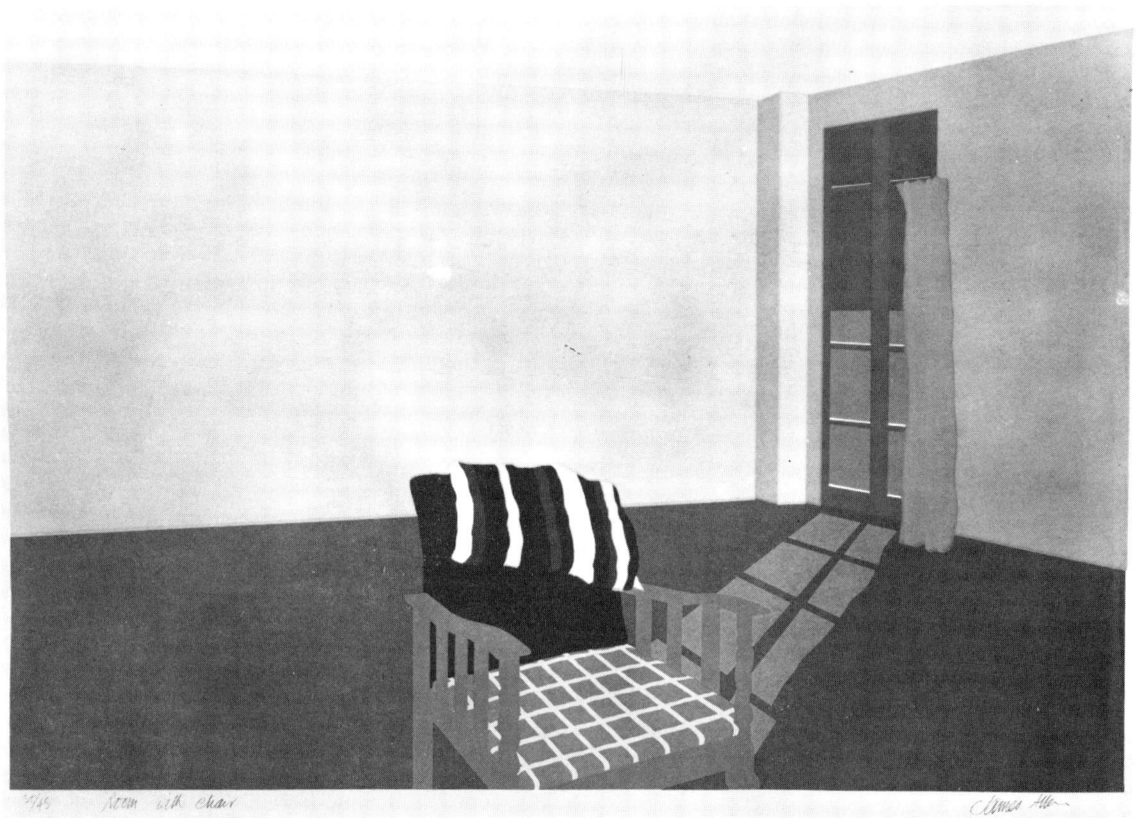

mystery that surrounds objects and places seen afresh. His works after he came to Ulster in 1962 began with delicately representational studies of decaying or merely stopped machinery. The water colours among these were derived from the surreal images that Paul Nash had created out of his paintings of crippled Luftwaffe aircraft and the general detritus of war. Oakley's *Princess Maud* of the mid 1960s showed the beached and broken ship's engine room stranded in an empty landscape lit by a Paul Nash sun. In the early 1970s his style became more naturalistic, but the effect was anything but natural. His ruined cottages have already been discussed (see page 32) but he also did a series of graveyard scenes at least two of which, entitled *A View of Ulster '71* (no 37) had ironic local overtones not discernible from the straight-faced image. Charles Oakley's preoccupation with the unheard resonances of place may be understood from the title of one painting — *The Room in which Van Gogh died, 29 July 1890*. Using a technique and motifs which more and more echoed Renaissance models, he produced interiors with empty boxes,

37 CHARLES OAKLEY
A View of Ulster '71
1971; acrylic on canvas; 122 x 122 cms; Arts Council of Northern Ireland collection

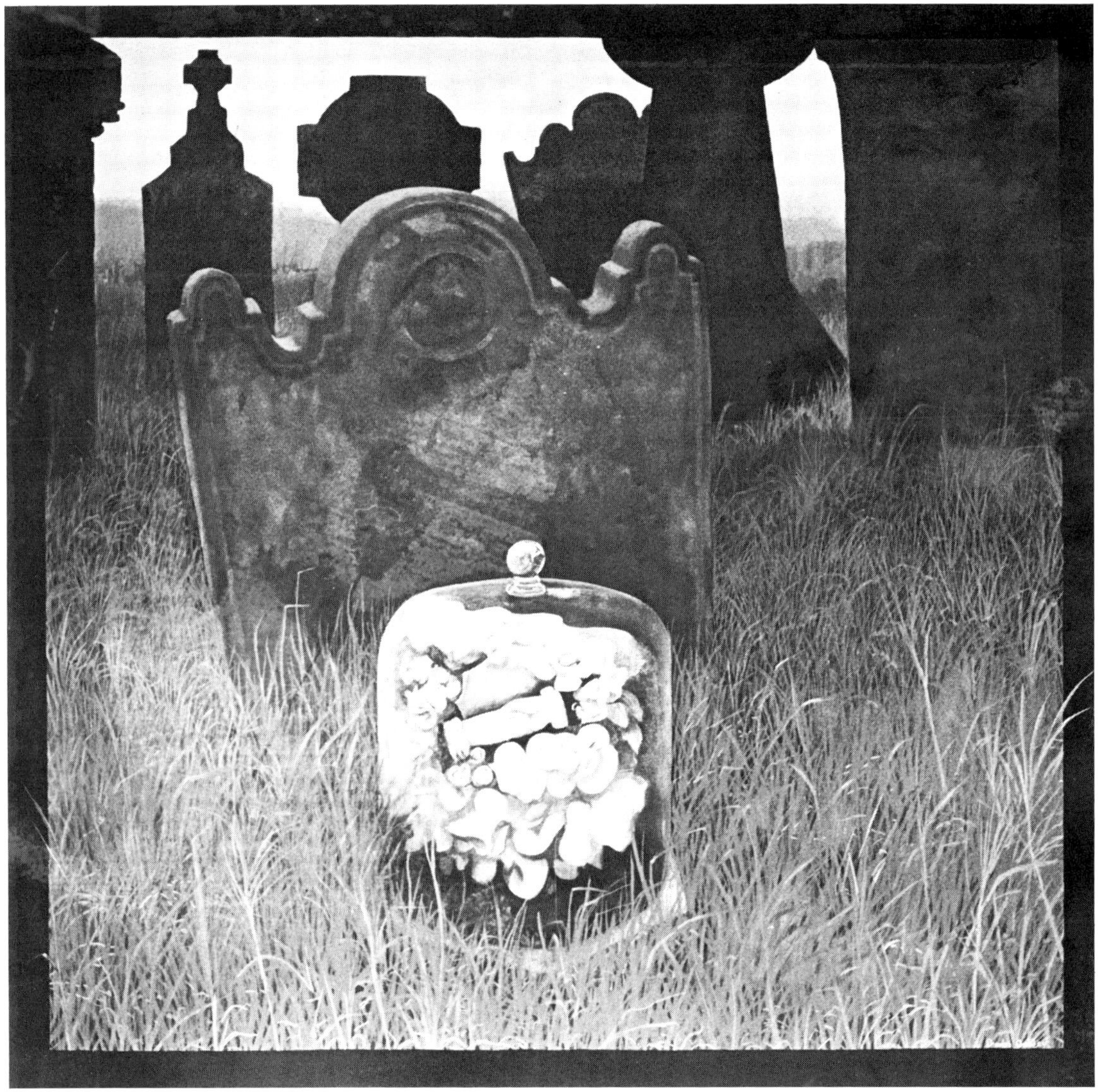

38 CHARLES OAKLEY
I Don't Want to Go Any Further
1970; acrylic on canvas; 122 x 91.4 cms; collection the artist

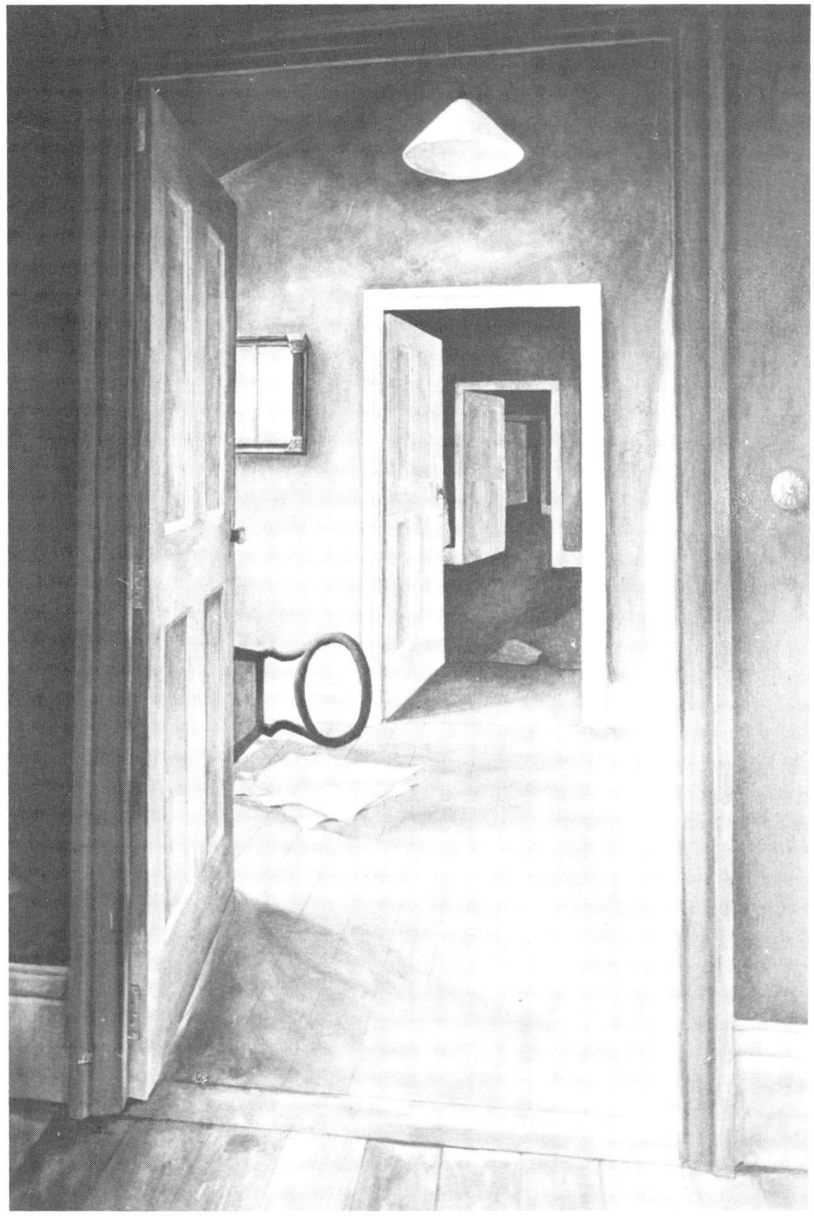

discarded papers and doors ajar. The silence and the ambiguities surrounding the subjects were oppressive as may be seen in illustration number 38. Another artist with the same surrealist sensibility is Pat Coogan (see page 132) who was a student at the Art and Design Centre, Belfast during the time that Oakley taught there.

Now that abstract and post-representational art is common (if not yet totally accepted), paradoxically it is representational and hyper-realistic art that seems to be new, especially as this style is used to focus our attention on details or angles of view and attitude that were not part and parcel of the academic aesthetic. Another young ex-Art and Design Centre graduate, Carol Graham (born 1951) works in an almost Pre-Raphaelite style but her framing of the subjects she paints is determined by the angles and perspectives created by camera lenses at varying focal lengths. This, a *Goat's Head* (available as an Arts Council poster), is seen in extreme close up, while *The Girl's Skirt* (no 39) shows a cut off view from above. Several of her works have been of dolls and dresses in gingham checks. Ulster can boast at least one artist who was producing seemingly realistic paintings before the pendulum swung back to accept figurative works into the artistic canon again. Michael Baird (born 1928) has exhibited little in over a decade but the paintings he showed between 1957 and 1965 were deceptively simple but actually complex studies of elemental landscapes, and nature smoothed stones, animal skulls and bones. These were highly-charged Romantic works and Baird's nearest local equivalent in this decade is Stephen Harper, who paints and draws table top still lifes of sprouting potatoes, shells, boxes and feathers with considerable intensity. The strictly representational mode may be used to various ends including the scientifically descriptive. Even with all the advances in colour photography the artist may still be called upon to illustrate medical, zoological or botanical subjects. Raymond Piper is a skilful, conventional portraitist, but for the past ten years he has pursued and painted orchids. Botanical illustration is a highly exacting discipline yet artistic beauty (and even symbolism) need not be sacrificed despite the objectivity that the discipline requires, as may be seen in Piper's study of *Marsh Helleborine* (no 40) done in 1972.

So far the works and careers examined have generally derived their depiction of figures and space from a Western tradition, although, as already noted, Cubism looked to non-European prototypes for reference. At the level of convention the Middle East provided the Romantic artists with subject matter like odalisques, sheikhs and wild eyed Arab stallions but it was not until the end of last century that artists began to learn from the handling of pictorial space, anatomy, symbolism and artistic aesthetic of civilisations as diverse as Japan and Polynesia. Since then many artists have looked to the East for inspiration; an inspiration that extends to religious beliefs, life styles and philosophy as well as to the different artistic lessons that can be learned. Eastern art may be representational but it can also be so formalised and symbolic that its subjects seem abstract to Western eyes.

In the 1968 Open Painting Exhibition the English artist and scientist Peter Lloyd-Jones won a supplementary prize for a painting entitled *An Illustration to the Indian Musical Mode Madhmadvani Ragini*. It was of a few coloured

39 CAROL GRAHAM
The Girl's Skirt
1977; acrylic and oil on canvas; 39.4 x 39.4 cms; An Chomhairle Ealáion collection

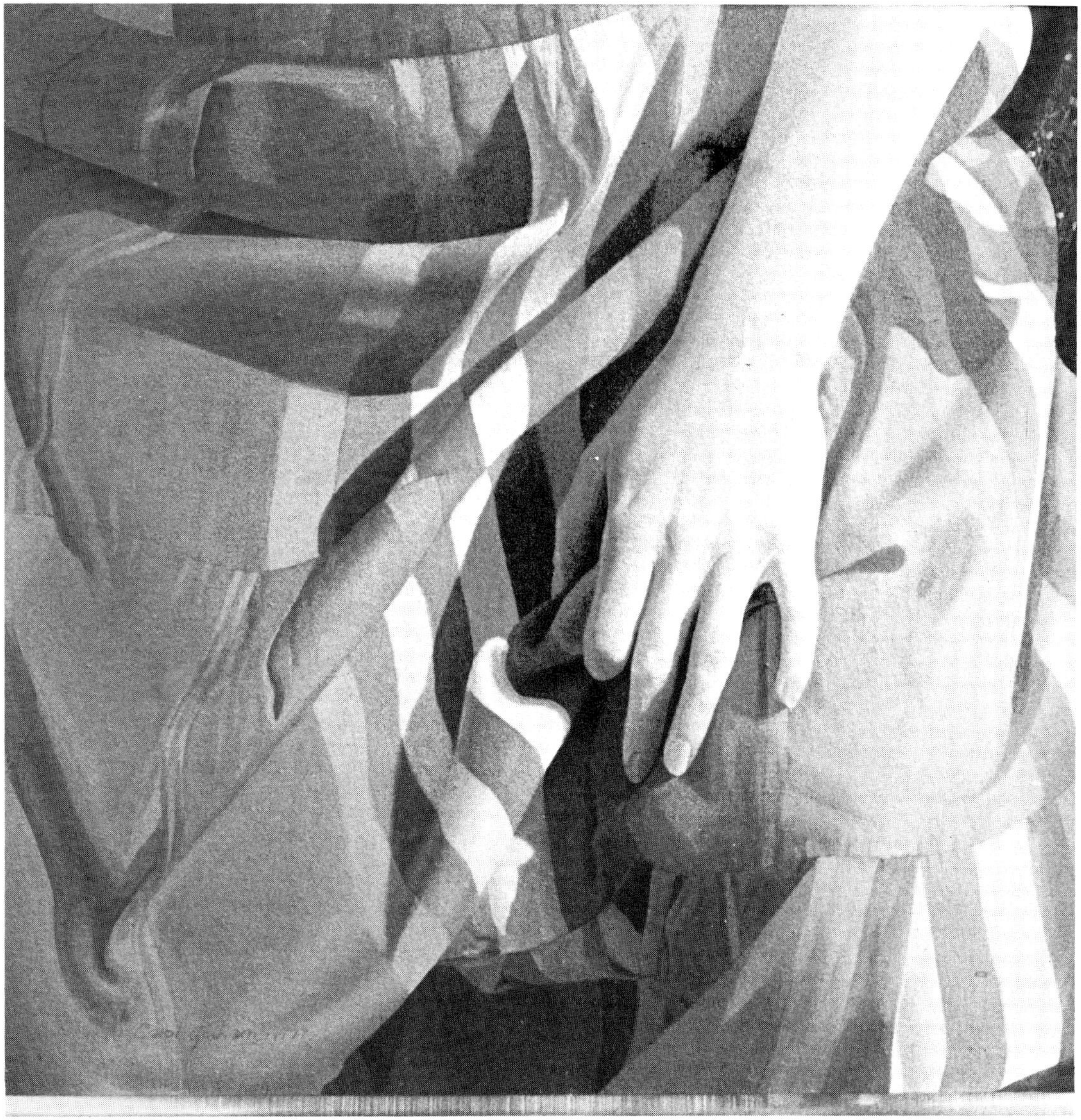

40 RAYMOND PIPER
Epipactis Palustris [*L*] *Cranz* [*Marsh Helleborine*].
1972; pencil, watercolour and body colour on white paper; 49.8 x 30.9 cms (sight); Ulster Museum collection

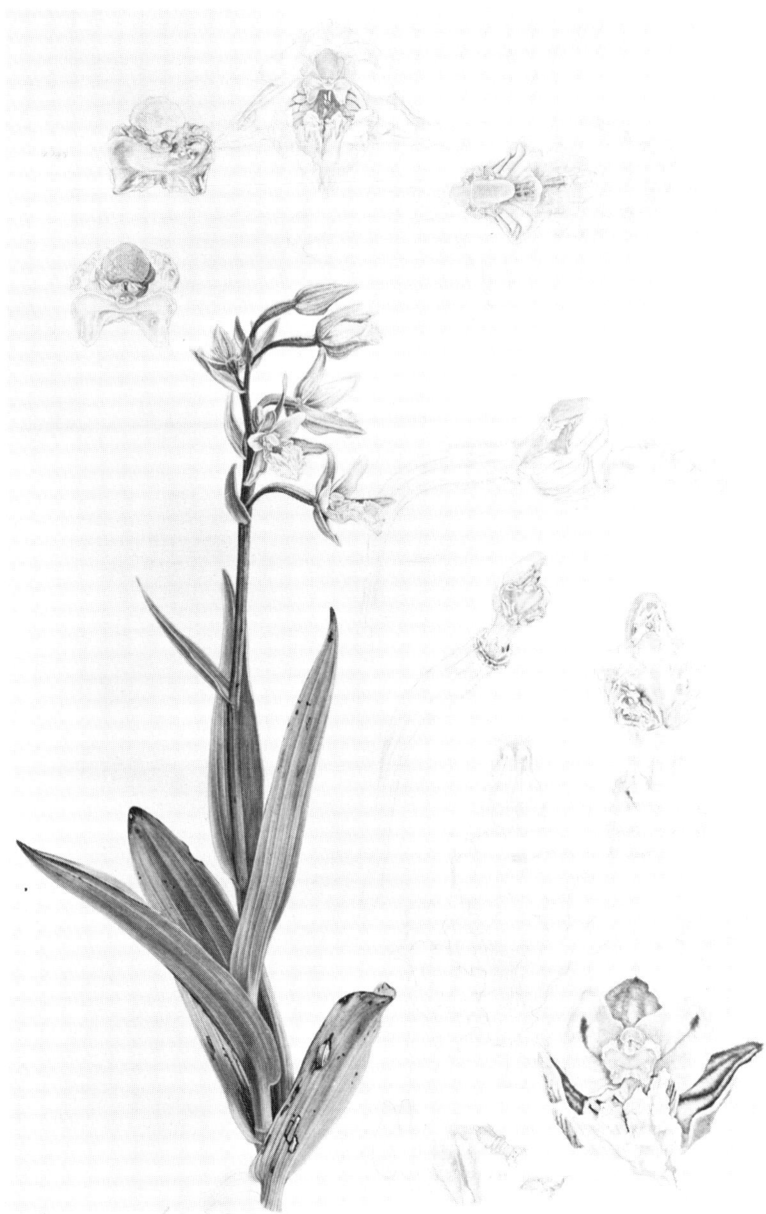

V DAVID BARKER
ainbow Tower
973; screenprint; 45.5 x
5.5 cms

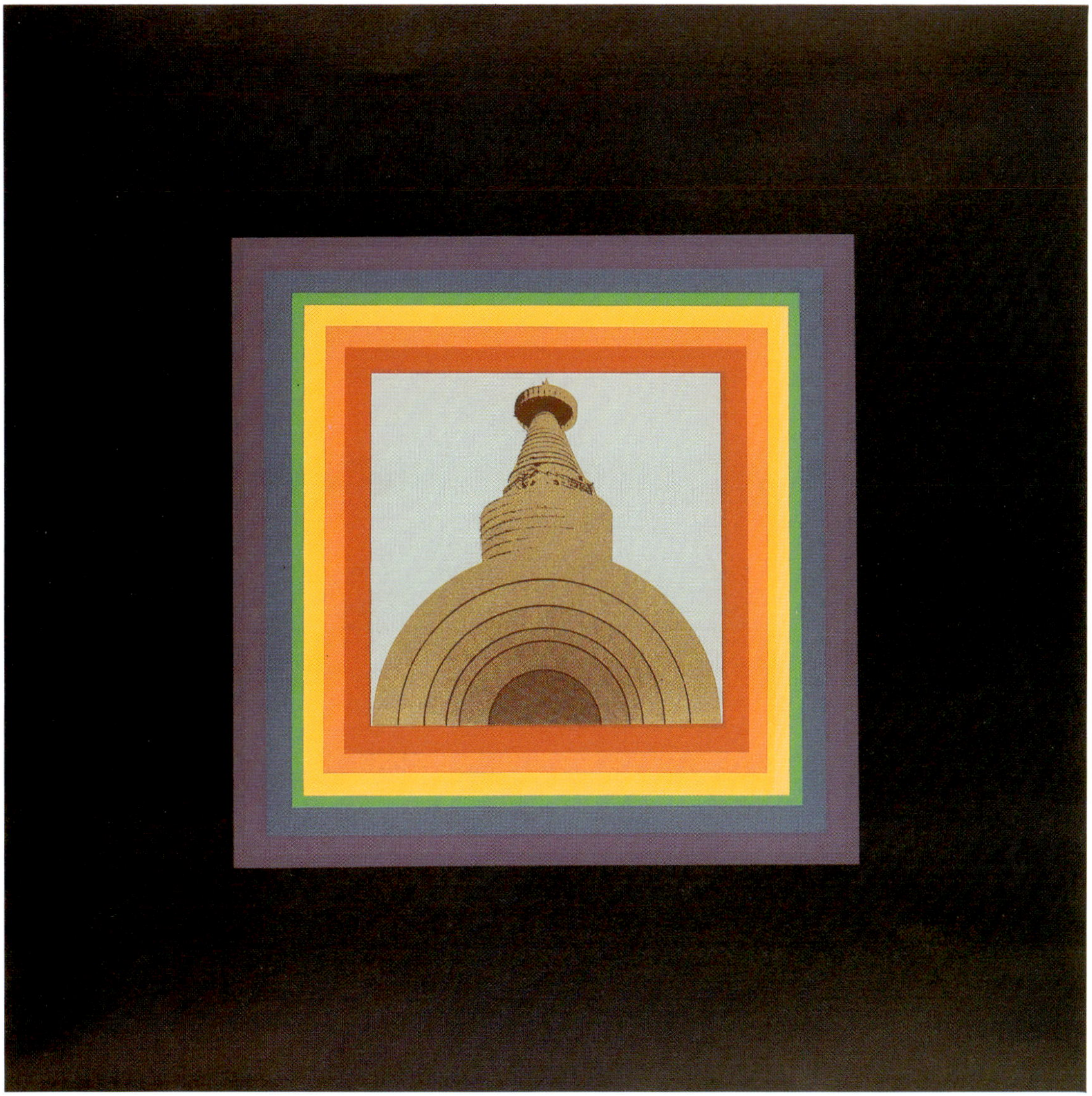

icing page 76

geometrical shapes and lines, and appeared to be totally abstract yet it was, in fact, a very close transcription of the colours and shapes to be found in provincial Mughal paintings of the 18th Century. These prototypes often used various musical modes, *ragas* and *raginis*, the abstract musical notation personified as men, women, architecture and colour. Thus it might be argued that the visual arts cannot be truly abstract like music, just that the terms of reference need not include the illusionistic and the representational. This may also explain why artists give their works scientific, mathematical, musical or non-European titles. Here in Ulster can be found artists whose stimulus may be oriental symbolism or computer programmes with end results that are not dissimilar.

For John Middleton (born 1945) the philosophy that determines both the content and the form at his work is that of the yin and the yang, 'the manifestation of the two antagonistic and complementary forces which are at work in the universe, centrifugal force away from the centre and centripetal, towards the centre, or yin and yang respectively as they are known in the east'.[13] If one accepts the universality of these two polar principles then Middleton's work may be said to be representational but not illusionistic, for it represents sets of values rather than exterior likenesses. Indeed, the artist would maintain that his works are 'real' rather than mimicking reality because everything is dynamic and changing, and illusionistic art is formal and static. John Middleton (Colin's son) works with shapes that are simple but with complex symbolic overtones: *tau* crosses, the classic shapes of *tantra* and so on, and his colours, like those of Peter Lloyd-Jones are often very subtle variations of tones. For this reason they do not always reproduce well; and since the paintings are closely inter-connected, by virtue of their philosophy, this schematic transcription, by the artist himself, of all the paintings in his 1972 one man show may serve to explain his ideas rather than simply to reproduce examples (no 41). John Middleton is also a graphic designer and a fine printmaker. It may be that the various print media (especially screen printing) suit his forms and the serial nature of their changes.

Another artist whose work takes its cue from the symbolic languages of oriental art is David Barker. He too is a printmaker and has produced etchings and engravings in addition to silk screen prints. David Barker (born 1945) extends his interest in Eastern art and aesthetics to language itself. We write words composed of individual letters; Chinese and Japanese are language systems in which ideas are expressed in ideograms or picture writing. That is to say there is a closer link between calligraphy and the visual arts in the East than in the West. Barker came to this province in 1968 and his work at this time was strongly calligraphic in style, and 'weathered' in appearance. By 1971 he had evolved a style in which geometric, architectural shapes were filled in with busy, linear details usually in the form of triangles, diamonds and chevrons. *The Death of Ti-hsin* (1971) is one such work (no 42). The tower-like form has no background, what happens within it and the octagon shape beneath does not conform to Western laws of perspective. The spatial ambiguities recall the work of Maurits Escher, while the symbolism is unfamiliar, although that does not prevent the viewer from appreciating such a work. The tower motif with its stepped

41 JOHN MIDDLETON
Diagrammatic representation of his paintings in catalogue of one man show
1972

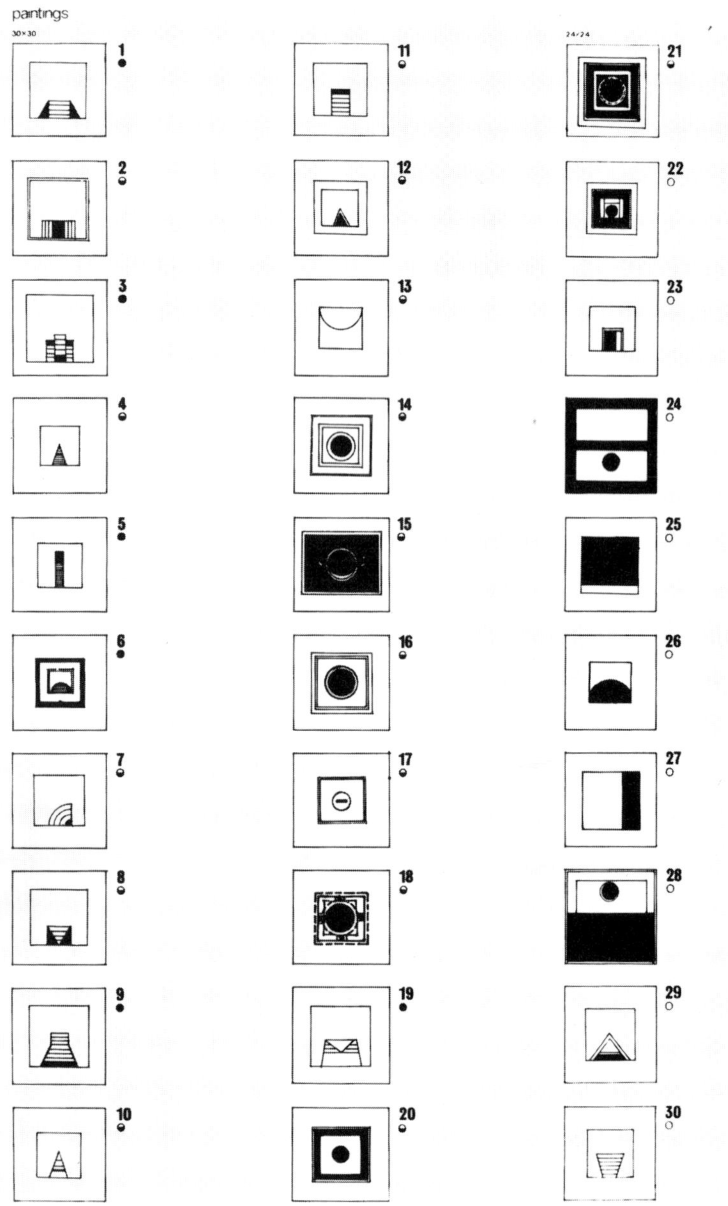

sides re-appears in his silk screen *Rainbow Observatory* which is one of a series which explored a particular theme and the medium of screen printing itself. For many years the screen printing process was mainly used in industry, for example in textiles. It is a surface process, no plate is necessary. It is basically a stencil, and with the development of photo-sensitive screens it was possible to re-print photographic images of some complexity rather than relying upon simple hand-done shapes. The Pop artists seized upon the medium, possibly deriving satisfaction from the fact that they were using a commercial, mechanical process to produce images themselves probably derived from commercial and mechanical objects. Andy Warhol's ubiquitous *Campbell's Soup Cans* and his re-worked pin-ups of Elvis Presley, Marilyn Monroe, Liz Taylor etc are all photo-screenprints. Each colour requires a separate screen and the more screens used the more difficult it is to line up the registration of one screen on top or beside another. From the early 1960s onwards the screen-print process (the term silk screen is now a misnomer) became one of the main standbys of all students in art colleges. Many of these prints had only one or two colours plus black and the effect, although powerful, could seem mechanical and restrictive. David Barker is one of the printmakers who shows that the screen print can produce images and tones of sophistication and subtlety. *Rainbow Observatory* and *Rainbow Tower* of 1973 (no iv, colour) use many separate colour screens, in fact some other works by Barker use well over a dozen screens to give minute tonal graduations, the nuances of which are not always apparent to the viewer. The subjects of these works are reminders of the complex astrological and astronomical heritage of the East and also of the fact that the architecture of these observatories is as beautiful as it is functional.

It is difficult to know exactly what the word 'abstract' means when applied to art, especially as it is used as an umbrella title in the same way as 'modern' has an implied pejorative meaning in the phrase 'modern art'. It is equally hard to find a synonym for the word abstraction which will have any precision. 'Experimental' implies dynamism and open-endedness, but in *Art and Illusion* E H Gombrich notes that one of the conditions of public and critical acclaim is the disappearance of the 'experimental' status of a work. We may be left with negatives like 'non-objective', 'non-figurative' or 'non-illusionistic' to describe what is a positive process. Certainly, what Vasarely described as the move from an external to an internal vision requires effort and patience on the part of the spectator before full comprehension can be reached. Of course, all good art, whether figurative or not, requires repeated viewing for all the nuances to be understood. Some artists change from a figurative to a non-figurative mode and back again several times in their career, and their so-called abstract works can often be seen as a synthesis or refinement of ideas and motifs which are present in their figurative works.

An example of this consistency of theme or vision may be seen in the work of Brian Ballard (born 1943). He began with a figurative reference expressed in terms of landscape painting. Ballard's landscapes were not highly imitative but rather a simplification or stylization of landscape elements. The works were really colour essays in which the vertical structures of trees and hedges were complemented by hori-

42 DAVID BARKER
Death of Ti-hsin
1971; engraving; 52 x 26 cms; Arts Council of Northern Ireland

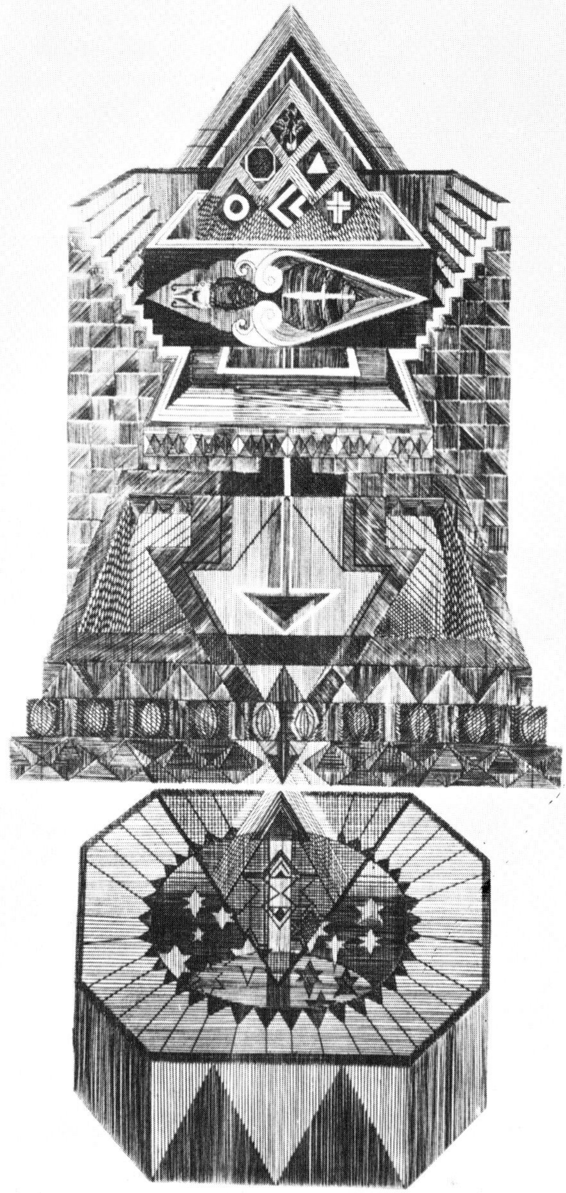

zontal or diagonal shifts of light. Gradually the examination of this filtered light became the actual subject of his paintings. *Light Strips (Purple)* (no 43) shows the progression of his art by the early 1970s. Bars of strong, even artificial, colour tones vibrate and shimmer against a dark background. The mesh motif that can be glimpsed in this reproduction is more apparent in paintings like *Catch* (1971) and *Spring March '70*. The net-like shapes 'catch' and anchor the pulsating light forms giving them a reference point without which the resonance would lack stability. The net might also be seen as the final remnant of the horizontals and verticals of the landscape. By 1975 Ballard was disengaging himself from such a formal system and was producing what appeared to be conventional still life portraits and landscapes, and in 1976 he had a one-man show mainly of tree studies. These works, many only about 18 x 25 cms generally focus on vertical tree trunks between which slanting light filters. Illustration no 44 is a typical example of this series and the affinity with *Light Strips (Purple)* is apparent even in a monochrome reproduction. Viewing the originals would show that the flickering blues, purples and yellow of the 'abstract' are just as vibrant in the 'figurative' work. One of the reactions against the exuberance of Abstract Expressionism (especially that aspect of it dubbed 'Action Painting') was the cool geometry of the so-called Hard Edge painters. Masking tape, ruled lines and air-brushed paint replaced flung pigment and torn canvases, yet the effect could be as exciting and sensual as anything that had gone before. In some cases, for example Frank Stella, this type of painting led to shaped canvases which destroyed the notion that a rectangular picture 'frame' is the norm for a painting. Other artists such as Kenneth Noland, Barnett Newman and John Hoyland emphasised the flatness of the paint and the picture-support. Even so, the critic Clement Greenberg reiterated that the first painted mark on a surface destroys its virtual flatness and for several artists an illusionism crept in. It might be a literal illusion based on the canvas being stretched into recession and projection; or it might be a depicted illusionism based on optical illusions of line and colour.

The work of Ulster artist William Collins (born 1938) represents a concern for the latter plus a minimal figurative illusionism. Like many artists today he uses the new synthetic pigments, acrylic and PVA. These new paints can be used like oil paint, but thinned, they can be used like gouache or even in a manner similar (but not identical) to watercolour. Acrylic paint may be used with brush or palette knife but it can also be airbrushed on to a picture support to give both a flatness and (if required) a soft, diffused, spray edge to tonal areas. Collins' paintings tend to use a framing motif like a grid or window 'through' which hazy forms may be glimpsed. A large number of his paintings from the end of the 1960s have, as their starting point, the landscape as in the Lough Neagh series. These cannot be described as landscape views, rather they are re-constructed interpretations of the perception of light seen atmospherically. *Coastal Dolmen* of 1974 (no 45) is a monoprint, a technically difficult medium which Collins frequently uses for its ability to produce subtleties of form and tone. While it lacks the geometry of some of the Lough Neagh series it does have a quality which may be read as two or three dimensional.

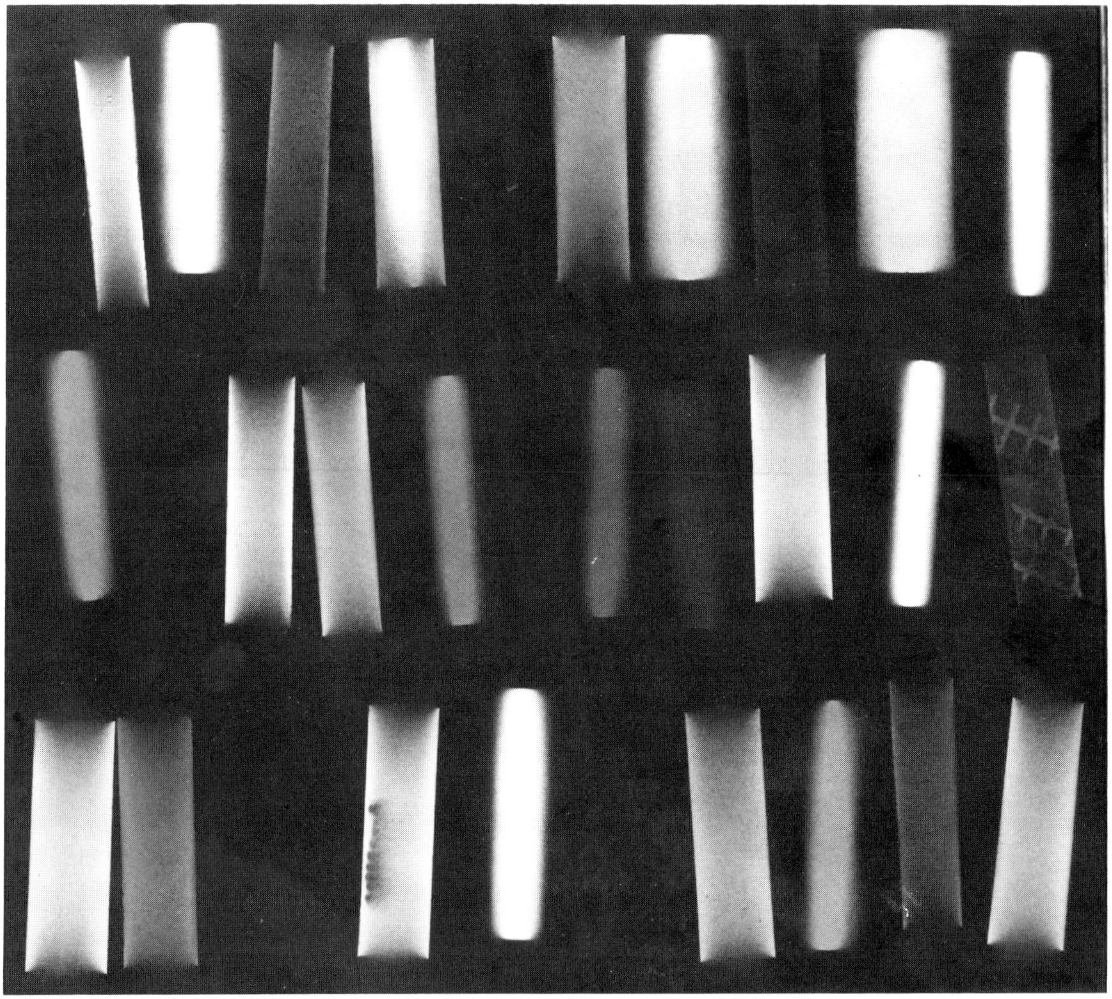

43 BRIAN BALLARD
Light Strips [Purple]
1972; acrylic on canvas; 91.5 x 101.6 cms; Ulster Museum collection

Gordon Woods (born 1938) also produces work which has the immediate appearance of geometrical abstraction but which, like that of Collins, Ballard and others, is a response to both the *perceived* world and its *conceived* counterpart. An example of this is *Skullscape* of 1974: working from a cleaned animal skull Woods produced a work which, by use of the close-up, transforms the ridges and sockets of the skull into a landscape and at the same time into a metaphor for the world beyond the exterior. The underground film maker Ed Emshwiller made an experimental film called *Relativity* in which the camera not only travels over a body but passes

44 BRIAN BALLARD
Forest
1976; watercolour; 50.8 x 76.6 cms; collection the artist

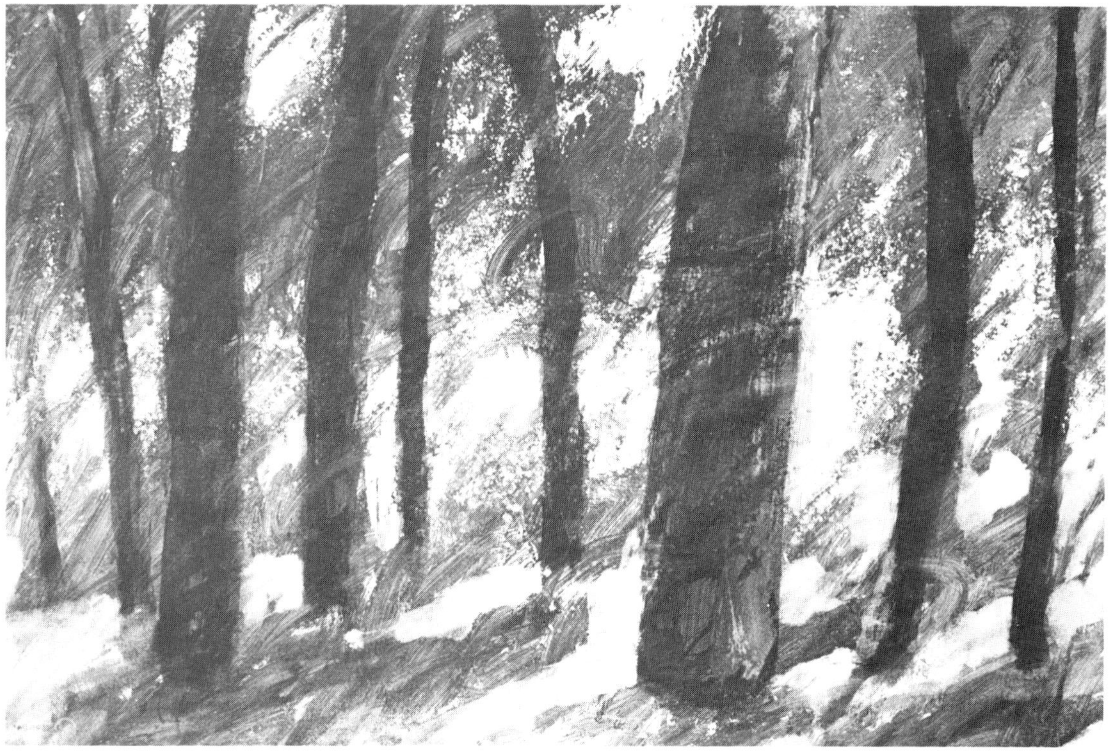

inside to reveal a universe not normally visible or even dreamed of. As Woods put it, 'the core of my work is now based on an increasing interest in concepts and ideas being disseminated from the enquiries made by scientists into the physical and chemical nature of the universe, both microscopic and macroscopic'.[14] *Microaction VII* (no 46) is one of his works whose title and geometric forms convey scientific discipline but whose colour, paint surface and general aesthetic is Romantic. His works are generally small in scale but within the picture 'frame' he builds block forms whose megalithic appearance (reminiscent of Robyn Denny or Cecil King) is contrasted with the busy surface of the paint strokes which in density resemble the lichen which was the subject of one of his 1977 paintings.

Certain photographic terms have crept into this narrative, for we use terms like 'focus', 'close-up' and 'zoom' outside the medium, to imply that photography has allowed us to see the world from new angles. This has already been noted in the work of Carol Graham, but unusual angles which create visual uncertainty are found in the paintings of many artists. Quizzes often present images of familiar objects from un-

45 WILLIAM COLLINS
Coastal Dolmen
1974; monoprint; 30 x 25 cms; Arts Council of Northern Ireland collection

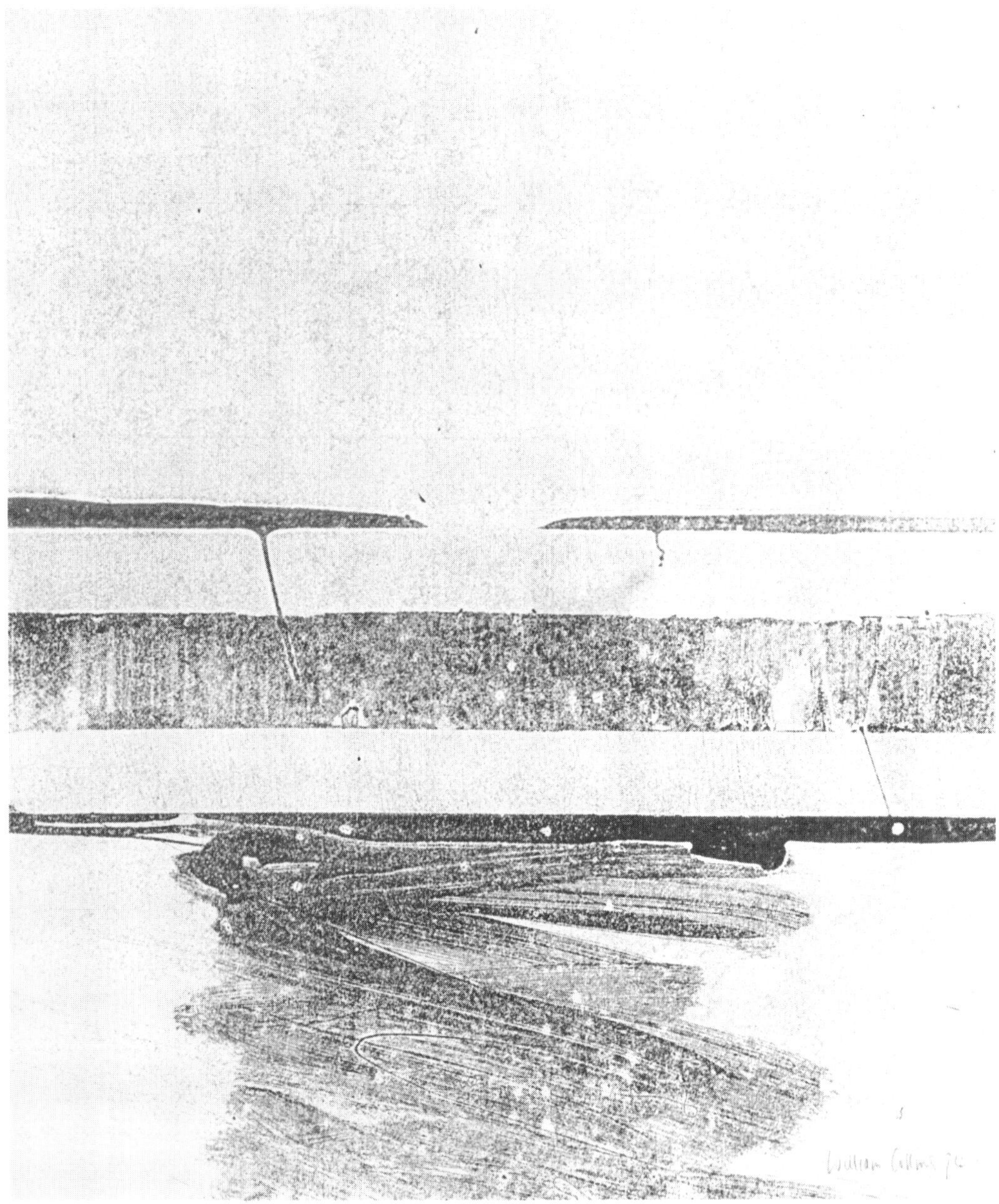

46 GORDON WOODS
Microaction VII
1976; oil and fixotropic medium; 70.5 x 52 cms; Arts Council of Northern Ireland collection

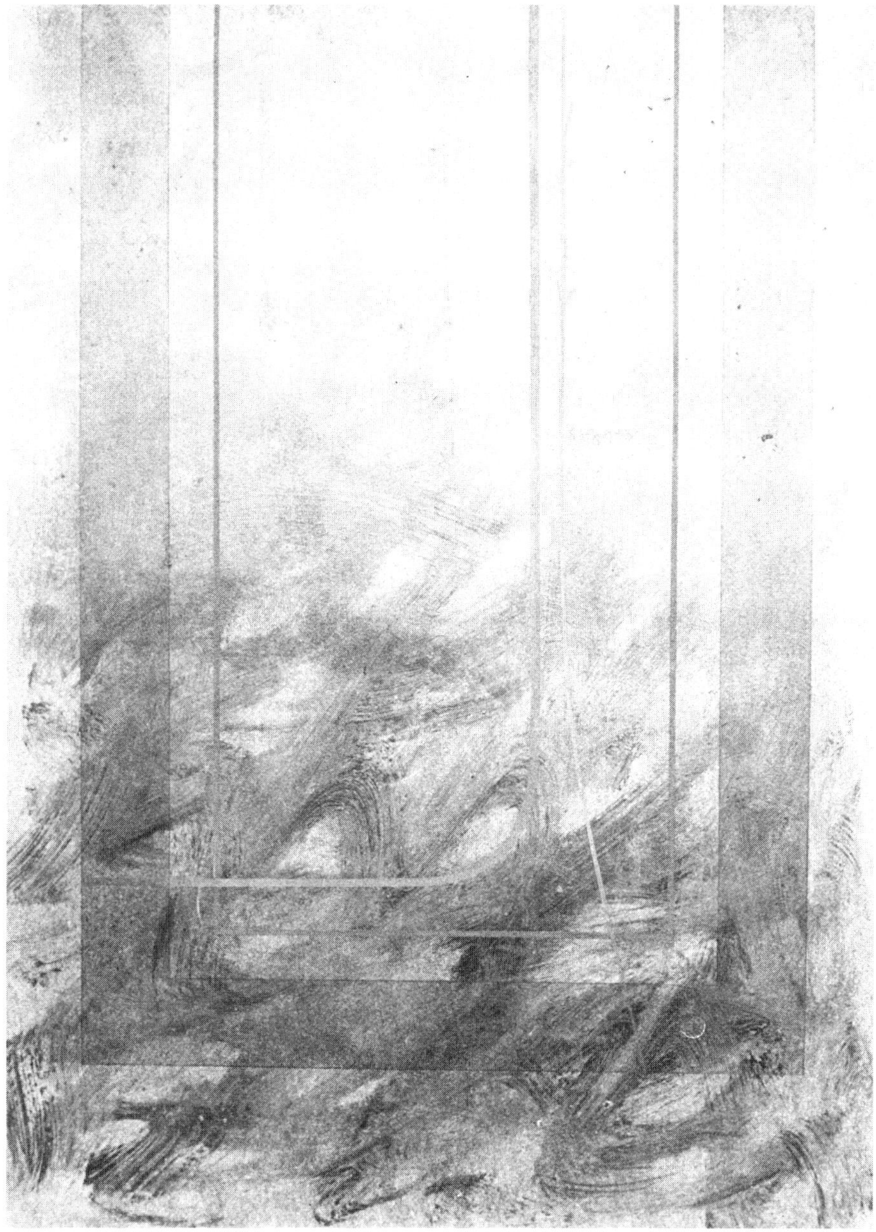

47 JOE McWILLIAMS
Rendezvous with a Rainbow II
1976; mixed media; 160 x 140 cms; Etain Nugent collection

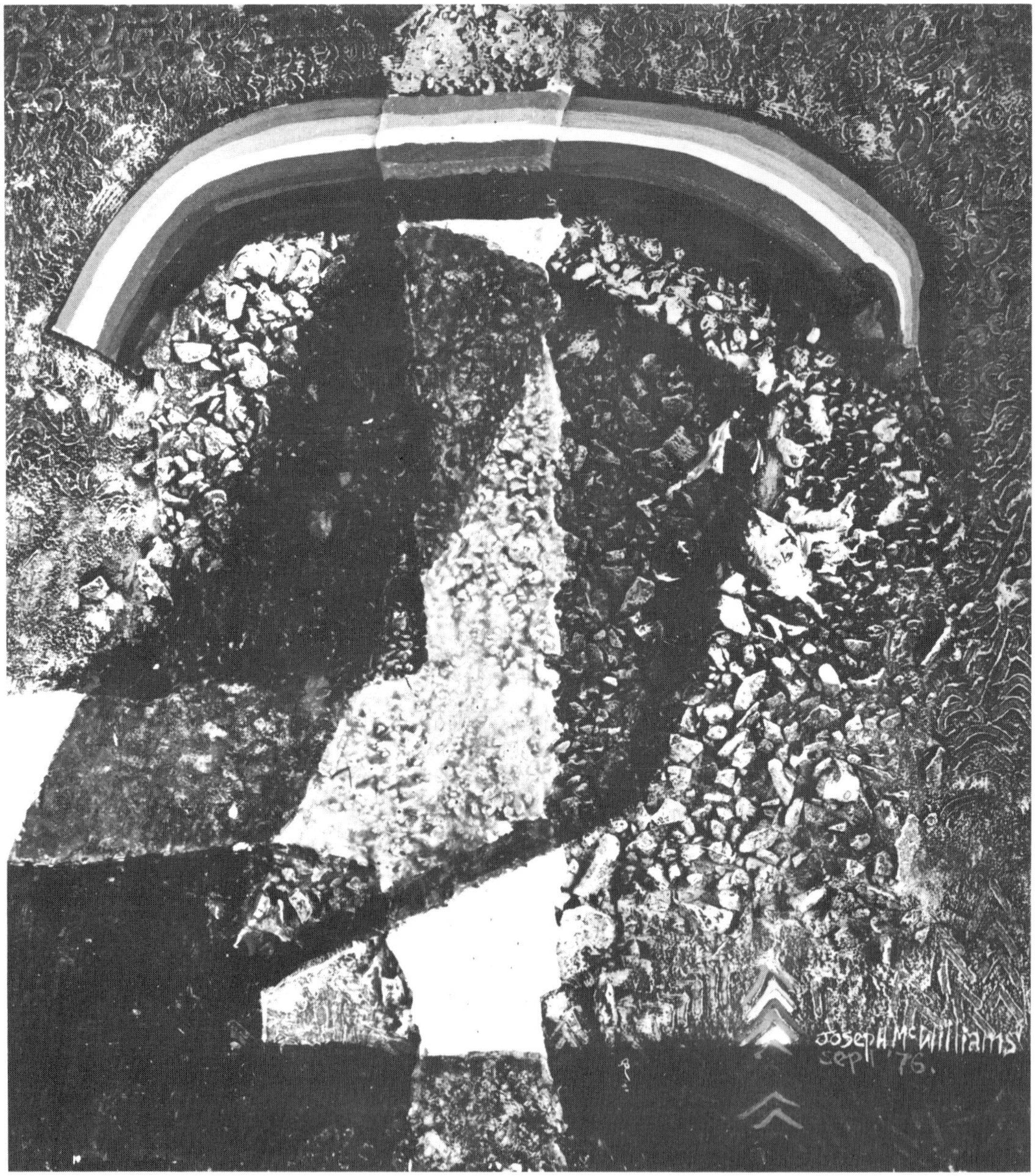

familiar angles and without the normal frames of reference these objects are frequently unrecognisable: they became abstract shapes. Look at this painting *Rendezvous with a Rainbow* by Joe McWilliams (no 47). Even in monochrome the rainbow is recognisable, for we accept the visual shorthand which conventionalises that most ephemeral of light effects. The rest is less obvious, yet it too is concerned with light, in this case the shadow of an opening car door across the shaft of light from another open door. The ground on which the light falls is literal, gravel mixed in with the pigment. His work is still broadly based on figurative works as a piece of pure pattern. And like the rainbow which has become a personal symbol, the chevrons are often given a free rein of colour which extends beyond the conventional picture space. In some recent works, notably that based on Picasso's *Joie de Vivre* (the title is as significant as the forms) the bands of colour spill happily on to the mount and right over to the frame. Along with the use of collage and inclusion of objects in the picture this extension of picture space both defines and questions the nature of picture making.

The joyful sense of pattern making can be seen in Colin Middleton, Denis McBride and Joe McWilliams although there is normally a figurative basis to it, and with some other artists their abstract phase was a period of freedom arrived at only after an apprenticeship during which the figurative elements were refined down until the original reference vanished. Neither Robert Linton nor Noel Millar has exhibited much in the past decade but their work in the early and mid 1960s showed a flair for rhythmic composition. Linton (born 1930) studied in London under Louis Le Brocquy and Victor Pasmore after his Belfast college training, and his work showed a reductive quality which pared away subjects such as boats, buildings and landscapes until only the essential elements were left, often interconnected by the merest thread. Thus liberated, the shapes became colours and these floated off against simple backgrounds; indeed as Linton experimented with different materials (often three dimensional) the shapes could find their identity on more than one actual plane. Noel Millar (born 1936) was for a short while connected with Group 63 and the Irish Independent Artists group in Dublin and in his works (for example, illustration number 48) organically rhythmic shapes intermingle and connect with precisely geometrical shapes (which in some cases meant the edges of the paintings themselves). The colours were bright and buoyant and the way in which he exercised a control between the colour and the snaking forms recalled some of Bernard Cohen's work.

Alice Berger Hammerschlag (1917-1969) was an Austrian who came to Belfast and who became an influential figure in the arts here. Her paintings not only brought a first hand European influence to this province but also her tireless work for the arts, including acting as administrator and guiding spirit of the now gone New Gallery, was a source of real encouragement to Ulster artists, young and old. Her work in the early 1950s had the kind of soaring architectonic cubism associated with Lyonel Feininger. These paintings were still sometimes figurative in elements but the subjects, often concerned with dance, water or crystalline matter, were expressed by means of sparkling facets of light which were genuinely abstract in spirit. Although these

48 NOEL MILLAR
Untitled
n d; gouache on paper; 73 x 49 cms; Arts Council of Northern Ireland collection

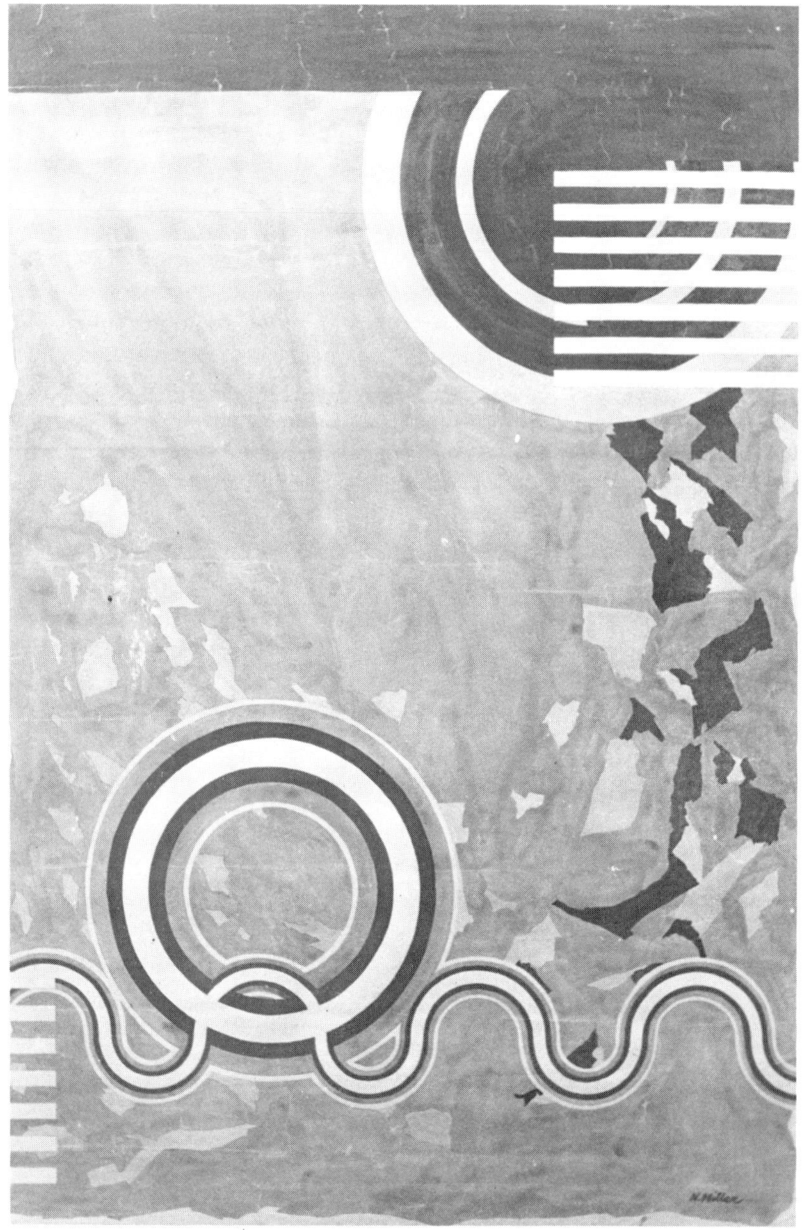

works were generally modest in physical size the paintings were heroic in scale because the very gestural vitality of the forms and colours seemed to magnify the canvases. From 1956 to 1962 her work lost nothing of this freedom of expression but the swirling atmospheric shapes which spread across the canvas began to lose their joyous overtones and instead became intensely personal statements about the anguish of mankind. Alice Berger Hammerschlag's apocalyptic Expressionism was extremely moving to watch: dramatic light would shoot through dark cloud forms in these works, and they were pictures of contest in which light always struggled with darkness. The titles give some hint of the feeling and personal experience which had gone into these paintings: *From the Seven Words: It Is Finished — Concentration Camps 1945* (1962), *Elemental Force* (1961), *Mood Study from Yeats' Deirdre* (1962) and *Calvary — Old and New* (1961) which is illustration number 49. The latter may be read as the last vestige of figurative forms but of course the forms are purely symbolic representations of, on the one hand, suffering and darkness, and on the other freedom and light. In the mid 1960s her work became more sculptural with rounded shapes seeming to move rhythmically in studies of balance, interaction and penetration. Gradually the lines which had provided the counterpart in these paintings came to the foreground and in her last two years they speeded up until they were like atomic particles hurtling through space. A lighted object whirled around in a darkened room leaves an afterimage of line rather than of point, and these swirling patterns of Alice Berger Hammerschlag's were harmonious, joyful and works which not only revealed the structure of light but also said something about time as well. Illustration number 50 is a fine example of this development; it is also one of the last works she did before her death in 1969. She is remembered not only through her paintings (which curiously owe nothing stylistically to her country of adoption) but also through her help for artists which continues after her death in the form of the Alice Berger Hammerschlag Trust (see Chapter 5).

Even though individual artists or generations have sought to deny the link, art and science have often gone hand in hand. For the classical Greeks as for the men of the Renaissance, proportion, harmony and beauty were goals to be sought through a study of geometry as much as through a grounding in the visual arts. The older universities today still teach mathematics as an Arts subject, while in the new establishments of learning the computer may be used to draw pictures and patterns. Significantly, those art movements of this century which embrace the rigorous purity of geometry, the precision of mathematical composition and the abstract beauty of numbers are those whose works are often best expressed in terms of the three rather than the two dimensional image. Indeed, Suprematism, De Stijl, Neo-Plasticism and Constructivism are all movements which themselves produced or influenced the basic forms and design concepts of modern architecture and applied design. A basic aesthetic of such movements was a quest for 'purity' of form, that is to say, decoration (ie figurative elements) was declared redundant and the functional was held up to be the ideal.

Roy Johnston (born 1936) is an Ulster painter whose present work seeks to combine the discip-

49 ALICE BERGER HAMMERSCHLAG
Calvary — Old and New
1961; oil on canvas; 101.8 x 127.2 cms; Ulster Museum collection

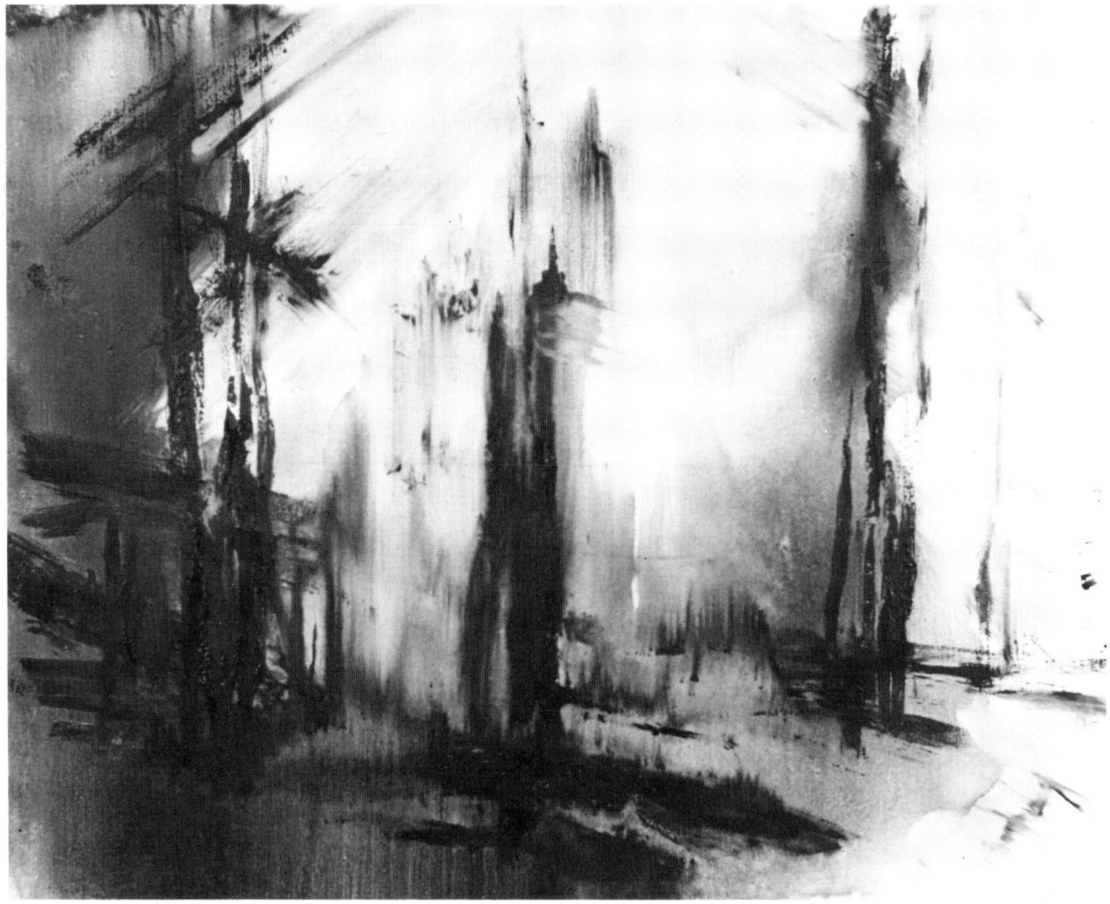

lines of order and sequentiality with the dynamism that is found in abstract patterns. Until the late 1960s Johnston produced works in which geometric shapes were contrasted with freely applied 'busy' accents of paint. Despite the careful articulation of the basic forms the effect was highly painterly. Obviously seeking a 'cooler' technique and a wider range of formats Johnston abandoned this style and evolved a series of works which employed a contoured canvas. That is to say that the cotton duck surface was shaped over supports thus allowing for spatial projection, regression and expansion. Naturally the relief effects were geometrical in nature and the reductive process was continued by the simplification of the texture of the paint (as well as of the painted forms themselves) leading to a highly organised abstraction in

50 ALICE BERGER HAMMERSCHLAG
Painting '69
1969; mixed media; 96.5 x 76.2 cms; Arts Council of Northern Ireland

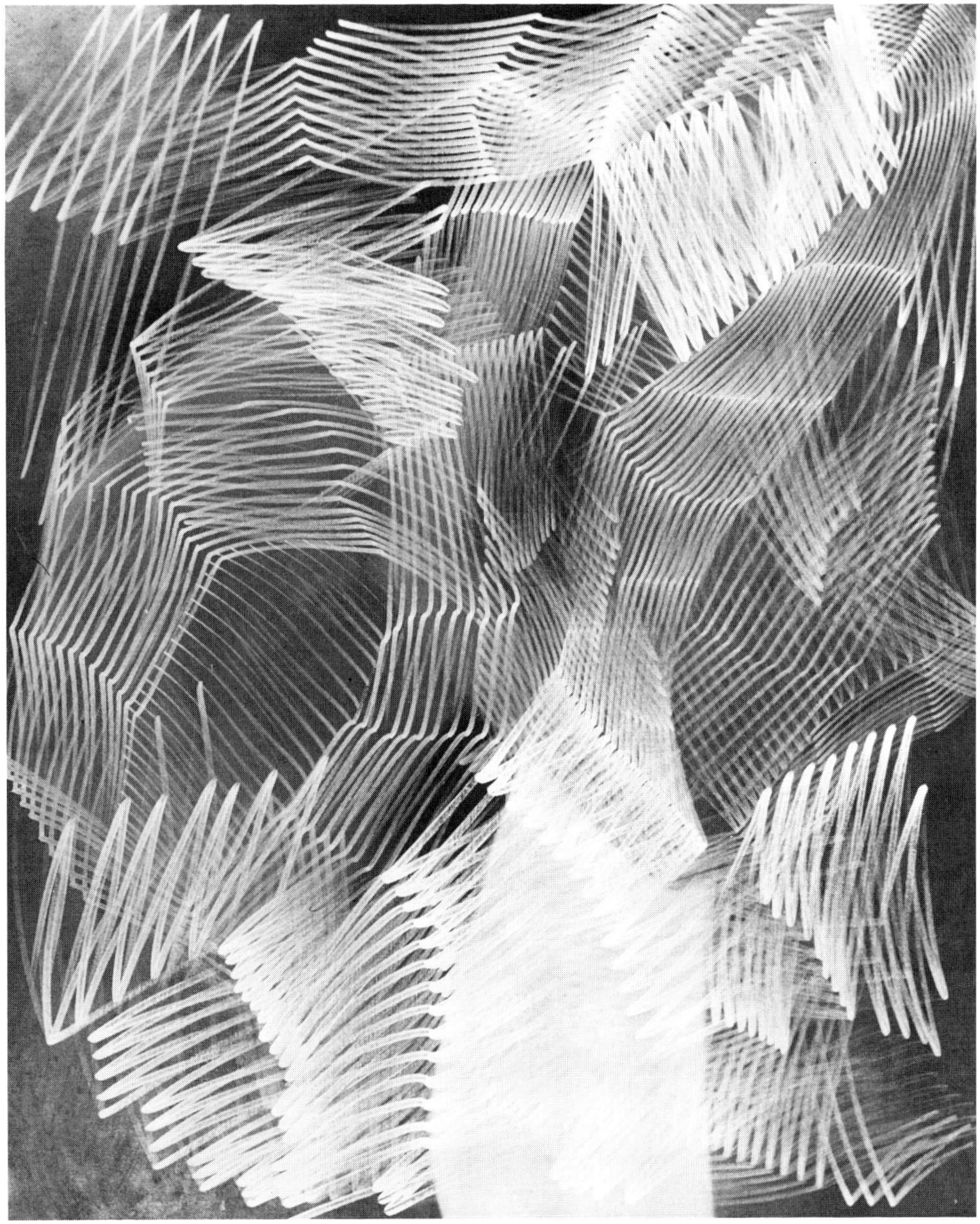

51 ROY JOHNSTON
Overview
c1971; acrylic on canvas; 274.3 x 213.4 cms; Ulster Museum collection

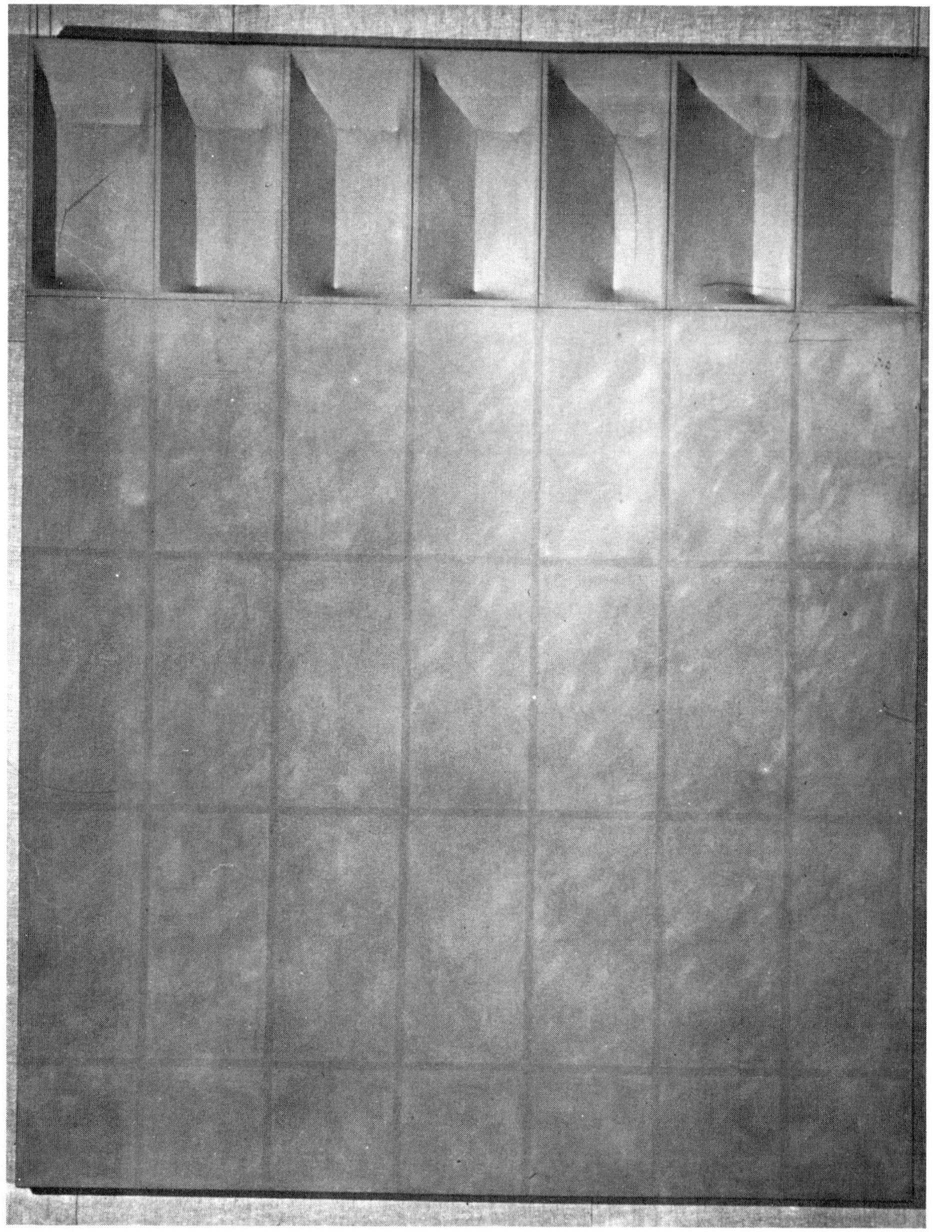

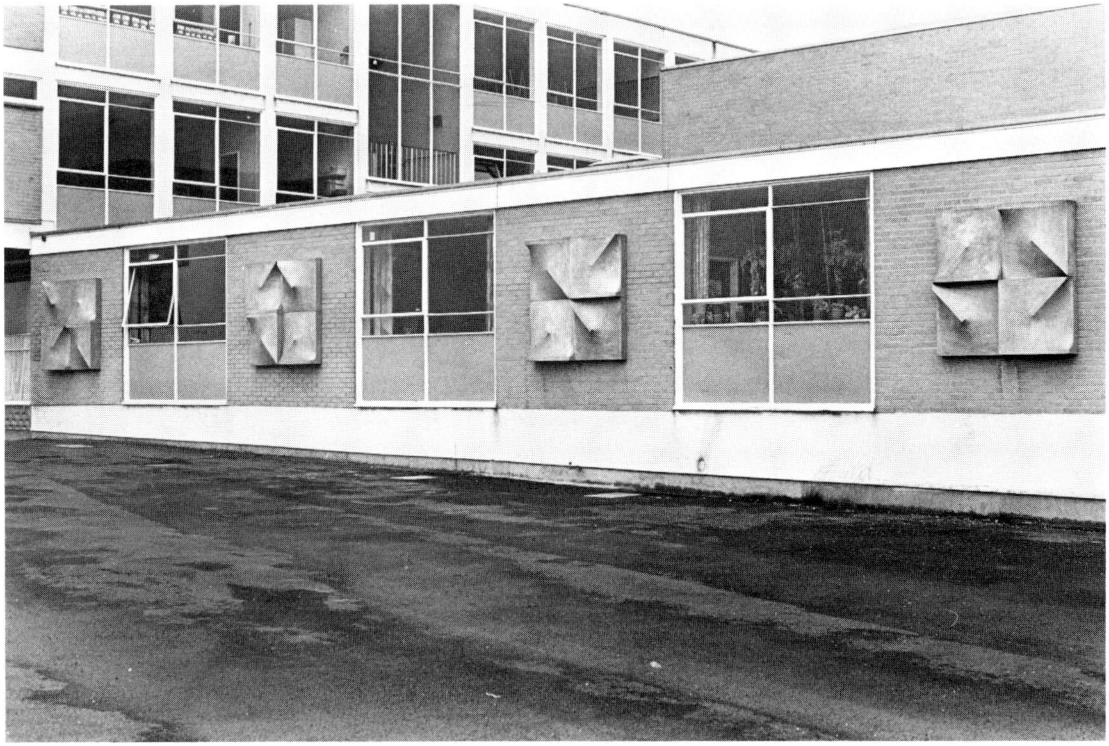

52 ROY JOHNSTON
Modular Relief
1974-75; mixed media; 122 x 122 cms each; Cross and Passion School, Glen Road, Belfast

which flatness of paint contrasted with literal depth in the canvas. Illustration number 51 shows one of these contoured canvases of the 1970s, works which recalled the shaped canvas experiments of Richard Smith, Trevor Bell and others. More recently, however, Roy Johnston has pushed this constructivist technique further, employing what is for him a logical, mathematically derived style and aesthetic belonging to the Systems Art movement.[15] 'System' implies order and structure, while in architecture and design the phrase 'system building' implies the use of modular units in repetition. Johnston's work involves both aspects of the word, being permutations of arithmetically and geometrically simple shapes which achieve complexity by being produced in multiples. This may be seen in his relief for the exterior of Cross and Passion Secondary School, Belfast (no 52). In square one, a raised diagonal goes from the centre to one corner; in square two, one side is raised; in square three, two sides, until by square four, three sides and the original diagonal are thrown into relief. Then 'a rotation principle is introduced to activate the potential dynamic of the diagonal'.[16] This modular multiplicity is close to the work of Kenneth Martin, Malcolm Hughes and Anthony Hill.

Lest it be thought that work produced out of a mathematically programmed system must, of necessity, be geometrical in format, the most recent work of Norman Fraser shows that computer generated and derived shapes can have an extraordinary capacity for freedom and creativity. Fraser (born 1943), when a student in the early 1960s, painted representational works with a strong emphasis on broadly defined architectonic shapes. In 1965/66, study in London brought him into contact with the work and ideas of Peter Sedgley and Bridget Riley, the Op artists whose dazzling canvases were the result of extremely patient research into colour and form. Such non-figurative work, concerned with perceptual and spatial phenomena expressed two dimensionally involved artists in extremely laborious and precise work. Fraser's output between 1967 and 1974 was derived not only from the Op artists but also from a new awareness of the intricacies of Celtic *entrelac* design. His work became diagrammatic, exploring multiple facets of line expressed on a flat plane. Gradually, with the introduction of hatched line and dots the forms assumed a squared or rounded three dimensionality. *Faceted Units* of 1974 (no 53) is a late example of this complicated and rhythmic style. As the artist said, 'These explorations of the mathematical elements in structures:- tessellations, permutations etc, became extremely time-consuming to produce and a need to find a quicker means of production was the initial reason for looking towards the computer.'

Computer generated art may be initially enlisted as an aid to the human artist, but as Norman Fraser learned by the time he went to America to study this new art form, the computer could be used to produce almost infinite variations. Programme it to trace the possible paths between, say, three points and the permutations run into the millions. Nor need these lines be rigid, images of immense flexibility and delicacy can be produced, a modern equivalent of Klee's 'the eye taking a line for a walk'. While making full use of his access to a computer, Fraser still remains the master allowing himself to make subjective decisions from images produced and also utilizing random elements of chance. For example, by using the 'artificial intelligence' which can be a feature of modern computers he designed programmes which allowed the machine to make sequential decisions and a kind of 'freehand' drawing technique. His latest work is painted by hand, a realisation of his need to paint linked to the recognition of the limits of available technology here. Rather than being individual units, his recent paintings explore boundaries (like maps) and relationships between forms. These relationships, as in *Tagged Flags* of 1977 (no 54) involve chance, and the association of ideas (by the spectator) with the images produced, not unlike the open-endedness of the Rorschsach ink-blot test.

Although it is difficult for many to accept, a lot of painters do not paint just as many sculptors do not sculpt. Given the freedom to put whatever one wants on the canvas (subject and medium), the next step is to discard the picture space of the canvas and to produce objects anywhere. Then one may choose not to produce but to document natural phenomena and produce statements and propositions concerning the nature of art. This area of Conceptual Art known as Art Language is an amorphous mixture of lingustics, formal and symbolic logic, structuralist criticism, philosophy and a good measure of polemic thrown in. Like most post-object art it is

53 NORMAN FRASER
Faceted Units
1974; pen drawing; 42 x 59.4 cms; collection the artist

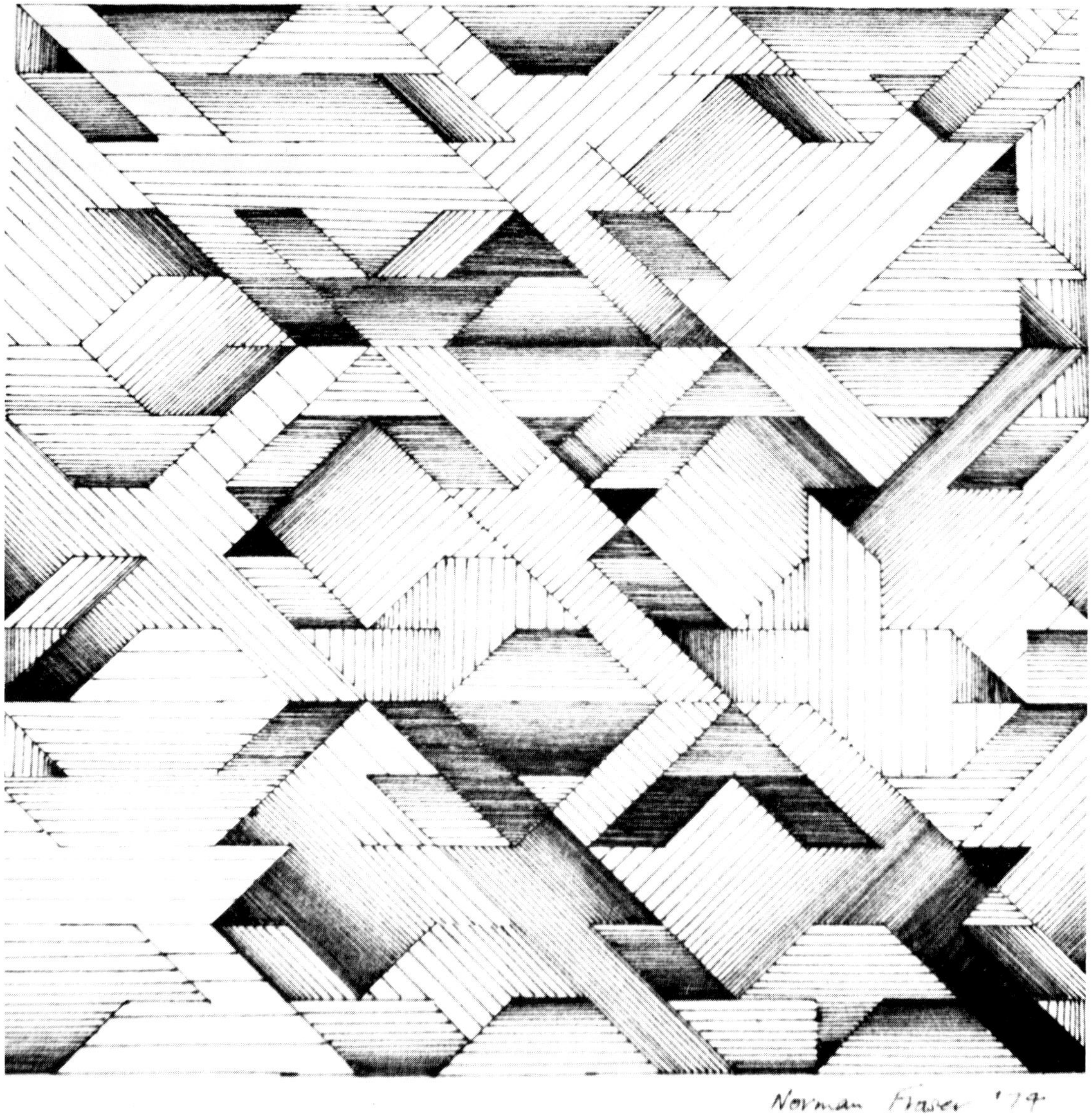

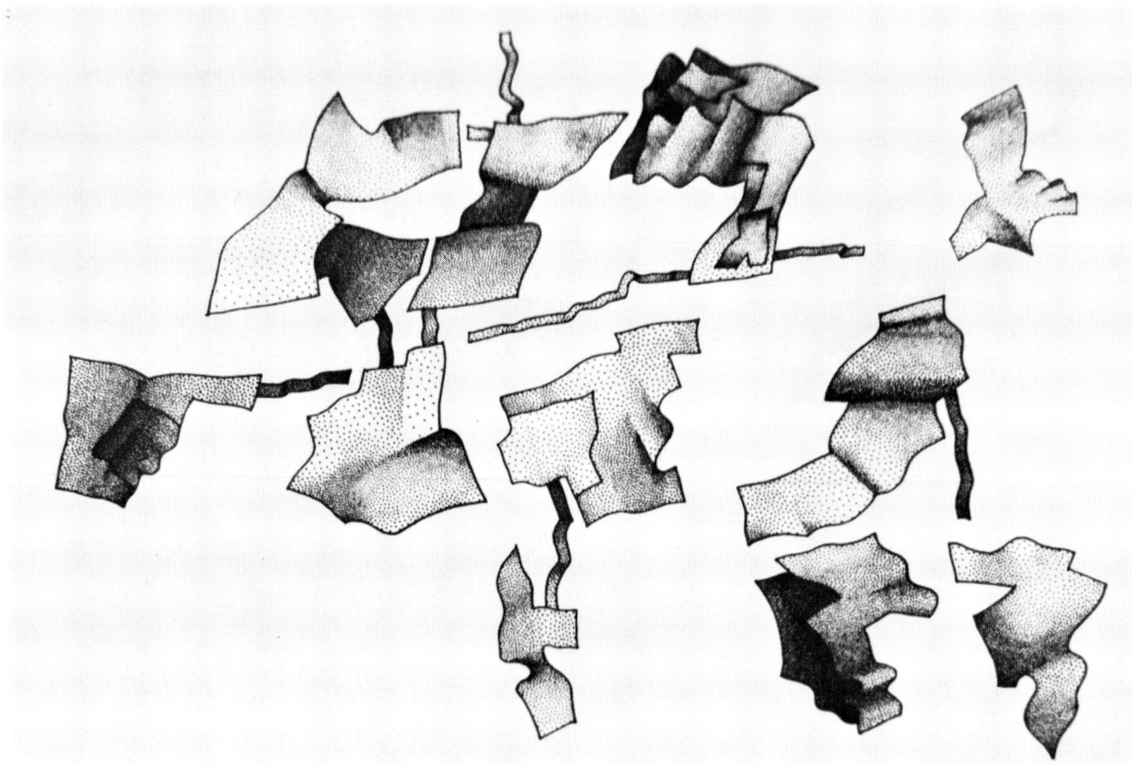

54 NORMAN FRASER
Tagged Flags
1977; pen drawing; 42 x 59.4 cms; collection the artist

radical in intent and like all art movements it produces a few original and influential examples and a vast number of derivative and not fully worked out pieces. One common theme running through most avant-garde art today is the desire to question existing concepts and aesthetics of art. There is nothing new in this; all new art questions and re-defines its progenitors and it is almost sixty years since the cry 'Art is dead, long live Dada' was heard. Whether the present questioning of artistic identities will be seen as art in itself or as a series of 'Notes toward a possible Re-definition of Art', time alone will tell. One thing is certain, it won't go away if one closes one's eyes and in the midst of the bewildering variety of objects, performances, manifestoes and bluff there are extremely serious individuals who are getting on with the business of re-definition in the face of public and professional hostility.

Since much of this work is not concerned with gallery art, saleable pieces, art as product or whatever, it is sometimes invidious to single out one artist and use him as an exemplar. But out of the several young art school graduates in this province whose work is essentially different from the framed paintings which form the bulk of the

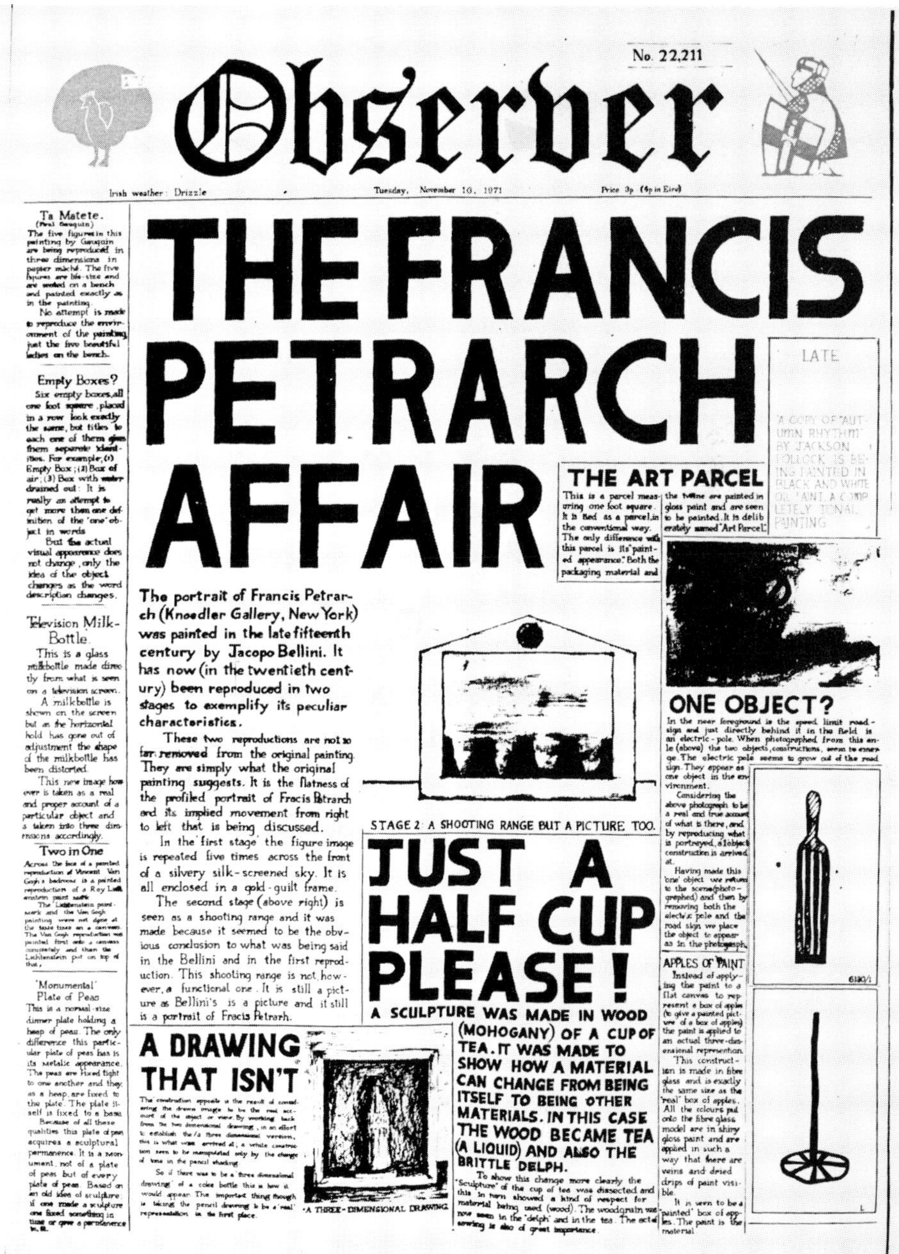

55 PADRAIG MURPHY
The Francis Petrarch Affair
original 1971; Arts Council of Northern Ireland poster 1974; original: ink and paint on paper; poster: screen-print; 76 x 51 cms

work discussed here, Padraig Murphy has pursued a path which is deeply concerned with placing contemporary activities and attitudes in a context of the whole history of art. In this poster for the Arts Council of Northern Ireland (no 55) Murphy, who was born in 1949, examines the various media used in art and also tackles the notion of what is 'real' and what is 'constructed'. Lichtenstein did paintings in which the comic book shorthand style of drawing was used to describe an actual painted mark, and Claes Oldenburg with large scale soft sculptures questioned the nature, size and uniqueness of objects. *The Francis Petrarch Affair* is about illusions and illusionisms, procedures, and that first massive step of making a mark on paper or canvas. He once took an ordinary, dirty, used apple box from a stack of thousands of identical boxes. He painted it white, then *painted* on simulated marks of dirt and general wear and tear: the box was then simply returned to the stack, a unique object only because its marks were illusionistic rather than 'real'. No attempt was made to sell it or in any other way to identify it with an 'artist' but it is a good example, like his proposal for having an exhibition of specially painted canvases shown face down on a gallery floor, of a contemporary approach which is tantalising, iconoclastic, witty and yet deadly serious.

Attitudes change as do styles. In the summer of 1977 Arthur Armstrong has exhibited new still life paintings in Spain whose crisp lines and glowing colours are Quattrocento in spirit, and yet the sense of composition and the emotive nature of the colour is in accord even with his dark, lowering landscapes (see page 22). During the period June to August 1977 the author has seen enough to suggest that considerable changes in style, or subject may be expected to emerge soon from the studies of several Ulster painters, proving that the idea of a 'typical' style or medium must be viewed with caution.

NOTES

1. From the introduction by Derek Kinnen and Mike Catto to the catalogue *Art Spectrum Ulster*, Arts Council of Northern Ireland, 1971.
2. *The Arts in Ulster*, eds Sam Hanna Bell, Nesca A Robb and John Hewitt, Harrap and Co, 1951.
3. Statement by the artist in *Artist's Choice*, Ulster Museum, 1973.
4. Letter by the artist quoted in entry for *Anne and the dog*, *Irish Art from the Ulster Museum* catalogue raisonné, Belfast 1978, quoted here by courtesy of the Ulster Museum.
5. Available as a colour reproduction and published by the Arts Council of Northern Ireland 1977.
6. 'My composition of the Connemara landscape was influenced by my study of the Celtic Crosses. On the crosses I'd see figures encompassed by squares. So in my Connemara landscapes I'd use the fields as the squares, stand them upright and paint my figures within them. Then people would say back in Belfast: "That ould eejit can't draw at all, he even has fields standing on their heads."' Gerard Dillon interviewed by Wesley Boyd, *Irish Times*, 28 January 1968.
7. In 1965 George Campbell acquired a tape recorder and he and Gerard Dillon recorded portions of Samuel Beckett's *Endgame* done in strong Belfast accents.
8. Colin Middleton interviewed by Michael Longley, *The Irish Times*, Dublin, 7 April 1967.
9. *ibid.*
10. Reproduced by courtesy of Appletree Press, Belfast.
11. Catalogue statement *Penta Exhibition* Octagon Gallery Belfast 1977.
12. Review by Hilton Kramer of Scott's exhibition at the Martha Jackson Gallery, New York, January 1973, reproduced by courtesy of the *New York Times*.

13. Personal statement included in the catalogue of John Middleton's one-man show, Arts Council of Northern Ireland, 1972.
14. Personal statement included in the catalogue of Gordon Woods' one-man show, Belfast and Dublin 1977.
15. See the article by Roy Johnston entitled 'System and Art' *Introspect* No 1, Dublin 1975. For a fuller history and analysis of this type of art see the catalogue by Stephen Bann, *Systems Art*, Arts Council of Great Britain, 1972.
16. Johnston, *ibid*, page 4.
17. Letter to the author 1977.

THINKING IN 3-D SCULPTURE

'Of sculpture there is little to tell.'
John Hewitt 1951 [1]

'If sculpture has scarcely been referred to in this survey it is because little has been produced in Ulster over the last two decades.'
Kenneth Jamison 1971 [2]

For a variety of reasons the picture has changed little since these two assessments were written. That is not to say that sculptors do not exist in this province or that no new ones are being produced, for every year the Art and Design Centre in Belfast has a number of graduates whose qualifications show that they have specialised in sculpture. Very few are heard of again. Certainly not every graduate painter continues to paint, any more than every graduate potter sets up a ceramic studio. The reasons why graduates fail to produce finished works after college are numerous and often very valid. Teaching is a tiring vocation, both mentally and physically and it takes a lot of determination to do creative work in the evenings. But many artists do, and the painters need only the minimum of space and equipment. A proper studio, huge canvases and a multitude of paints and brushes are laudable aspirations but in their absence a sketch pad on the kitchen table may suffice. The sculptor has a different story: sketch pad and table may be enough to help produce ideas, even small maquettes may be made in a confined space, but for full size three dimensional works (in any medium) not only is a generous space needed but so too are raw materials and specialist equipment. Supposing the young sculptor *does* invest in these things, and finishes a piece, what then?

'You can't even give sculpture away,' commented one disgruntled local sculptor. Even a very large modern canvas can find a wall somewhere, at home, at friends, at the local school; but no-one seems to have room for objects which occupy a lot of three dimensional space. A canvas may be rolled up, painted over if necessary, but unless a piece of sculpture is of the kind that can be dismantled and stowed in the garage, storage becomes a real problem. It also appears that modern sculpture provokes more public antagonism than modern painting, possibly because sculpture seems so permanent. Paintings can be ignored, sculpture tends to make its presence felt, and since it is often public sculpture, the public produces some pungent, grass roots criticism.

The Futurist Manifesto of sculpture in 1909 had called for an end to the unique position held by bronze and marble in the making of sculpture. The Futurists felt that sculpture of the twentieth century should reflect the materials of that century and that wood, metal, electric lights, even horsehair could be used together in a work, especially if the subject was not descriptive. Half a century later little real evidence of these or later theories of sculpture was to be found in this province. Even at the art college, great emphasis was still laid on the traditional skills of carving, modelling and casting. This is not to disparage these skills, the artists who taught them, or the works that were produced from them, but certainly most of the modern sculpture movements had little impact here. The subject matter of sculpture in Ulster may have shown an assimilation of motifs from movements such as Cubism, Surrealism and Expressionism, but, as in the case of *The Mystic* (no 56) by Newton Penprase (born 1888) who taught at the Belfast College of Art from 1911 to 1953, the actual medium and technique are traditional. The themes tackled by a sculptor like George Galway McCann (1909-1967) inclined to the religious and even the classical although with the simplification of form practised by sculptors like Moore and Epstein. If not actually given the title Madonna and Child, the sculptural subject of mother and child runs throughout much of the figurative sculpture of this century and a glance at catalogues and sculpture lists in Ulster shows the popularity of this motif, even in the 'eroded' small sculptures of T Ian Friers (1909-1975). His works in wood, mainly of birds and animals were filed, sandpapered and polished. While showing an awareness of, for example, the elongation of form that was applied to modern figurative sculpture, Friers' sculptures are modest in scale and concept and are the antithesis of public sculpture such as is found in, on and around architecture.

The public or private commission is still one of the main outlets for the Ulster sculptor, and not surprisingly, a great deal of it is intended for ecclesiastical rather than secular buildings in this island. Many interesting free standing and relief sculptures, normally with some figurative and iconographical or liturgical elements, have been produced for churches here. At the same time, a lot of banal works have been produced as well. Secular commissions are less frequent even with the encouragement given to and by industrial concerns and local authorities. It is interesting to read the comments in the local press (by critics, journalists and vox populi) as recently as 1958 when F E McWilliam's *Princess Macha* (no 57) was erected at Altnagelvin Hospital, Londonderry. In retrospect this powerful but figurative piece is a typical example of the elongated, almost spiky shapes of British sculpture of the 1940s and 1950s but it is nowhere near as revolutionary as its supporters claimed. Nor is it the kind of work which deserved the derision which some correspondents directed towards it.

56 NEWTON PENPRASE
The Mystic
n d; plaster; 65 x 39 x 46 cms; R N Penprase collection

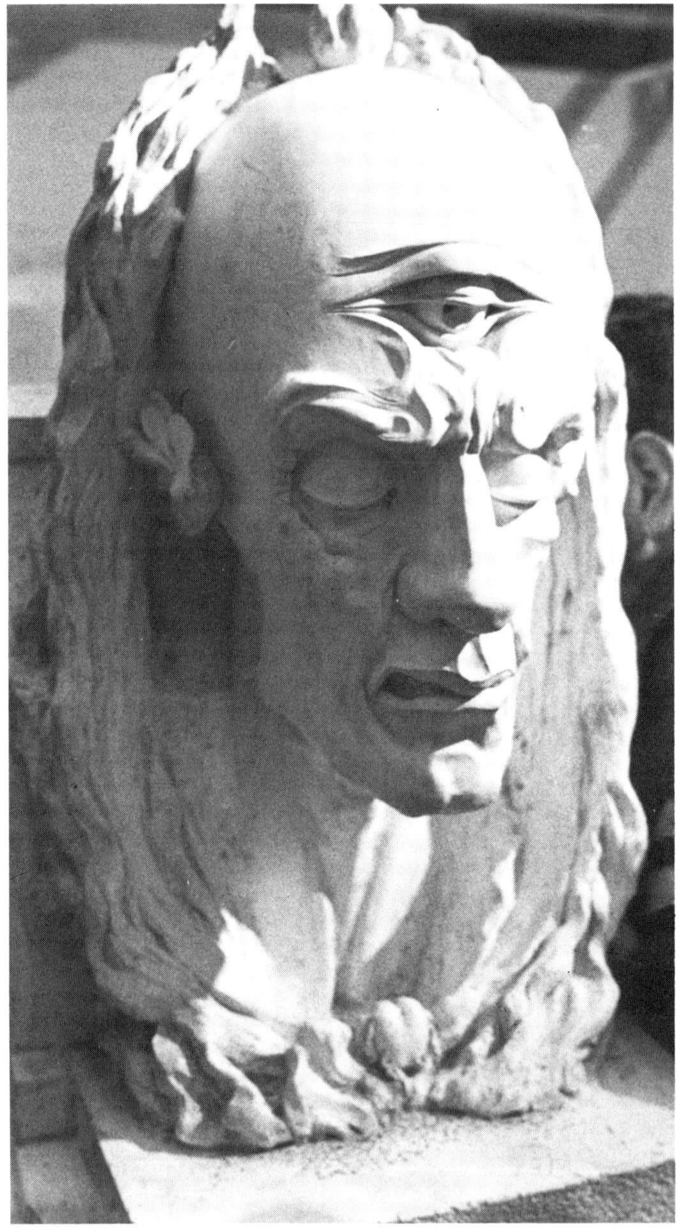

It must be viewed as a work of its time by an Ulster sculptor who had to leave the province to make a name for himself. *Princess Macha* may also represent the coming of age of twentieth century Ulster sculpture.

In British, European and world terms F E McWilliam is the most celebrated Ulster born sculptor. Born in Banbridge in 1909, he left the province at eighteen and his subsequent development was motivated by what he saw and learned in London and Paris rather than by anything that Ulster sculpture could teach him. McWilliam is also discussed in *Art in Ulster 1*, but of the influences on his work in the 1930s and 1940s two examples are worth citing here because they affect his vision throughout his career. The great Romanian artist Constantin Brancusi, who McWilliam met, represented two aspects of modern art, one the purity of form (abstract or not), the other being the national, emotional appeal of a sculptor who understood the tradition of carving in his own country. From Brancusi McWilliam therefore not only learned of modern sculpture, he learned about the forms and symbolism of ancient Celtic carving. The Surrealists also influenced him, not only with the energy of their work, but also by showing him the power of the subconscious and the way in which modern art might be literary, even representational, without having to sacrifice its modernity. Works like *Princess Macha* or *Triad* (1961) show an awareness of Celtic form, a great feeling for texture and a kind of primitive power. McWilliam has worked in many styles from abstract surrealist to representational portrait busts. In the last fifteen years he has gone from abstract bronzes like *Crankshaft Figure* of 1963, a reclining figure reminiscent of Moore, to figurative work whose point of contact with the ground is minimal. *Crankshaft Figure* 'sits' on three points and some of the works of the sixties are elevated above the ground, held up sometimes by one rod only. At the same time a greater sense of contained tension replaced the static, hieratic monumentality of some of the work of the previous decade. Yet even some small works in the late sixties could suggest heroic scale: these were bronzes of reclining women with one side cut away to give a flat, almost drawn feeling which contrasted with the rounded fullness of the other side. In the early 1970s McWilliam combined the themes of movement and turmoil with the reclining women as he looked back to the province of his birth. He strove to find a metaphor for the senseless violence that had erupted again, and he found it in the series *Women of Belfast*. This series and his latest small figures are discussed in the following chapter.

While F E McWilliam has experimented with many materials and techniques, he is at home with that traditional and costly medium, cast bronze. Bronze is an eminently respectable medium, it allows every nuance of the original modelled clay to achieve permanence, but it is very expensive and a sculptress like Carolyn Mulholland has to go to John Behan's foundry/ workshop in Dublin for bronze casting. Like many others she uses a more modern medium, bronze fibre-glass, which achieves the same appearance but is both lighter and cheaper. Carolyn Mulholland (born 1944) is a contemporary sculptress whose work embraces both modern and traditional materials and themes. She is an accomplished practitioner of portraiture in which area her bold but sensitive portrait bust

57 F E McWILLIAM
Princess Macha
1957-58; bronze; figure 237.49 cms, plinth 3.81 cms, pedestal 100.33 cms; Altnagelvin Hospital, Londonderry.

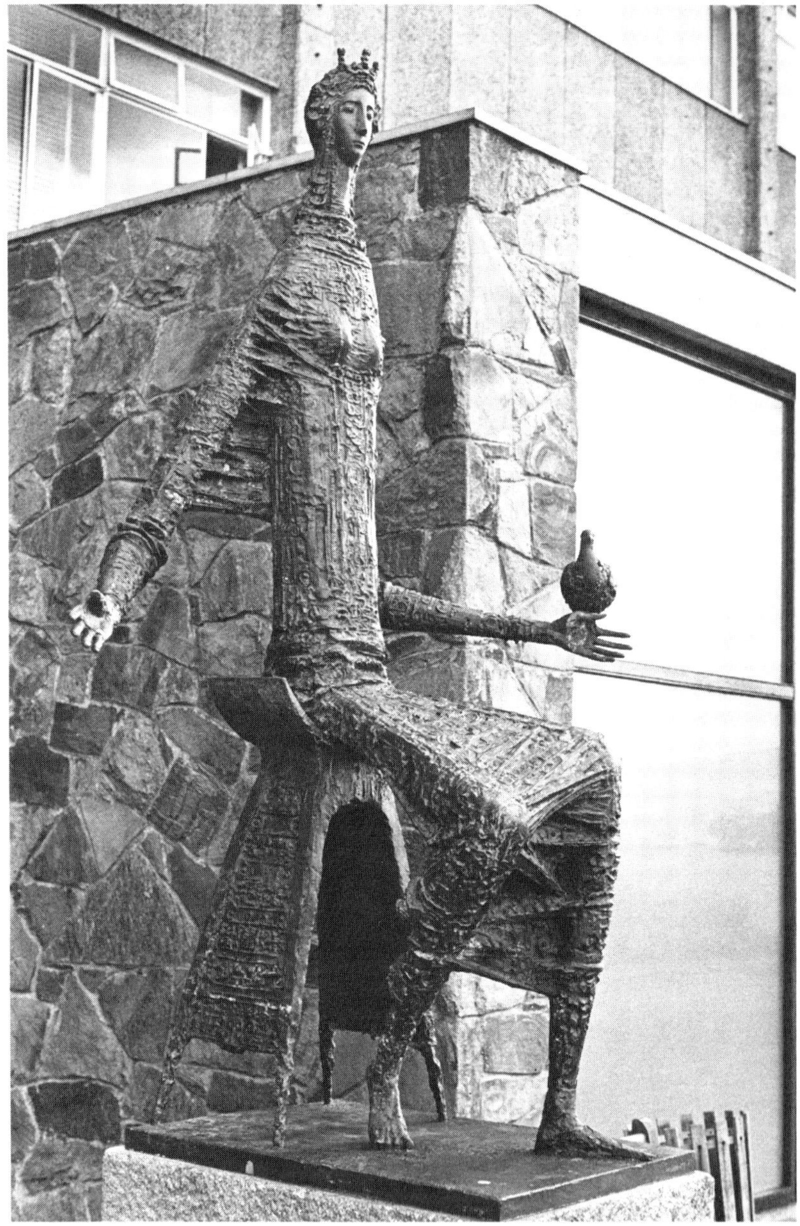

58 CAROLYN MULHOLLAND
Stretch
1971; mild steel and fibreglass; 152.4 x 30.5 cms; Martin Dillon collection

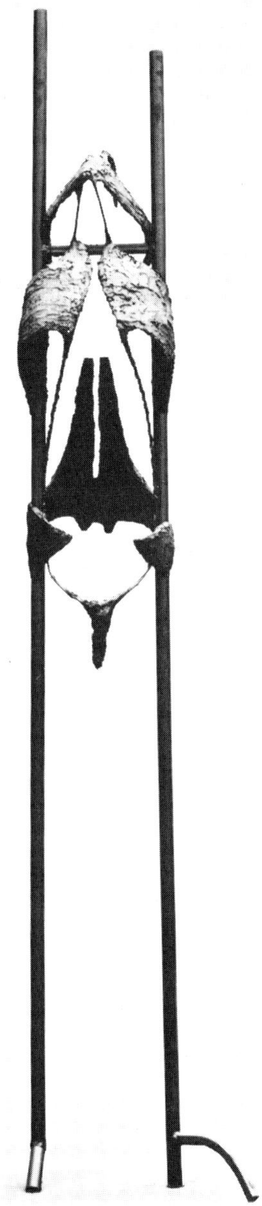

of R H McCandless represents a resounding success. Her life size portrait of Ulster athlete Mary Peters seems less successful. In formal terms the likeness is fine and the tricky problem of balance in the stance of the figure is handled well, but it lacks the sense of movement, of energy, of tension which one normally finds both in the work of Carolyn Mulholland and in the subject of this piece. Her more abstract work like the figurative sculpture exudes a sense of directed movement and controlled energy. *Stretch* (no 58) a Giacometti like construction is a convincing analysis of vertical and lateral movement, the two opposing forces held in check by the skeletal cage. In recent years she has exhibited a number of very small pieces of tumblers and acrobats seen in the act of performing. Figures pile up, one on top of another creating axes of vertical, horizontal and diagonal movement. Each little figure was a unit and it seemed that they could be interlocked to create a variety of poses and thrusts, similar in spirit to some works of John Behan in which flights of birds are connected wing to wing to form a rhythmic screen in space. These small works of Carolyn Mulholland were also the starting point for the large scale group of balancing figures which she made as part of the Arts Council of Northern Ireland's Art in Context plan to site work in public places. This group (no 59) stands at the Antrim Forum.

The work of Deborah Brown might be located as legitimately in a chapter on painting as in this one on sculpture, for her creations successfully bridge the gap from two dimensions to three, and even today her fibreglass sculptural pieces have a tactile quality which is extremely painterly. 'I wouldn't like to work in... bronze,

59 CAROLYN MULHOLLAND
Figures
1974-75; fibreglass bronze; approx 168 cms each; The Forum, Antrim

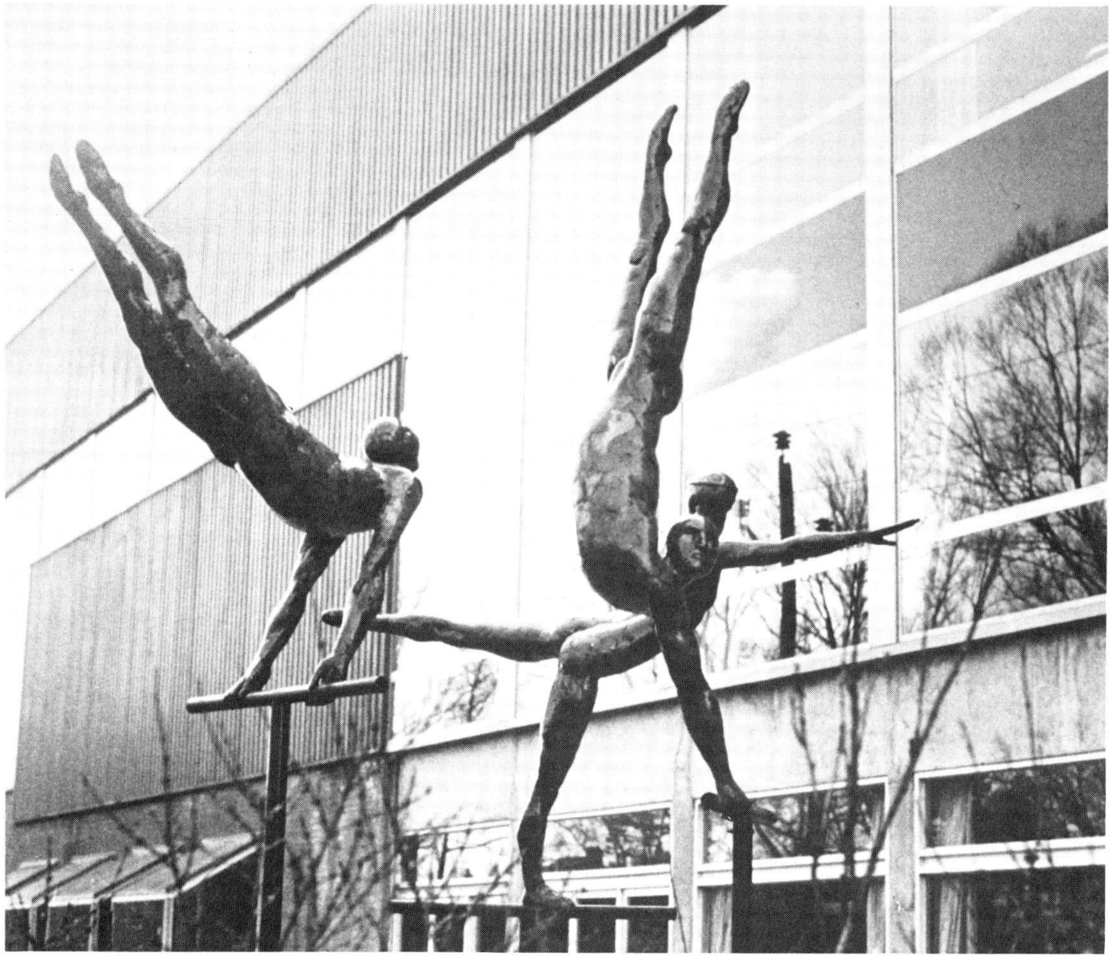

as it's a much more solid material than those I use, or maybe it's because I still think of myself as a painter.'[3] Born in 1927 her initial works until about 1957 were of spare, elemental landscapes and objects. Her exposure to art in Paris and the whole range of international painting at that time led her towards abstraction and specifically to the exhilaration felt in the act of painting. This manifested itself in a number of large Abstract Expressionist works which by 1958 were strict (but remarkably joyful) explorations of mark making and the variety of experiences deriving from brush strokes, line, tone, etc. Her forms were either of swirling cloud line shapes, for example *Painting* of 1962 (no 60) or of thin, energetic lines which defined the

60 DEBORAH BROWN
Painting
1962; brush strokes on canvas; 102 x 76 cms; Gordon Lambert collection

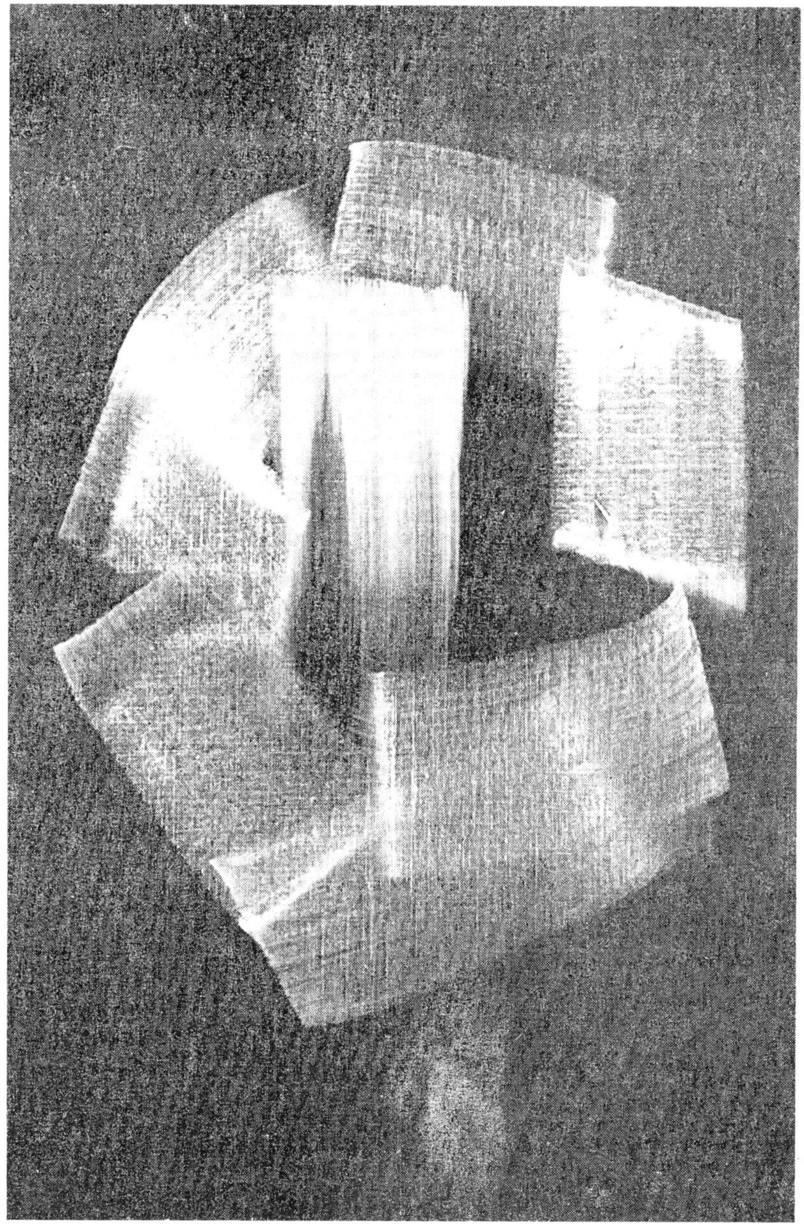

space around them. Although a common bond of form and energy exist between the paintings of Deborah Brown and those of Alice Berger Hammerschlag, the work of the former was different in that her work was not intended to convey symbol, metaphor or representation. Her titles are descriptions of medium and technique: a work entitled *Canvas nailed on wood* is that. The last mentioned work, of 1961, is one of her first essays beyond the painted surface. Her admiration for the simple but expressive shapes of William Scott and Mark Rothko and her own, often large, paintings of the late 1950s show her understanding of the relationship of all the elements in a work. *Canvas nailed on wood* (no 61) she described as follows:

> 'The variation and sense of space made by the darkness of the lines formed by the planks nailed down at uneven intervals.
> A further space created by the transparent quality of the thin canvas on the wood texture.
> The contrast between the irregular line of the edge of the canvas on the board and the hard lines of the planks.
> The tension felt between the wood grain and the weave of the canvas.'[4]

This is almost a manifesto for her work since then. She moved on to a series of relief paintings with the canvas cut and re-assembled and other materials such as string, cane and wire added to give a solidity in which the skeleton or structure became visible and integral to the effect. Papier maché made them even more sculptural and by the mid 1960s she was working in fibreglass, a move which resulted in the relief forms by which she is best known now, but also allowing her to produce some works in the round. Fibreglass gave Deborah Brown the chance to continue her critical analysis of form and relationships, as noted above, but it also heightened the effect that light could bring to bear on the work. Light not only plays over the forms; the dips, bumps and ridges, it penetrates the forms themselves creating new relationships of form to form and form to background. Colour is also a feature, since even nominally white fibreglass creates subtle colour effects for the viewer and this can be developed by the use of coloured fibreglass, coloured background or both. On several occasions she has spoken of her love of the landscape, especially that of the glens and coastline of Antrim where she grew up, and something of this sensibility for the textures, light and sheer physical presence of the earth may be felt when looking at a work like *Fibre Glass Form on Tinted Tempered Masonite* of 1969 (no 62), of which a detail is also given (no 63). This is not an illustration of a landscape, but it is almost a reconstruction of its component parts. Truly abstract, the work of Deborah Brown is not austere, not is it 'samey' even if many of her forms are similar. It does have a remarkable constancy of purpose.

A major turning point in British sculpture came in the early 1960s when the so-called New Generation sculpture became critically recognised. Henry Moore, Barbara Hepworth and others had pursued traditional values of modelling, carving and casting. Even the 1950s 'generation' like Reg Butler, Lyn Chadwick and F E McWilliam had continued to cast, though they were more concerned with welded forms with surrealist overtones; figures that were *almost* birds, *almost* animals. The New Generation (now, only fifteen years later, an old

61 DEBORAH BROWN
Canvas Nailed on Wood
1961; media as title; 122 x 91.4 cms; collection the artist

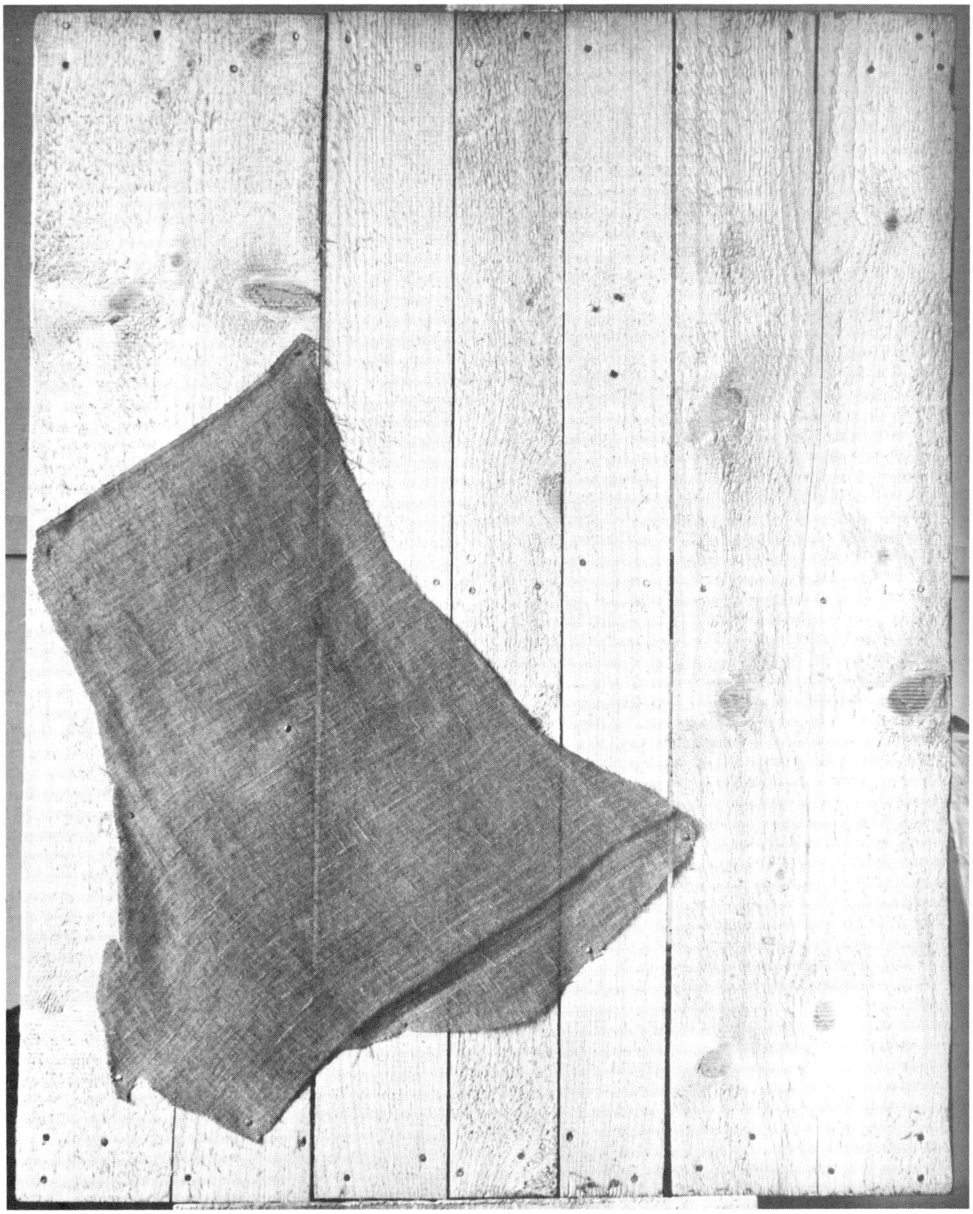

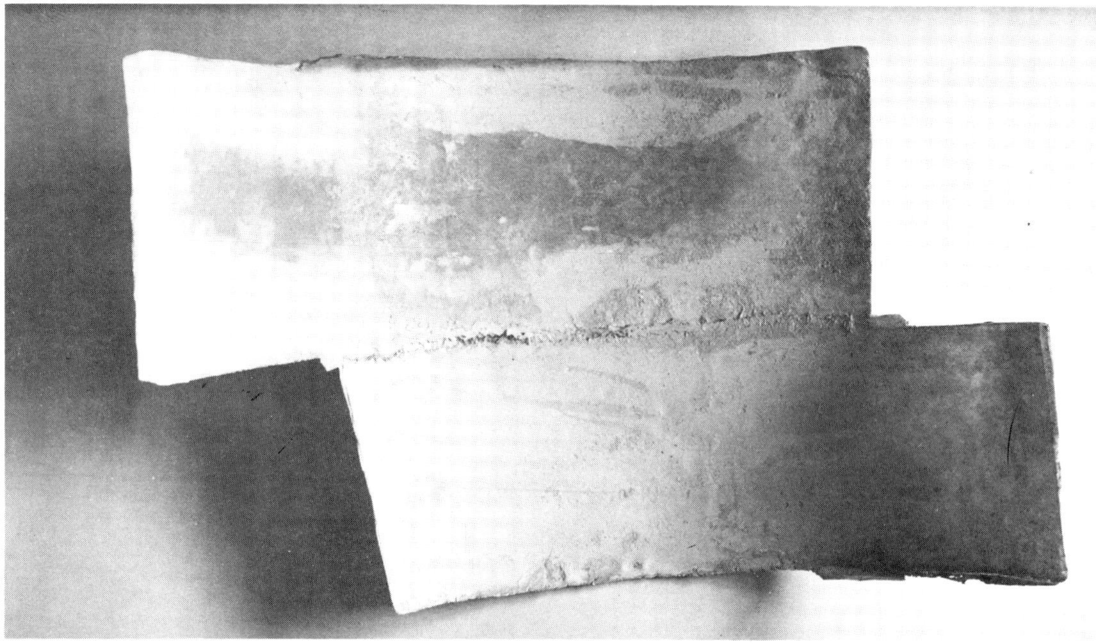

62 DEBORAH BROWN
Fibre Glass Form on Tinted Tempered Masonite
1969; media as title; 122 x 193 cms; collection the artist

generation) of sculptors like Anthony Caro, Philip King and William Tucker produced uncompromising sculptures constructed out of sheet metal, girders, mesh and industrial tubing. Some were brightly painted, and some were left with rivet and weldmarks. These had little to do with the vaunted idea of 'truth to materials'; materials were brought into service as required, not for aesthetic values. Much of this derived from the American sculptor David Smith who had not only utilised industrial materials in a manner closer to engineering than to art but had also suggested the move away from the sculptural 'object' to the use of sculptural elements to manipulate quite large areas of land and air. Open constructions, devoid of stand or pedestal, might snake across the floor and occupy all the space of a room.

Space and scale and materials might be set head over heels by the Pop-influenced sculptors who used found objects, or re-made objects in new scales or materials. Different again from Anthony Caro other, younger artists in Britain and America actually returned to the idea of 'truth to materials' exploring the hardness of hard things, the softness of soft, the differences between a roll of felt, a brick and a twig. In short, by the mid 1960s the idea of sculpture as being an object, solid or pierced sitting on a pedestal in a gallery had finally been dispelled.

In Ulster a number of artists tried to keep abreast of the unceasing number of innovations which

63 DEBORAH BROWN
Fibre Glass Form on Tinted Tempered Masonite
1969; detail of no 62

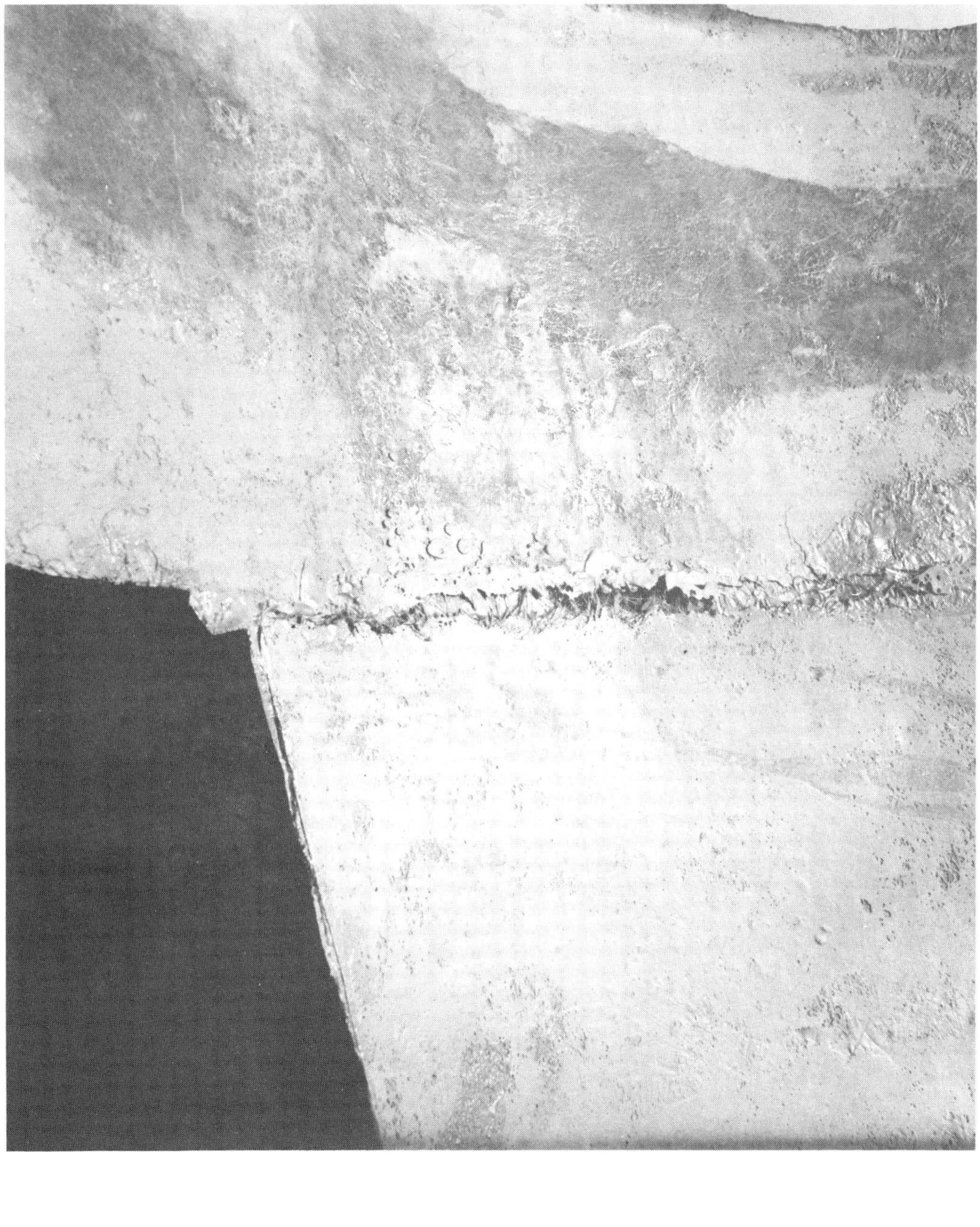

were being announced monthly, it seemed. It is impossible to say who in Northern Ireland exhibited the first Anthony Caro-type sculpture of welded, riveted or bolted sections, the first minimalist Don Judd cube, the first pile of sand or whatever. Nor is it particularly relevant: what is relevant is that these were adopted into the language of sculpture with considerable alacrity after the mid 1960s and were soon adapted to the particular sensibilities and talents of local practitioners.

David Winters (born 1942) was fortunate in having spent three years at the Royal College of Art in London at a time in the 1960s when many of the new sculptural forms and theories had evolved from staff and students there and at St Martin's School of Art. On his return to Ulster he showed a concern for space as well as materials. The wood sculptures that he produced around 1970 were sometimes skilful carvings which sought the essence of wood and sometimes they used wood in assembled, modified ways, such as the use of strips, planks and so on. But he was also experimenting with sculpture which did not sit upright. *Triangle, Gesture and Mark* of 1971 (no 64) was a large flat piece which manipulated the space within it, that beyond it and also the surface on which it might be laid. It is a contrast piece: geometry (triangle, circle and so on) against organic shapes; rough texture against smooth; solid against the hollow; the

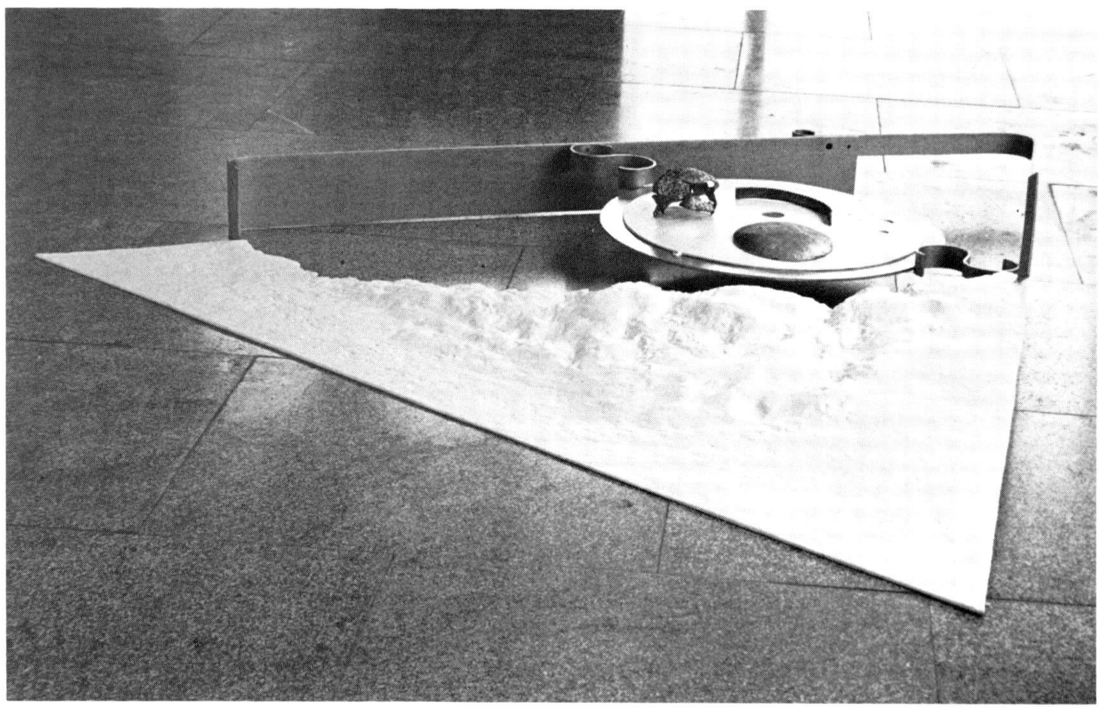

64 DAVID WINTERS
Triangle, Gesture and Mark
1974; glass reinforced plastic, cast aluminium, painted steel; 249 cms equilateral triangle rising to 22.85 cms; collection the artist

V ADRIAN HALL
Sculptogram
1975/6; photographic print;
50.8 x 76.2 cms

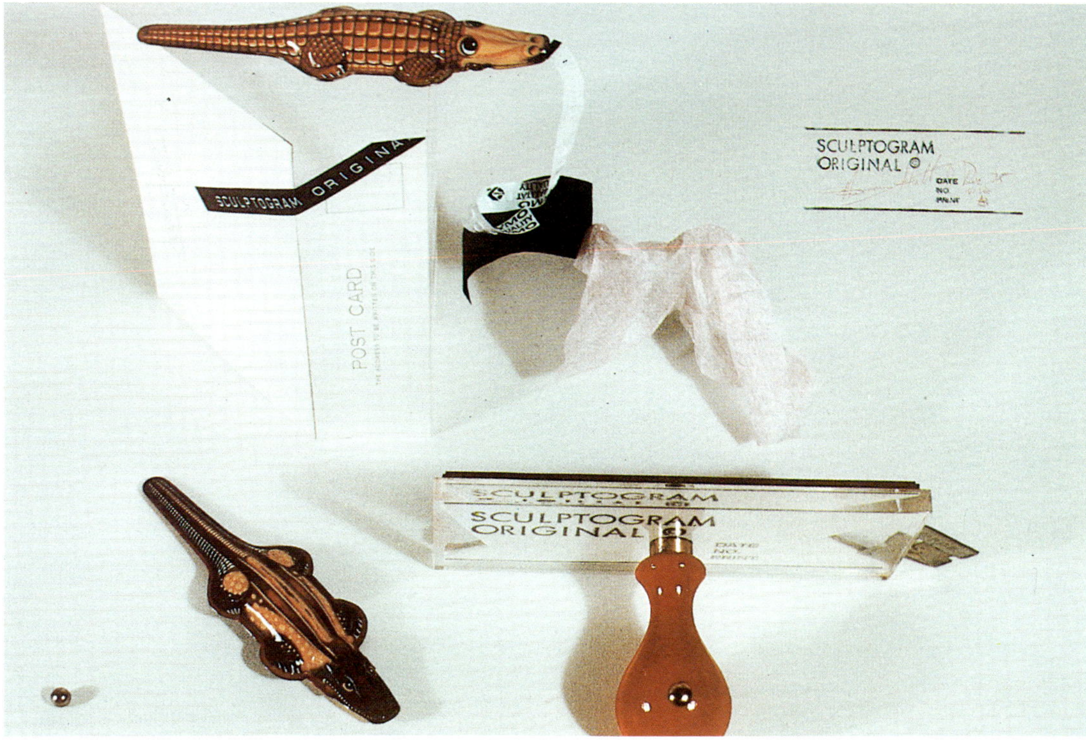

facing page 112

65 DAVID WINTERS
Land of Hearts
1974; glass reinforced plastic, cast aluminium, steel and wood; 122 x 122 x 18.4 cms; collection the artist

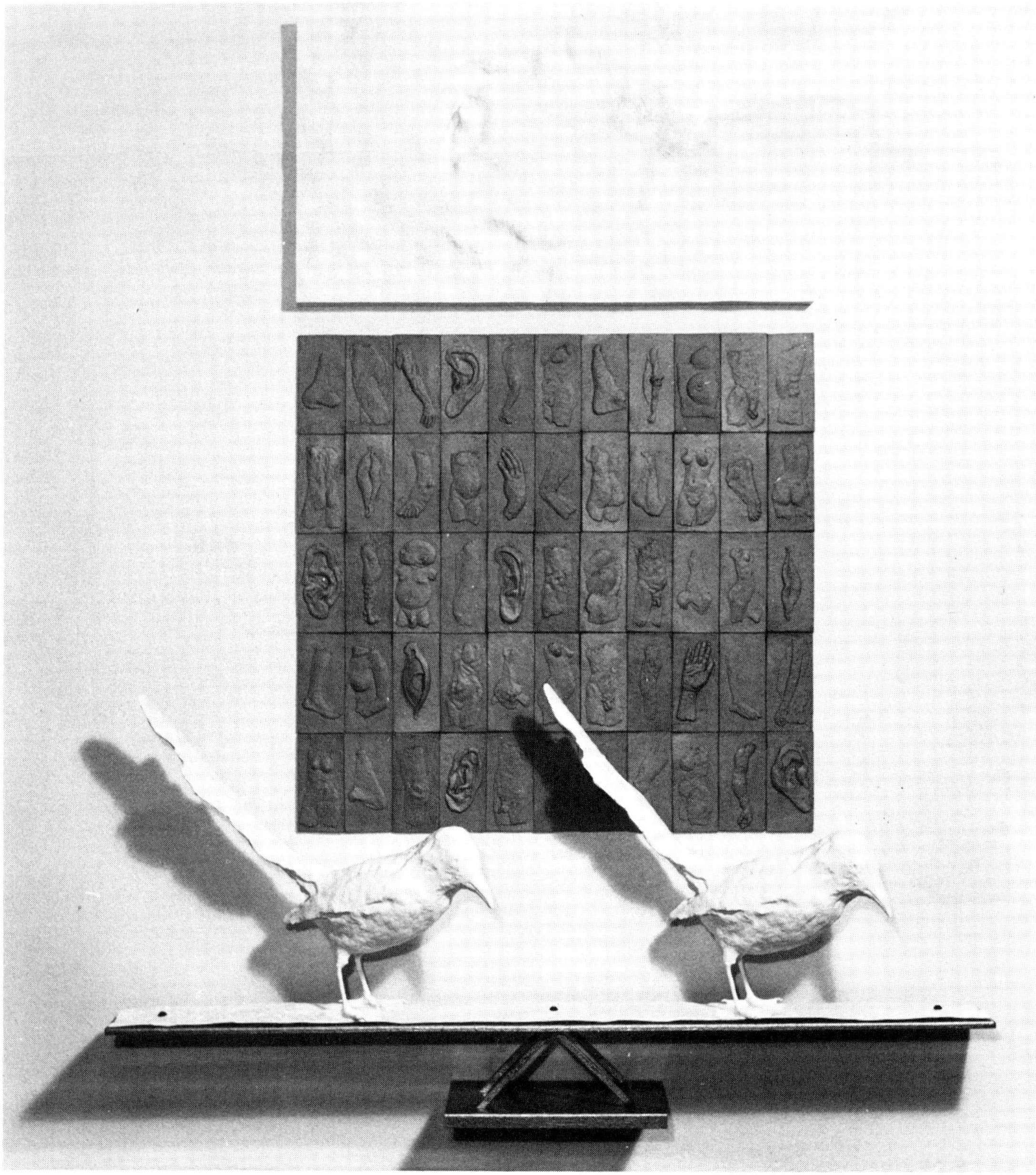

66 CLIFFORD RAINEY
Palm Springs
1974/5; glass, copper, brass, marble; 53.3 x 30.5 cms; Arts Council of Northern Ireland collection

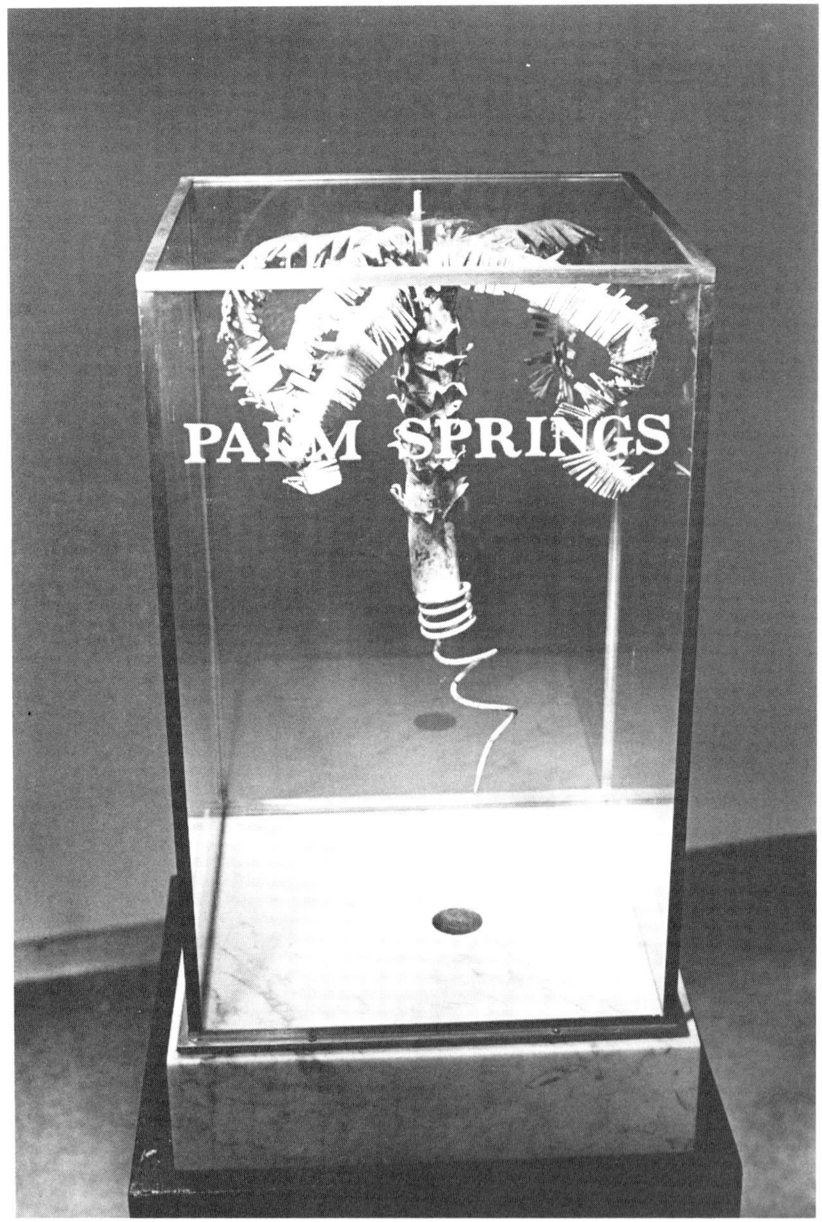

whole piece against its surroundings. Even the words 'gesture' and 'mark' in the title suggest the exploratory nature of the work. In contrast, *Land of Hearts* of 1974 (no 65) is in the nature of a bas-relief, an assemblage of recognisable elements; birds, anatomical parts set out in a fashion which seems both explanatory and illusive. Such a work derives its spirit of private mythologies from constructions and assemblages made in the late 1950s and early 1960s by artists like Jasper Johns and Robert Rauschenberg. The fact that both these artists are as much painter as sculptor shows that strict categories are misleading. David Winters too produces work that is two dimensional, mainly in the form of prints which sometimes give additional graphic information to the themes explored in his sculpture.

There are many reasons why sculptors work in two dimensions, just as there are plenty of valid reasons why painters make excursions into the realms of sculpture, textiles and pottery. Some drawings by sculptors exist as preparatory studies for three dimensional pieces but as the drawings of Henry Moore show, the sculptor is eminently capable of producing drawn or printed images which add to our knowledge of the artist and his work rather than remaining as two-dimensional substitutes for 'the real thing'. Just as it is difficult to categorise Deborah Brown, it is also difficult to say whether Clifford Rainey is a draughtsman who sculpts or a sculptor who draws. Most probably the answer is that both aspects are equally important to him, especially when there are so many similarities between the two media as handled by him. Rainey's drawings (see page 48) are meticulous and 'clean', and his sculptures are executed in steel and glass, materials which allow for the purity and precision seen in the drawings. His sculpture training not only includes art colleges but also time spent at important glass works in Denmark and Finland, so that his handling of glass, and its use in sculpture, is masterly. His sculptures, which often include miniature versions of ordinary objects are pieces of superb craftsmanship and throughout his work, as in *Palm Springs* (no 66) with its Hockney-like tree, there is a vein of humour.

Something of the clarity which is found in Rainey's work may also be seen in the preoccupation that Andrew Sheils has for moving water. Andy Shiels was born in Sunderland in 1943 and has been teaching sculpture in the Department of Foundations Studies of the Ulster College of Art and Design (now Art and Design Centre, Ulster College) since 1966. The water theme appeared in some of his work in the 1960s except that since these were constructed from metal (aluminium, polished brass and chrome plated steel) the reflective nature of the material expressed the surface quality of water. Seeking to explore the inherent transparency of his subject Shiels moved on to acrylic as a medium. Both Rainey and Shiels would agree that working in glass is a costly and complicated process involving equipment and skills which are available in only a few European centres. Clear and coloured acrylic are available commercially and in theory it is simple to manipulate, although in fact it is extremely difficult to bond without leaving unsightly marks. Using, as a basic unit, a sandwich construction column Shiels produced a number of *Waterfall Columns* between 1974 and 1976, half of them dealing with surface characteristics of moving water, the rest concerned with differences below the

67 ANDREW SHIELS
White Water Box
1977; acrylic; 40 x 11.5 x 11.5 cms; Arts Council of Northern Ireland collection

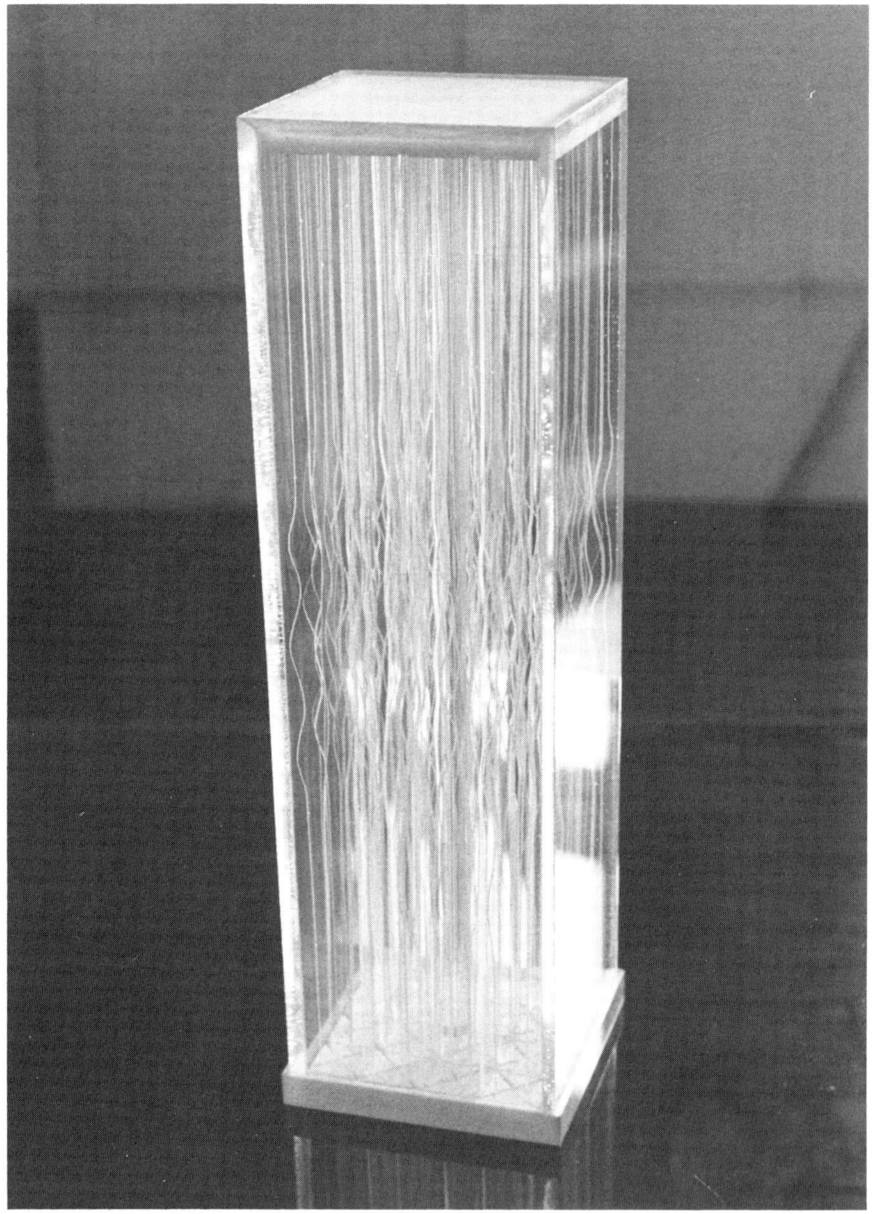

surface. The latest works, *White Water Boxes*, one of which is reproduced as illustration number 67, continue this theme. The light transmitting properties of acrylic (the basis of fibre optics) allow for a gentle but constant shift of light (which creates implied movement) within a deliberately formal framework.

The painter is rarely faced with technical problems that need to be dealt with by industry (although the computer artist is dependent on sophisticated equipment he could not build himself) but the sculptor is constantly faced with this fact. When Gianni Colombo and Rory McEwan independently turned to acrylic sculpture in the 1960s they discovered that if they wanted the material polarised and sandwiched correctly it would have to be sent to a firm in Lichtenstein. Mention has already been made of the lack of bronze casting facilities in this province, and commercial casting of other metals for sculptors is often a very low priority in foundries. Bob Sloan (born 1940) another lecturer in Foundation Studies at Ulster College, recognises this problem and is setting up his own casting facilities so that he can have an even more personal control over materials and processes. His cast metal pieces show the relationship of the nature of the medium, the surface textures and problems of weight and balance. His large constructed pieces use elements like corrugated sheet metal, wood, wire and ropes to open up the sculptural space and to show the inherent nature of the actual materials and how they work with and against each other. They are frameworks, a kind of scaffolding which both surround the subject and become it as well. Tension is integral to these works; actual tension of objects balanced against each other and metaphorical tension in the way in which objects, obstacles and materials surround us in daily life and influence our patterns and behaviour. This can be seen in *Connector* (no 78) which is discussed in the following chapter.

Adrian Hall (born 1943) came to this province in 1973 and his work in Ireland builds closely on preoccupations with space, time, scale and physical material which had been with him even before his teaching periods in the USA and New Zealand. Early works created environments in which the human spectator gave scale to the pieces and also reacted to the space and materials. *Water Tunnel*, a metal tunnel over a tank of water, seemed large indoors, small outdoors. Moving it outside also allowed time and the elements to change the appearance and 'reading' of the piece, showing a theme that many sculptors have worked with; the lack of permanence in a sculpture, a direct contrast to the traditional concept of a piece of sculpture being for all time. This also comes out in *A Hole My Size*, a framework of bricks held together by tension and not by mortar. Its scale, as the title suggests, relates to the size of the artist and its eventual placement in an outside environment in New Zealand draws attention to the piece itself, the way it acts on the environment and the way in which, given time, the environment would be able to re-assert itself by closing in on the brick frame. The concentrated tension which articulates the shape may also be noted in Hall's wall pieces in which clear vinyl was stretched so that the actual points of stretching and their effect on the material was the focus for attention.

These are not arrogant pieces; Hall is concerned with measurement, the way in which we define ourselves by relating everything to natural or arbitrary scales such as length, weight, duration, beauty, value as if these can either give us identity or re-affirm its existence. *Plumb Rite* (executed in a gallery space in Auckland) involved white cord being stretched from the door of the gallery, up and through rooms, tautly crossing itself and ending in two plumb bobs. Simple as this seems, it serves to create a self sufficient 'shape' (lines in space) and also identifies the architecture it is in, and the fact that gravity is a component part of *our* identity. In that same exhibition in 1971 he showed a piece which in form and concept relates to some of the large scale pieces (such as *Slow Rise: Mount* at the 1976 Irish Exhibition of Living Art) by which he is known in Ireland. *Pyramid* was just that: a large pyramid with electric light bulbs up the four diagonal edges. A simple geometric shape, its size indoors again causes problems of scale and identity for the viewer but it was more than a simple shape. A pyramid has connotations of place and history which exist outside its place in geometry and this pyramid had a timing device inside to regulate the intensity of light to the bulbs. The 'programme' fed to the device was linked to the passage of the sun over the Great Pyramid of Cheops. At high noon there the bulbs were at their brightest in Auckland (when the gallery was empty of spectators, it being local night time).

Memorial to a Friend Not Quite Dead (no 68) was shown at the Project Arts Centre, Dublin in 1975, and it is almost a checklist of items in Hall's aesthetic. It is big, and its size gives it an emotional impact. The diagonal beams are perfectly balanced against the wall: Hall admires natural laws and balances. It had electrical components (bulbs and vacuum cleaners) and Hall has a penchant for what can be done with electrical energy and hardware. This also relates to his sense of respect and craftsmanship towards his materials as he has been both carpenter and electrician. The swastika has so many connotations: Hall invites the spectator to give it whichever identity he wishes but if he chooses the one which includes Nazism and Adolf Hitler (not quite dead, if the torrent of books, films, plays and even musicals are anything to go by) then the effect is softened by having the swastika covered, in part, by reflective material, which, linked to the bright lights and noisy vacuum cleaners, gives the ensemble almost a fairground appearance. As with much of Adrian Hall's work (and this is what some people find infuriating about aspects of modern sculpture) it is both witty and totally uncompromising. Nor is his work so outrageous or difficult to understand; like a lot of modern art it seeks to get back to fundamentals and work forward from there. For example the very large piece that Hall showed as part of the Oasis Sculpture Exhibition in Merrion Square Dublin in 1975 was made of bright clean scaffolding and measured 61 metres by 9.1 metres by 3.05 metres and was dismissed by Brian Fallon as being 'a piece of broken fencing'. In fact its form, two long, folded back, fence like shapes, created a lane down which the environment could be viewed afresh. Its open structure did not hamper or dominate the environment but allowed the eye to see the trees and buildings much in the same way as views were constructed in eighteenth century formal garden landscapes.

Not all Hall's works are so large and he can find sculptural qualities in the juxtaposition of even

68 ADRIAN HALL
Memorial to a Friend Not Quite Dead
1975; plywood, galvanised steel, pine, electronic hardware and other space age wizardry; 2.9 x 2.9 x 2.44 metres

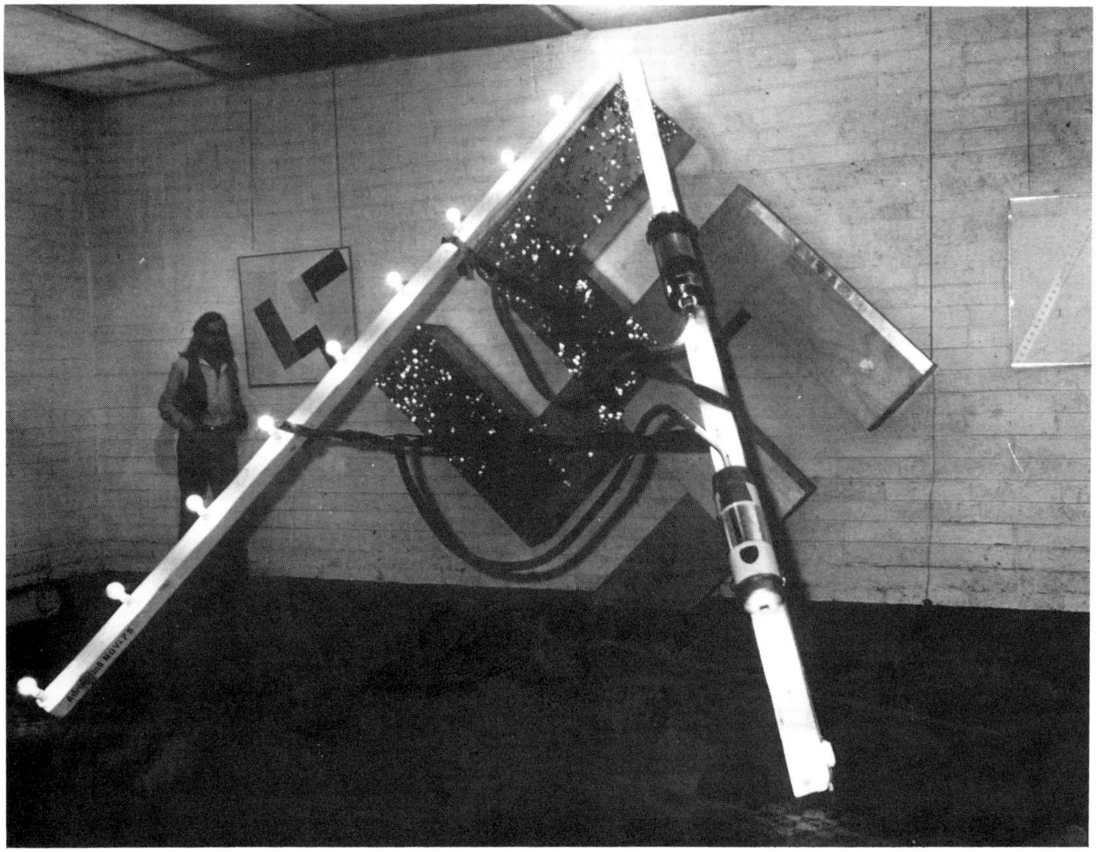

the most ordinary objects. That is part of a long tradition of 'finding' sculptures but where Henry Moore's shelves are full of shells, pebbles, twisted roots and animal skulls, Hall's are full of the detritus of commerce and industry, from badges to an Airfix model of a Stuka. These and prismatic light and drawn marks form the basis of his *Sculptograms* one of which is reproduced as colour illustration number vi. Hall's copyrighting of the term *Sculptogram-Original* and his use of stamp and signature is in the tradition of Edward Kienholz and the N E Thing Co's artworks which are art work, definition and provenance all in one.[5] His description of the procedure used to arrive at the chosen image[6] shows that chance plays a part but also that the artist exercises the final control. The language which is partly legalistic, partly subjective is a piece of description which is also a formal criticism of the work. The work is *not* the arrangement of objects but the print of them, in the same way as Laszlo Moholy-Nagy's film of his *Licht Requisit*

69 BARRY ORR
Industry
1974-76; metals; 5.18 x 4.19 metres; Queen's University, Belfast

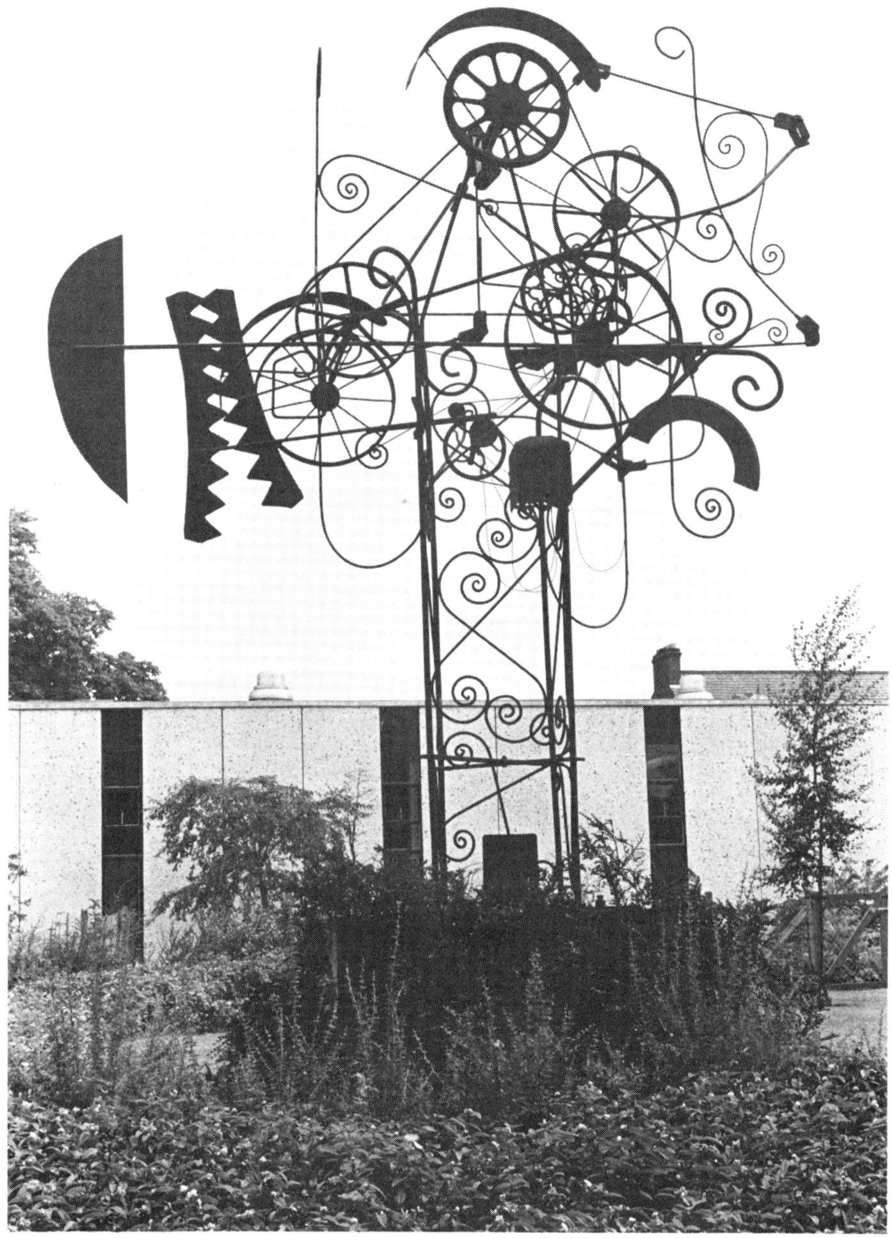

sculpture superseded the constructed piece and was designated as the final artwork by the artist himself.

Mention of Moholy-Nagy's *Licht Requisit* of 1922-30 serves as a reminder that the principle of kineticism in sculpture is hardly new, but its application by Ulster sculptors has been minimal. During the period of popularity of Op Art in the middle and late 1960s several kinetic sculptures were produced as extensions to paintings which relied on optical effects, but nothing lasting came of it. Possibly the only artist in Northern Ireland who works consistently with kinetic three-dimensional pieces is Barry Orr. Most of his works are very small, involved pieces of 'useless' machines; amusing spindly constructions moved by small electric motors whose purpose is to move through complicated but ultimately pointless tasks providing amusement by their very construction. The tradition here is that of Heath Robinson or Emmet and is amusing because of their intimate scale. The whimsy is a little less acceptable when constructed on a much larger scale as in this piece outside a science department at Queen's University, Belfast (no 69). What might have had the power of a Jean Tingueley meta-matic becomes a slight joke and might even be construed as an unfortunate metaphor for mis-directed science itself.

As John Hewitt points out in his companion volume, much of the outdoor sculpture previously produced in this province might be loosely termed memorial sculpture: statues erected to the memory of national or local worthies (often in the form of idealised portraits) or symbolic statuary commemorating events such as the Great War or the sinking of the *Titanic*. Such sculpture is often propagandistic, either generally or particularly so, and that must include the religious sculpture which appears as well. Obviously any such work may arouse emotions which have little to do with the artistic achievement of the actual sculpture. Until fairly recently there was little outdoor sculpture which might be termed sculpture for sculpture's sake, but today few industrialists or local authorities commission sculpture which must express a particular viewpoint. That is not to say that memorial sculpture does not exist but it can be produced in a form which is not overtly propagandistic. The 'memorial' to Marconi's wireless telegraphy experiments of 1905 at Ballycastle is not an individual piece of sculpture but intended as a sculptural environment which uses the landscape features and may be used as a picnic area. Designed by Ethna O'Kane who won the competition to design the piece while still a student, the Ballycastle/Marconi piece is worth citing here because the final version which has been constructed is a somewhat watered down version of the artist's original intention. Too often, sculpture designed for new environments ends up as a token gesture to modernity in the midst of the concrete flower pots, garden furniture and poorly designed objects which are found in pedestrian precincts, leisure areas and housing estates.

The Arts Council of Northern Ireland's Art in Context scheme is designed to 'marry' appropriate proposals with good sites belonging to sympathetic authorities. Not all authorities fully accept the spirit of the works which do well in the judged entries but some pieces (and not all are sculptural) are successful. Graham Gingles'

70 GRAHAM GINGLES
Concrete Trees
1972-73; cast concrete; 244 x 122 x 39.5 cms; St Colmcille's Primary School, Omagh

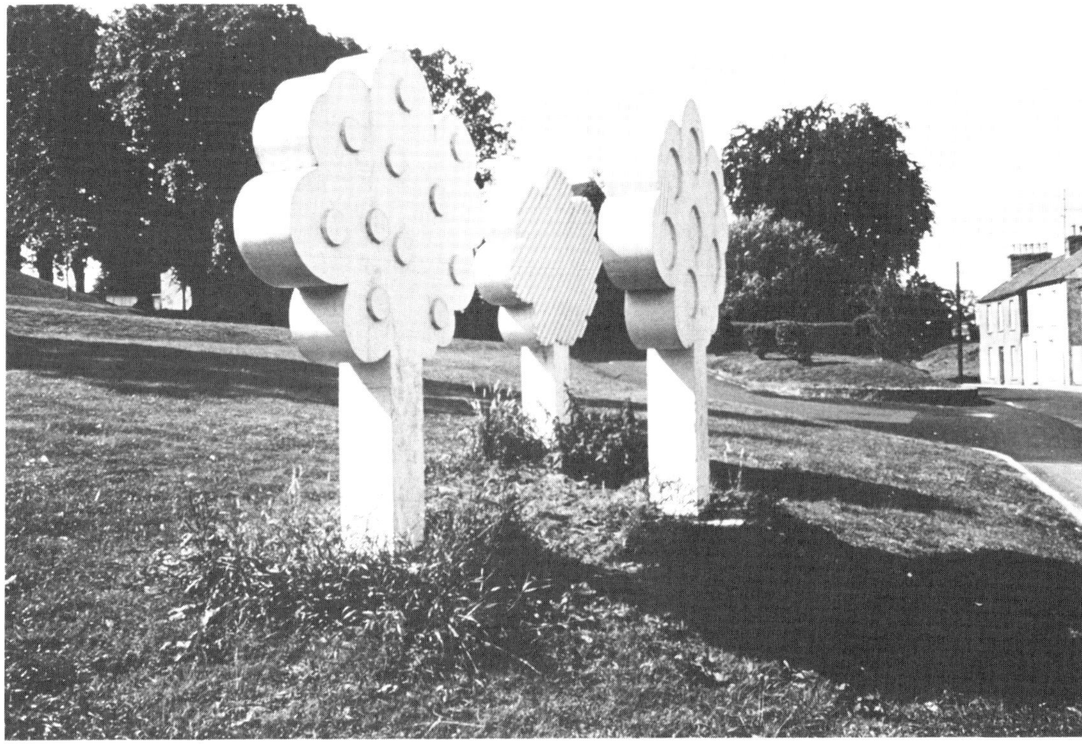

concrete trees (no 70) are trees reduced to their basic form and complement the landscape nicely, while Arthur Armstrong's play sculpture, made of concrete and fibreglass at Belmont House School, Londonderry (no 71) employs bold formal shapes and is designed to be used and not simply to be looked at. Lawrence Alloway, the critic, once proposed some rules for public sculpture one of which said that if a piece could be got at, and its meaning significantly altered (ie through vandalism) it was a rotten sculpture to start with.

As the definitions of sculpture change or expand we may see sculptural qualities in many things. It might be argued with some force that the best pieces of environmental sculpture in the province are in fact pieces of architecture and in this century Newton Penprase's remarkable self-built Bendhu House at Ballintoy fits the bill. This singular piece is in the great tradition of Simon Rodia's Watts Towers, Los Angeles or Clarence Schmidt's House in the Catskill Mountains. From the large to the small: much fine sculptural work is now again being produced in ceramics. The sculptor Eduardo Paolozzi has been teaching ceramics at the Royal College of Art since 1969 and this is symptomatic of the move to a new (or traditional) medium by sculptors so that now much of this fine art oriented, non-functional

71 ARTHUR ARMSTRONG
Playsculpture
1972-73; concrete and fibreglass; 183 x 183 x 183 cms; Belmont House School, Londonderry

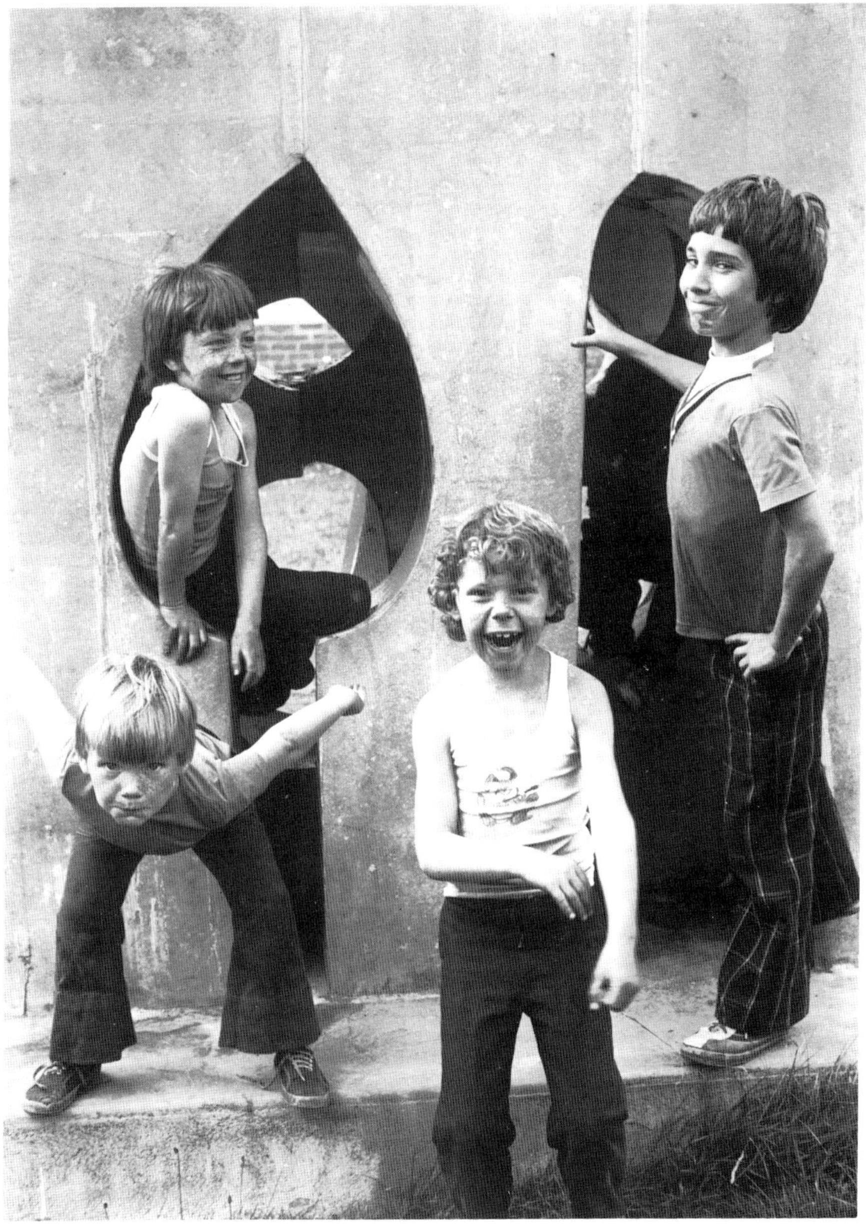

ceramic sculpture is being produced by people who are not normally associated with fine art work. True, some pieces are whimsical, but much powerful imagery is being made by potters... and jewellers and creative embroiderers.

NOTES

1. From an interview with Deborah Brown by students of the Ulster College of Art and Design, February 1971.

2. 'Why' by Deborah Brown, *Ferranti Journal*, Autumn 1966.

3. Article of Copyright, 24 August 1975:

   'With respect to the usage of the term "SCULPTOGRAM" and the meaning of this term as described below, and also to the compound term "SCULPTOGRAM-Original" and the following ascribed meaning:

   '"SCULPTOGRAM" = a mechanically reproduced photographically derived image of a contrived or chosen spatio-emotive situation of ephemeral nature, where the original form is further developed emotively by an adjustment of scale. These decisions dependent upon the variable perceptions of the sculptor, Adrian Hall, and whose applied signature upon one such "Sculptogram" shall constitute a "Sculptogram-Original", and thereby a bona fide artwork.

   'Signed, Adrian Hall.'

4. 'Each colour Print measures 20 x 30 ins horizontal or vertical in a limited possible edition of 13, lettered A-M.

   'The image occurs through a procedure formulated in the copyright lines, which only became redundant when they had been written. The procedure avoids gesture but allows for degrees of whimsy, sentiment, irony, chance and formalism. The references made include the self referential, the art historical, the socio-political, the subjective emotional and objective universal. The whole procedure becomes a hermetic analogue of a more general creative continuum.

   'The image is constructed monocularly through a 35 mm camera view finder, the situation to be photographed is arranged, illuminated and viewed in this way. There are no hidden tricks in the arranging and the photography is adequate in the manner of a saucepan advertisement. Expressive, dramatic, contrived photography is avoided, the scale of the print is a convenient standard, the proportions of which are those of a 35 mm transparency. (Fibonacci series 2:3). Many transparencies are taken of the situation and its subtle variants.

   'The film is sent away for processing and on their return some weeks later the transparencies are projected to the size of the finished prints. They are viewed and reviewed. On the basis of technical adequacy, formal interest, strength of evocation and relevance to this procedure, after long consideration one image might be selected from thirty or forty others. This one is then exiled once more and an internegative made. Prints are produced without any further control by the Artist. There is no cropping or retouching.

   'A rubber stamp imprint and a signature completes the Sculptogram when the colour print is returned. These two gestures, one formal, expedient, ubiquitous, the other autographic, idiosyncratic, eccentric, reaffirm the reality of the physical two dimensional against the illusion of the photographic image, and the dialogue between the past/three-dimensional/real and the present/two-dimensional/actual begins. The past conjunctive so making the present tense.

   'In spite of these notes being written to help the viewer on being confronted with the photographs which are not Photographs, of sculpture which is not Sculpture, in some cases using drawing which is not Drawing: everything in these notes may be deduced from the Sculptograms themselves, but everything in them may not be deduced from these notes.'

NOTES FROM A SMALL WAR ART AND THE TROUBLES

It is somehow significant that the visual image used to re-inforce the words 'Seven Years Are Enough' on the official government peace poster campaign at the end of 1976 should show the text as if daubed or sprayed on to a brick wall. This was a relatively sophisticated and professionally designed example of graphic design but it achieved its impact by being derived from the crude but direct technique of graffiti. These slogans, battle-cries, obscenities and dire warnings are among the less acceptable images by which the world knows contemporary Northern Ireland. I do not necessarily subscribe to the fashionable notion held by, among others, the authors of the book on New York subway graffiti, *Watching My Name Go By*, that such work is a valid form of folk art. However, there is no doubt that such imagery is tremendously powerful and represents an emotional desire to proclaim, to complain or, admittedly, just to deface. Here in Ulster graffiti is normally naked sectarian propaganda, but it sometimes employs the same words and symbols which are found in the various examples of popular art and artifacts of this divided community. Whether an image of iconic significance is sprayed by aerosol on a wall by a bored or embittered teenager or is painted on silk with great artistic merit by a skilled craftsman the actual content of the message may remain substantially the same. For this reason alone this chapter must differ from the rest by examining work done by often anonymous hands as well as by looking at examples of work by professionally accepted artists.

Generally, the former work may be termed propaganda while that of the latter more often seems to be a commentary on the futility of violence. When discussing the images created during the present troubles it must be remembered that there has long existed a popular folk art tradition paralleling the religious, political and social schism of this island. A great deal of valuable work has been done on such imagery by various researchers: some has already been published while still more awaits publication. [1] It is not my intention to trace the lineage or to detail the iconography of the popular arts of the various sections of the community and I must emphasise that such work is not inherently inflammatory. With the polarisation that can exist in this province such symbolic items can and do become the focus of extreme views.

Even the chronological period covered by the euphemism 'the troubles' is subject to debate. Sporadic unrest and violence has dogged this area even before partition and during the time covered by this book there has not only been the present period of violence and change but also a campaign of violent activity which lasted from December 1956 until 1962. It is worth mentioning this because outside the province the latter events were little reported. Explosions and killings occurred but they rarely rated more than a small paragraph in national or international newspapers. Those who analyse the impact of the various news media have maintained that the development of a world wide network based on television rather than on newspapers or newsreels has contributed to the theory that when pictures come into the sitting room all local news is international news and all international news is local news. Just as improved printing techniques contributed to the growth of quality art magazines and books, allowing artists anywhere in the world to plug in instantly to international art trends, so too television coverage of such events as the Vietnam war allowed the inhabitants of McLuhan's Global Village to be acquainted with the various viewpoints and images of current affairs in a fashion impossible at the time of Suez or of the Second World War. Regrettably, the media not only devour any and all news, but they also realise that images of violence have a greater immediate impact than a shot of two people debating issues in a reasoned manner. It is hardly surprising therefore that national and international press and media men were quick to cover the riots and protests which broke out in Derry, Belfast and other places in late 1968.

1968 was a year of protest throughout the world with manifestations ranging from anti-US demonstrations almost everywhere to the May student rising in Paris. The so-called innocence of the year of peace of 1967 was replaced by a political consciousness which in 1968 often found expression in the production of politically motivated art works. Much of this politicised art imagery was communicated not by one-off 'unique' paintings but by the cheap, speedy multiple printing processes which were by then available. One colour lino and screen prints were used methodically in Paris during 'les évènements du mai'. These wall posters, produced by, among others, the Atelier Populaire of the Ecole des Beaux-Arts, were simple, direct and even witty in their condemnation of the establishment. The visual images were frequently rather obvious; shackled fists, riot police as gorillas, but the visual and printed punning which existed on many of them showed a con-

72 ANONYMOUS
Judge, Jury and Executioner: Don't Fraternise
c1971; screenprint on paper, original paper size 76.2 x 50.8 cms; reproduced by courtesy of the Trustees of the Imperial War Museum

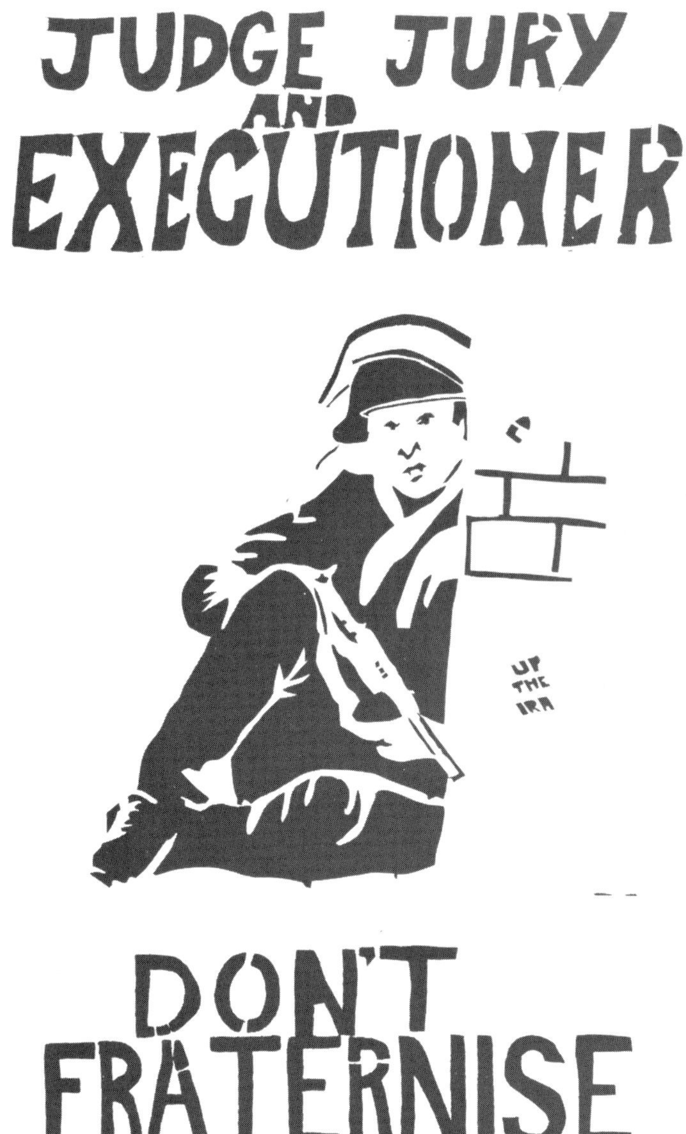

nection with elements of contemporary Pop Art. A link exists between such Atelier Populaire posters as 'Je suis Marxiste, tendance Groucho' and the same type of posters which emerged in Northern Ireland in 1969 and 1970. Given that the Paris 'revolution' was so well covered by the media it can be rightly argued that similar wall posters could be independently produced by anyone in Ulster who watched TV or read the right magazines. All the same it is known that some radical French students visited Ireland in early 1969 since they believed that the events here were (or should be) part of a world wide left wing 'battle of the proletariat against the imperialist aggressors'. I myself was introduced to two French student activists who had not only brought with them copious cyclostyled information on how to organise and sustain urban protest, but also carried examples of silk screen posters of June 1968 *and* instructions on how to create local examples. Perhaps they were ignored: after all the information was in French and local people probably felt that they needed little outside assistance, but whatever the outcome several wall posters did appear. These are ephemeral, designed to have an immediate impact and then to be replaced by another, more topical salvo. Being ephemera, few of these posters now survive, although the Linen Hall Library in Belfast has made a unique collection of publications and ephemera produced during the present unrest. One wall poster image which was a model of its type showed a black cloud (of CS gas) hanging over stylised rooftops. The wording simply read 'The Londonderry Air 1969'. An example illustrated here dates from late 1970 or early 1971 and is now in the collection of the Imperial War Museum (no 72). Such an image will be objectionable to many but it does represent a local version of agitational propaganda (agit-prop) art with a tradition as old as graffiti itself.

Such work allows for no artistic neutrality. It is of one side and for that side only and this propagandising continues in visual forms such as the politically influenced comics which have been produced in Belfast in the last few years. Using the medium of the comic strip, and based in particular on the methods of production and graphic styles of the American underground or alternative press comics such as *Zap!*, the Belfast equivalents have names such as *Resistance Comic* and they are light years away from the style and tone of *The Beano*. The content generally consists of an attack on the security forces and the powers that be, while the drawing style shows that the artistic influences have been R Crumb and S Clay Wilson and other American and Dutch practitioners of a kind of crudely sophisticated line. Despite the many chances for savage satire and expressionist anger, Belfast has so far not produced a local George Grosz who can see beyond partisan divisions to the universal stupidity, cant and surreal behaviour that accompanies the claim and counterclaim in any civil strife.

The political cartoonist does his best to expose such human folly and perhaps the best known local representative of this branch of the fourth estate is Rowel Friers. Friers, born in 1920, is a prolific artist having produced paintings, drawings and book illustrations in addition to the newspaper cartoons for which he is particularly well known. His style which has remained fairly consistent for the past twenty years, inclines normally to a gentle, not a savage kind of caricature.

73 ROWEL FRIERS
Miss Free Derry
13 November 1971; *Belfast Telegraph* cartoon

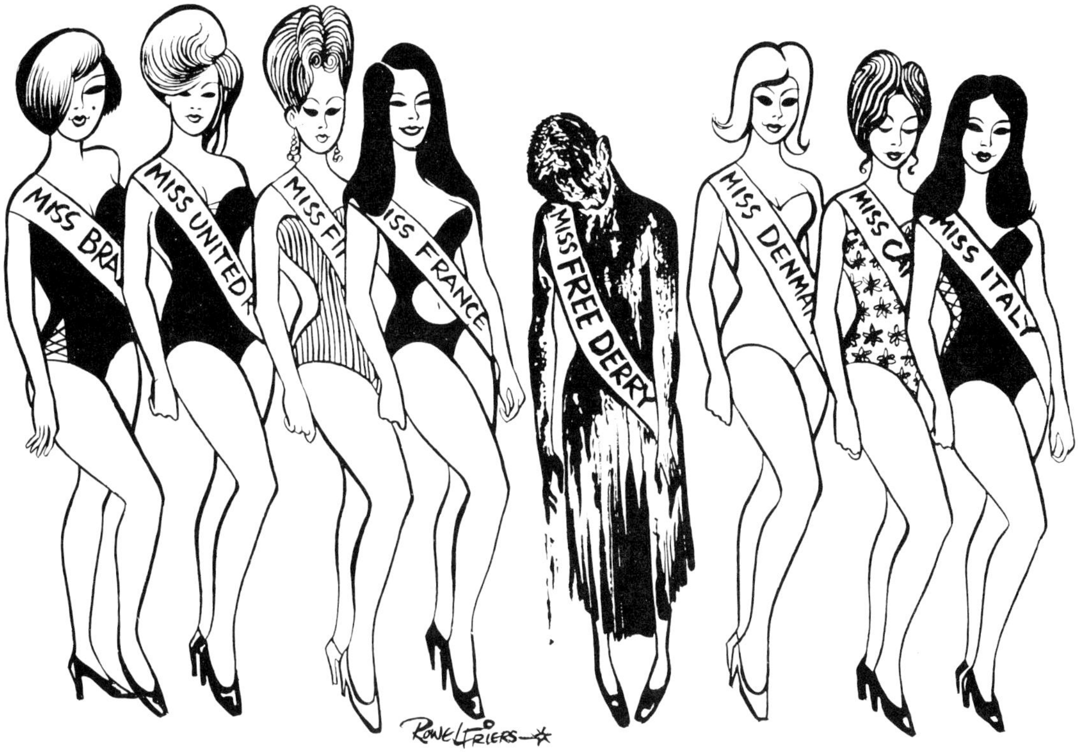

The example here (no 73), is typical of his style of draughtsmanship. His gallery of working urban or rural 'types' is generally a pithy form of human observation. Friers' political cartooning has a sense of fair play: it provokes a tut or a chuckle (in itself no bad thing) rather than giving the cruel flash of insight that one gets from commentators as diverse as Daumier, Scarfe or Heartfield. There have been some exceptions, notably the example illustrated, which is deservedly one of the most famous of the 'troubles' cartoons. Rowel Friers' art, however, is not specific to the troubles; for him this past decade probably represents yet another daft episode in the history of a fascinating but daft community.

Another Ulster artist who has specialised in cartooning with a political slant is Kenneth Mahood whose work appears regularly in *The Times* and *Punch*. Mahood was one of the young painters of promise in the mid 1950s but his subsequent move to London saw the spiky line of his paintings develop into an almost baroque graphic style which delights in curls and swirls. Although he has produced a fair number of scathing visual comments on the Irish situation, he has no great gift for individual caricature and his cartoons remain on a general rather than on a particular level. Perhaps the most acute political cartooning of the last six years here in the North comes from a non-Ulsterman, Martyn Turner, in his work for *Fortnight* and, more recently, for *The Irish Times*. Sometimes his work has a real barb of truth, possibly because a few years ago he was close to grass roots journalism.

I wish to end this section on graphic imagery by citing the example of a privately produced comment on the Ulster way of life and death. *The Hand* is a commercially printed illustrated story told by means of a kind of comic strip. It tells the cautionary tale if a young Belfast teenager who joins his similarly denim-clad pals for a routine evening standing on street corners and annoying the staff of the local Chinese take-away restaurant. The boy, who could be from either section of the community (although his name and the picture on his mother's parlour wall tell of a Loyalist environment) is casually gunned down from a passing car as he walks home. Illustration no 74 is taken from page 13 of *The Hand: A Tale of Old Belfast* (1975/76) drawn and published by John Kindness, one of a number of recent graduates of the Art and Design Centre in Belfast whose student and post-student work has reflected the effect of the violence of the last eight years. Kindness employs a low key tone in *The Hand*, using a deliberate sense of bathos in the page where the victim's last thoughts are not of his fatal wound but of the dog's dirt into which his head falls.

Most artists in Ulster tend to produce work which has little relationship to the troubles. That bald statement could be construed by artists in other countries as a sign of weakness in Ulster art. Some would claim that it is an artist's 'duty' not only to reflect contemporary events but also to be an activist and to shape events. I imagine that the average Ulster artist would reject this interpretation of his *raison d'être* and would claim that the troubles are merely a temporary aberration and that he doesn't need to produce scenes of bombing and shooting to prove that he is sensitive to what is happening. There is certainly an awareness of the causes and effects of the violence to be found in the lives and conversations of most of the artists resident in Northern Ireland, but in most cases it is not *obviously* reflected in works exhibited. That does not mean that the ambience of the troubles is missing from the work: far from it, many artists here have been deeply affected by the present unrest and have incorporated into their work motifs, symbols and personally relevant associations derived from the strife.

I can think of no image more obviously Belfast and more apparently innocent than the painting of a brick wall by Patric Coogan which is illustrated in colour on the back cover of this book. Yet in this and in the other works of his small but painstakingly painted output, Coogan invests the ordinary with malevolence and mystery. Lon Chaney once invited a journalist to examine his own reactions if was suddenly told that the comfortably chintzy sofa on which he was sitting had a dismembered body under it. The same reactions may be felt by anyone venturing out in Ulster today. Is that empty Cortina really a car bomb? How innocent is that tape cassette that someone is handling? Who is it signalling the car to stop? It is somehow natural to fear the unknown; it is more frightening to

74 JOHN KINDNESS
A page from 'The Hand'
1975/6; 30 x 21 cms

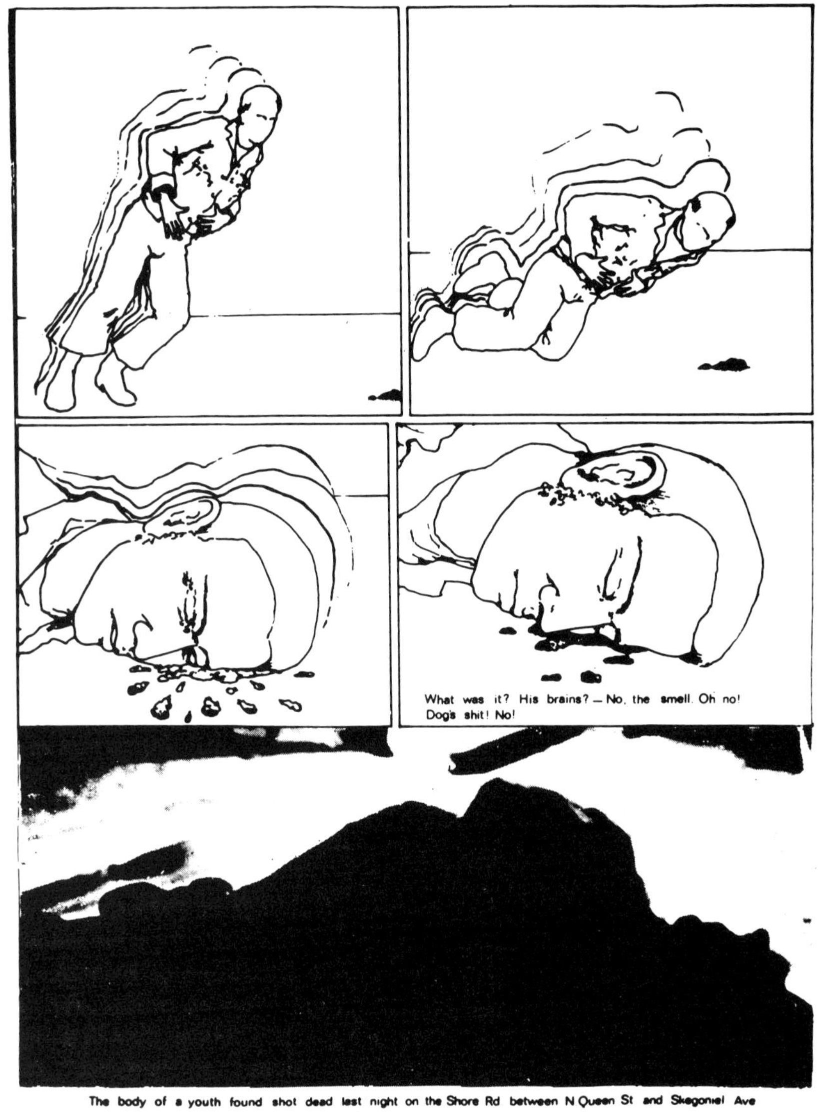

have reason to fear the known. The surrealist painter Giorgio de Chirico painted some urban scenes in which the shadow of someone unseen looms menacingly round the corner, and Charles Oakley, as we have already seen, played on the ambiguities that exist in objects and places in both his landscapes and roomscapes. Pat Coogan adds a particular Belfast flavour to this type of painting. That polythene bag in the work reproduced may just be a bag full of rubbish; it might be a bomb or even the remains of a body. Every supposition, every connotation is valid but Coogan gives us no clue to work on. Emotion is not suppressed completely but it *is* held in check. Someone who didn't know Belfast or who hadn't seen this work shown beside others in Coogan's diploma show some four years ago might be forgiven for thinking that this is merely a local variation of 1970s hyper-realism. That is not the case: Coogan rejects what is for him the superficiality of hyper- or photo-realism and employs a meticulously representational technique (a strong influence on him was the late John Luke) since he feels that abstraction or even a loosely painted divergence from a fidelity to what is perceived would be a betrayal of his personal philosophy and religious beliefs.[2]

Although he left college in 1973 Coogan was a good number of years older than his fellow students. The young generation of painters, printmakers and sculptors leaving college during the 1970s have passed their college days in a city full of sorrow and latent ugly violence. Indeed students entering art college in Belfast now were small children when the present disturbances began and what is for them a 'natural' way of life can be seen reflected in the drawings and doodles of Ulster's children. I have observed that some of the younger generation of artists have found forms and emotions in Expressionism which relate to their own experiences and fears and they have adapted to their own ends some of that movement's darker facets. Brendan Ellis (born 1951) is a young painter of disconsolate figures and scenes, and before he went to the Royal College of Art in London his work, not unnaturally, showed the influence of several artists. For a while he dallied with the lyrical fantasy of Chagall before embracing a dynamic Expressionism which strongly echoed the work of Max Beckmann, Oskar Kokoschka and even at times that of Fernand Léger. All students 'use' other artists, and the process of assimilating stylistic influences continues after formal education, so style spotting is often a futile exercise for the critic. What is relevant is how an artist fuses together many influences and experiences. Ellis defined his figures with a harsh, nervous black line and covered the surface with strong primary tones which are seemingly at variance with the darkness of the subject matter. He explored the new as well as the old urban decay, the environment of poverty as well as of violence. Where Conor might have shown cheerful street corner scenes, Brendan Ellis painted scenes of gaunt figures against equally gaunt surroundings. Winos, tired mothers and hard faced men stare out at the viewer and even his portraits, including one of Bernadette Devlin, offer no cosy comfort to subject and spectator alike. In a large horizontal format painting executed in 1973 he emphasised that a modern estate like Ballymurphy can be as desolate as any old part of the city, although there is a note of humanity in the gallery of figures who crowd the panel. These figures, among them Mother Theresa of Calcutta who had visited the area, seem to offer some hope through the perseverance of the people themselves. Just as the Expressionists had re-told many biblical stories in contemporary guise, Ellis has executed several paintings (among them some done in the traditional religious form of the triptych) in which local tableaux are seen in biblical terms. One of these is a kind of Belfast Descent from the Cross, or in this case, Lamp-post (no 75) and it has a kind of gruesome grandeur. It speaks of tarring and feathering, arbitrary 'punishments' carried out by self appointed kangaroo courts and as Baudelaire said of Delacroix's work, 'everything bears witness against the eternal and incorrigible barbarity of man... a hymn composed in honour of destiny and irremediable anguish'. Brendan Ellis's latest work still shows a very human concern with the born losers of society, but now the style is less linear and it is built up by means of small flickering slashes of paint.

An even darker, more nightmarish Belfast Expressionism was exhibited in 1977 by Martin Forker, another young local painter. Forker (born 1951) presented an uncompromisingly cruel view of local society and organised religion. Like James Ensor or Emil Nolde, Forker peoples his world with grinning, cackling masks and even the artist's own heroes, Vincent Van Gogh, Charlie Chaplin and Buster Keaton, who move through his paintings like holy innocents, have mask-like faces. While these paintings are not representations of specific events in the troubles they express some of its root causes and effects. This was particularly true of one painting in which Chaplin, as the policeman in *Easy Street*, is confronted by ghetto violence. Would the clown succeed in quietening the situation here when orthodox law enforcement officers have failed?

There was humour in some of Ellis's and Forker's works but it was a grim gallows humour. As a weapon for deflating pomposity, humour is used by painters as well as by political cartoonists. Joe McWilliams did a painting some five or six years ago of a member of the plethora of paramilitary groupings that have grown up here. This self-proclaimed hero, with the *de rigeur* outfit of combat jacket, rifle and dark glasses has a small body and huge block head, and looks like one of Sidney Nolan's Ned Kelly series. The ironic title is *God Protect us from our Protectors*. More recently McWilliams painted *Orangemen passing Unity Flats* (no vi, colour) which is both amusing and disturbing. Traditional Orange walks, with all their regalia and ritual, are a perennial feature of life in this province, although in recent years the changed environment has made them much more highly charged events. In this painting (actually a collage) the artist reminds us of the divisons, real and artificial that separate the communities. Peace lines, no-go areas or, as in this case, the anti-sniper screens erected by the security forces are all divisive in their effect. The background is sharply defined and the architecture is handled in a straight, representational manner. There is also a blue sky (the blue skies of Ulster which its supporters prefer to the grey skies of the Republic perhaps?) which contrasts with the spectral colours and forms of the figures in the foreground. Cutting through the dimness are the tiny doll-like feet of the Orangemen glimpsed beneath the screens. This relates to a personal memory I have of one of these Twelfth of July walks which have taken place since the troubles began. An hour before the Twelfth celebrators were due to parade their sashes and bright silk lodge banners, khaki clad army engineers carried drab canvas screens into

75 BRENDAN ELLIS
Untitled
c1974; acrylic on canvas; 181 x 122 cms; Ulster College collection

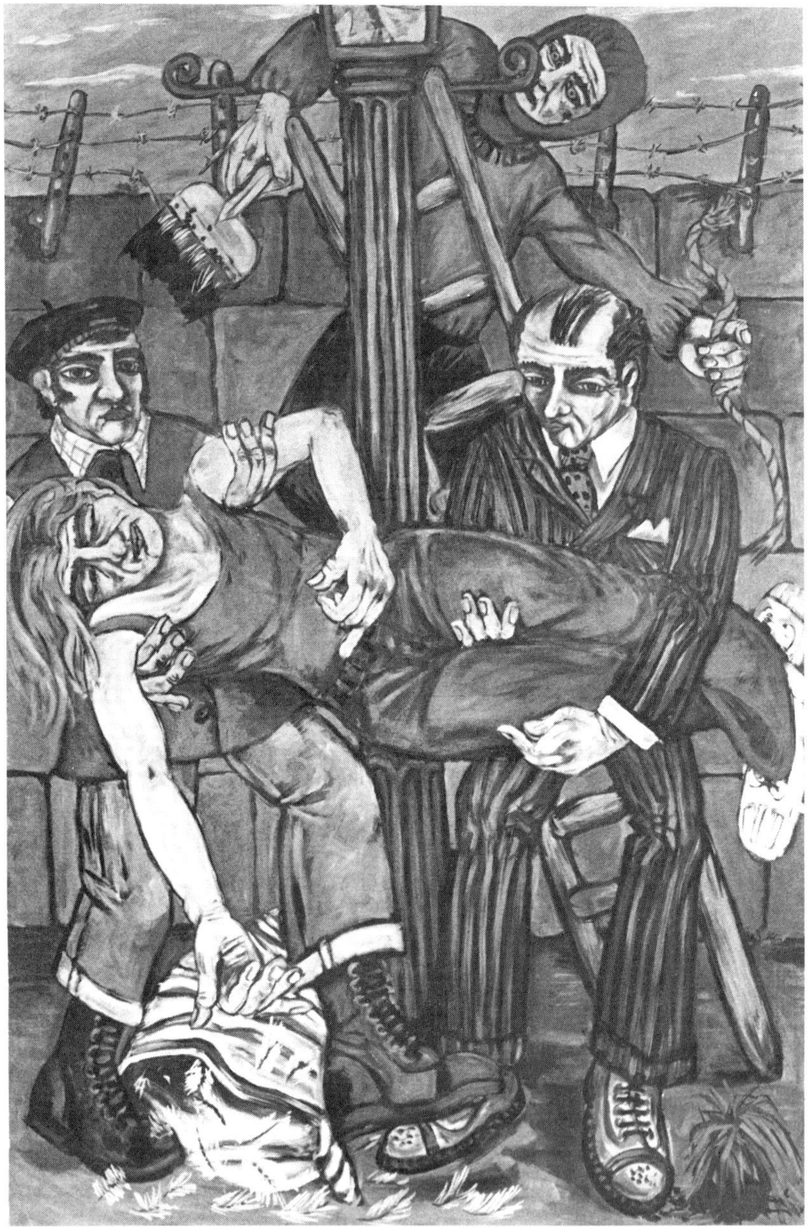

position in what seemed like a silent, monochrome parody of the walk itself. At the Kassel Documenta art exhibition in West Germany in 1977 McWilliams (as part of the Northern Ireland Workshop of the Free University) exhibited a firebomb charred door on and around which he painted the kind of rainbow and chevrons mentioned in Chapter 2. *The Community Door*, as this work is called, is not only an actual door from a much attacked community centre it is also a metaphor for the many roles that doors can play in Belfast. It can mean anything from sanctuary to the grim scene of the many sectarian murders that have shattered the security of domestic life.

Brian Ferran has also produced some works which have gently poked fun at the ritual and regalia of the factions. In one print entitled *Heroes* he again used the puppet-like figures, cruciform and striped patterns (see Chapter 2) to suggest the way in which these figures are not only bedecked by the icons of their history but are also manipulated by that same history. But again these images are not concerned with the violence as such, instead they help us to understand the potency that mythologies and symbols hold for this small island. At the kitsch level there is also a certain irony to be derived from the works produced by 'the men behind the wire'. Embroidered handkerchiefs, poker work plaques and small figurines are produced by both Loyalist and Republican prisoners and these are often sold as emotional mementoes. Although there seems to be such a void between the two factions many of the symbols employed in these works are curiously similar. For Tricolour read Union Jack or Ulster flag: for Green Ireland read Orange Ulster and for both sides there are hands clutching barbed wire. This is not a closed system of signs and almost daily there are new myths and new martyrs to be celebrated.

Jack Pakenham has also been deeply moved by the outward and inward effects of the violence here. Since 1976 he has adopted one of the figures from the *Swanage Honeymoon* series to create a figure who acts as a metaphor for all the people caught up in the civil strife. The little ventriloquist's doll who had appeared along with the Clown and Bride now comes to the foreground. As the artist himself put it:

> '... and so the doll with his inane optimistic grin even in death, his pathetic little body in grotesque positions, became for me both victim and terrorist... the ultimate manipulated little man whose words are only what someone else gives him.
> ... the friendly humorous Ulsterman who sets up his friend for an ambush with a Judas smile.
> ... the innocent faces his torturers, grinning in the hope that it is all some kind of game like those played by the school bullies and that he will be allowed to go home.'

In these paintings of the Belfast series, the ventriloquist's doll appears hanged, broken, tarred and feathered, knee-capped, left in dust bins and tortured in 'romper rooms'. Illustration no 76 is one representative painting from the thirty or so that he has done on this theme.

Because Northern Ireland has been a focus of world attention for several years now there has been a two way traffic in images and image makers. Some of the kitsch artifacts have found

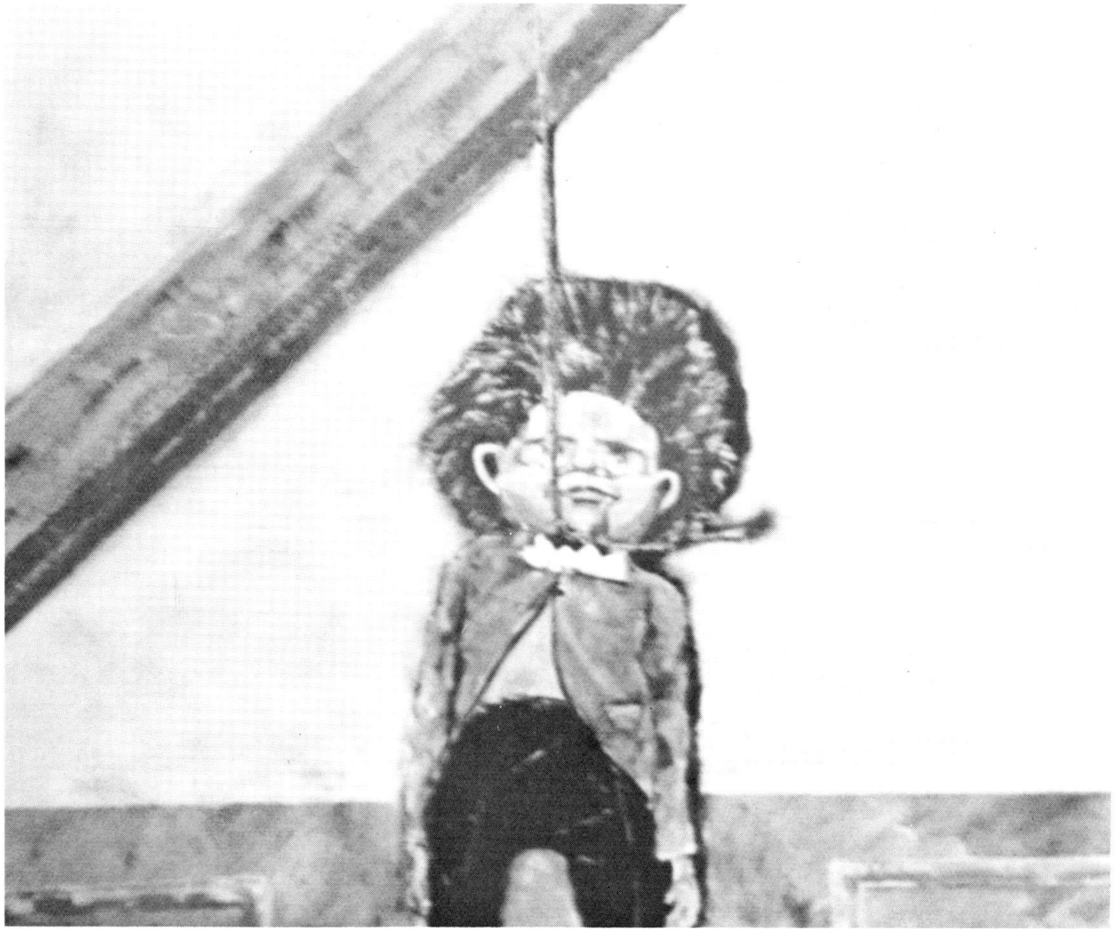

76 JACK PAKENHAM
one of the 'Belfast Series' [*detail*]
1975/6; acrylic and emulsion; 91.4 x 91.4 cms; collection the artist

their way to Europe and North America where they have a potent fund-raising value and in addition non-Ulster artists have based their work on aspects of the Northern Ireland scene experienced at first, second and third hand.

Some works have also been produced by expatriate Ulster artists such as F E McWilliam and George Campbell. The latter artist executed a series of dark works which explored the more obvious aspects of the violence. These included paintings of burning and burned out buses (no 77) and the pain filled faces of soldiers and civilians alike. During the Second World War Campbell had been moved to make a series of vivid works which were his personal response to the Luftwaffe blitz on Belfast. As he said, 'I think the blitz started me painting... I painted it

VI JOE McWILLIAMS
Orangemen passing Unity Flats
1975; mixed media; 40 x 66 cms; collection the artist

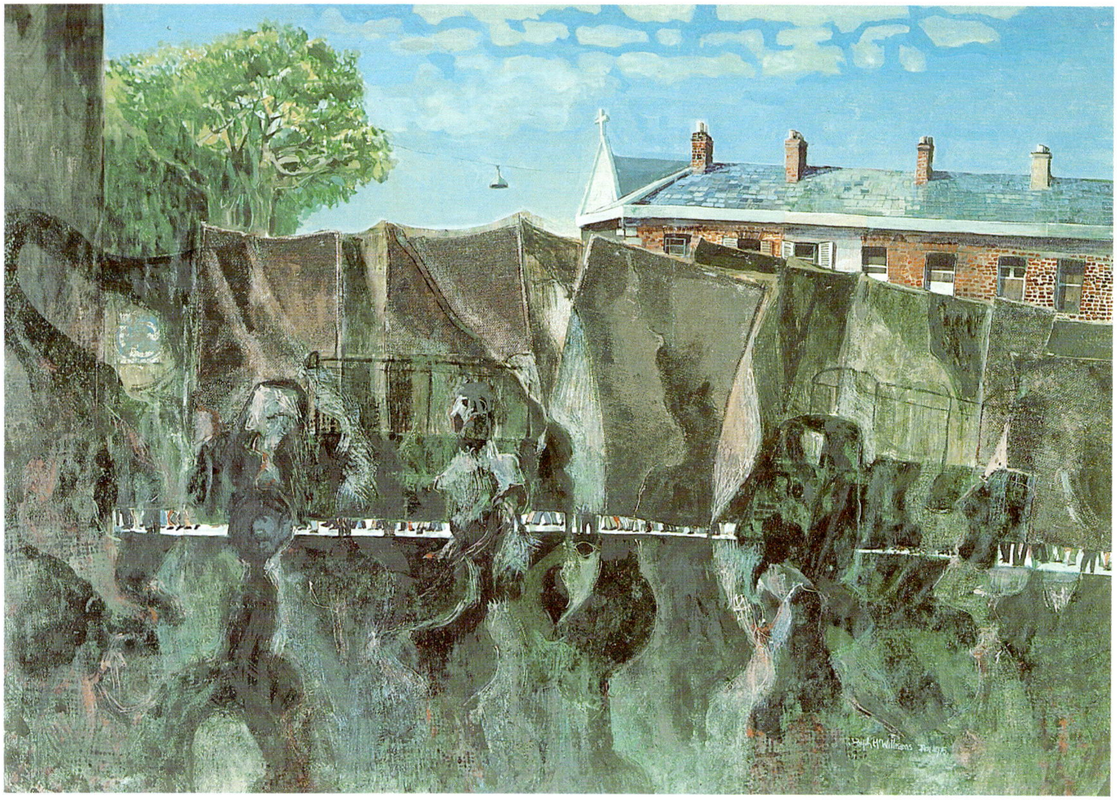

facing page 136

77 GEORGE CAMPBELL
Burned out buses
1971; watercolour and ink on paper; 26.5 x 37 cms (sight); Martin Dillon collection

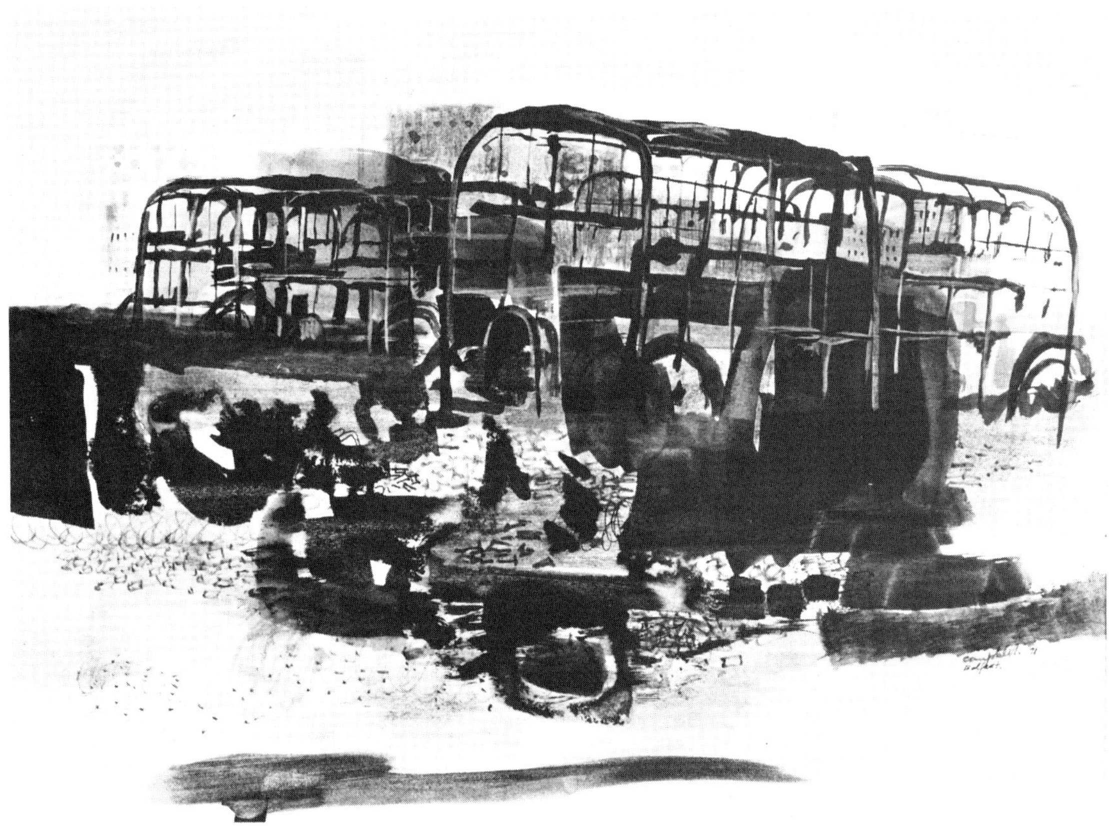

in watercolours and oils, all the burst girders and the crashed about streets.'[3] It must have seemed to Campbell that the blitz had come again, and the twisted frames of buses and the fiery glow on the stone strewn streets echoed back down the years.

Of course many of those who have derived their subject matter from the civil disturbances have no local experience and tradition to add dimension to their work. The final proof that this strife has the status of a war can be found in the decision in 1971 by the then GOC (NI) General Sir Harry Tuzo to commission an outside artist to reproduce scenes from service life and activity here. This was in the tradition of the work of the War Artists Advisory Committee in World War II. As a suitable civilian artist was not available the work was done by a serving officer who was also an artist. The result was thirty seven egg tempera paintings by Major Christopher Miers of the Royal Green Jackets, and these have been reproduced in book form by Denovo Press in 1973 under the title *Northern Ireland: A Soldier's*

View. These are highly representational records of active service in Ulster, worked up from on the spot sketches and photographs. Their main strength is not so much artistic as documentary. An entirely different approach, but one which also strove to explain and be balanced was the documentation exhibition *A shade of green, an orange edge* organised for the Arts Council of Northern Ireland and the Irish Congress of Trade Unions (Northern Ireland Committee) in May 1975. This exhibition of images, artifacts, documents and ephemera was undertaken by Conrad Atkinson, an English artist whose work has been based on studies of events of social and industrial conflict. He had previously exhibited documentation entitled 'Work, Wages and Prices' and 'Strike at Brannan's' the latter being named after a firm in his home town. All of these 'Exhibitions-as-works-of-Art' (as John Hewitt desscribed them in the booklet which accompanied *A shade of green, an orange edge*) were the result of a laudable political motivation and of an actual participation in the events documented. That is the key to the failure of Atkinson's Ulster project. He presented all the right images from para-military broadsheets to photographs of innocent victims but in his desire to offer a balanced view in which blame was apportioned to all parties he presented material which was overly familiar to local audiences and the various aspects of the material cancelled each other out. There is however one English artist who showed that the violence spawned here has spread beyond our own locale and in so showing she has created a series of elegant but frightening statements. She is Rita Donagan and her touring Arts Council of Great Britain/Whitworth Art Gallery exhibition was shown here in Belfast in 1977. In her themes she uses a kind of mapping technique to capture and explain minute resonances in chance found images. The method is precise but not sterile and this was seen to advantage in the series of paintings, drawings and collages based on car bombs and the effect of the 1974 explosion in Talbot Street in Dublin, when the newspapers showed photographs of a victim covered by... more newspapers. The effect was that of a slow motion film seen at the end of a long tunnel, and as the whole series derived from the emotional stimulus of terrorism in the North and South she achieved with success a sort of universal soundless scream against wanton brutality. As the violence has penetrated all corners of this island it is not surprising that many southern artists have been motivated by the situation in Ulster. In some works, such as in the bandaged, crippled prisoners of Charles Harper, the theme is generalised, while the work of others, for example the recent paintings of John Devlin, a more overt unilateral political stance is taken. At this point the work becomes propaganda.

As noted in the previous chapter, sculpture has long been used for propaganda purposes. Indeed the average man thinks of three dimensional work when words like 'memorial' and 'monument' are used. Yet most of these forms are figurative, conventionalised and didactic. Sometimes more avant-garde forms can be linked to social or political themes, for example Reg Butler's maquette for a monument to *The Unknown Political Prisoner* in the 1950s, or Zadkine's *Memorial to Rotterdam*. Even abstract sculpture can suggest human endeavours and ideologies. Recently some quite large scale work by Belfast sculpture students has confronted a selection of problems arising out of the con-

78 BOB SLOAN
Connector
1975-77; wood, marble, chrome steel, rope, sandbags; 84 cms x 4.25 metres x 50 cms; Arts Council of Northern Ireland collection

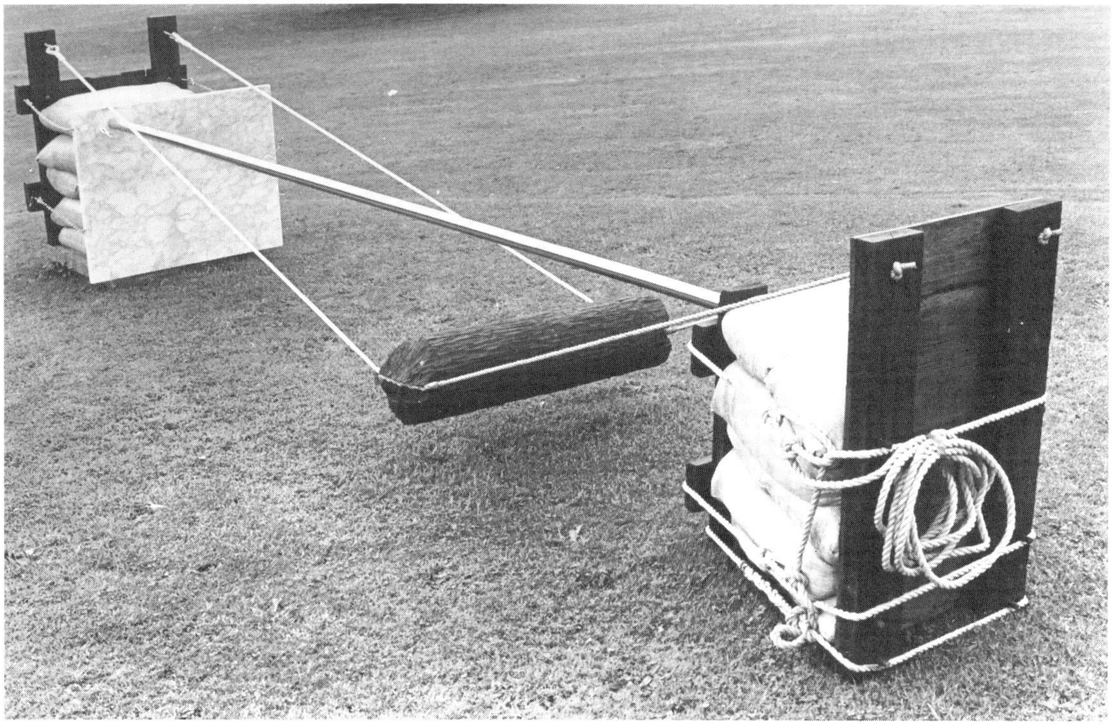

straints on life in this province today. One non-abstract piece was a George Segal-like life size transcription or reconstruction of the security barriers in Ulster towns, and it came complete with a fully clothed civilian searcher and white plaster shoopers queuing to be frisked. A piece which explores the same problems is *Connector* (no 78) by Bob Sloan. For the Kassel Documenta Sloan (born 1940) worked on a location piece based around the subject of obstacles and *Connector* symbolises the tension of daily life and also the tensions of the wires and ropes that divide off the segments of our environment. There is also a contrast of textures and materials: chrome steel versus rope; sandbags versus marble in the same way as permanent structures like buildings have been repaired or surrounded with makeshift materials. Barbed wire in particular is an obvious metaphor for division and violence and it crops up as an image on posters, on Long Kesh hankies and even in the normally abstract sculpture of Deborah Brown, who has produced at least one fibreglass piece in which barbed wire was embedded into the surface of the relief. The wire is coiled into a rough spiral which reinforces the structure of the work while at the same time suggesting nothing less than a crown of thorns.[4] Oddly reminiscent of this use of the wire are some recent paintings by T P Flanagan of which *Bog Water and Bull Wire* is a re-

79 F E McWILLIAM
Woman in Bomb Blast
1974; bronze; 56.5 x 139.2 x 57 cms; Ulster Museum collection

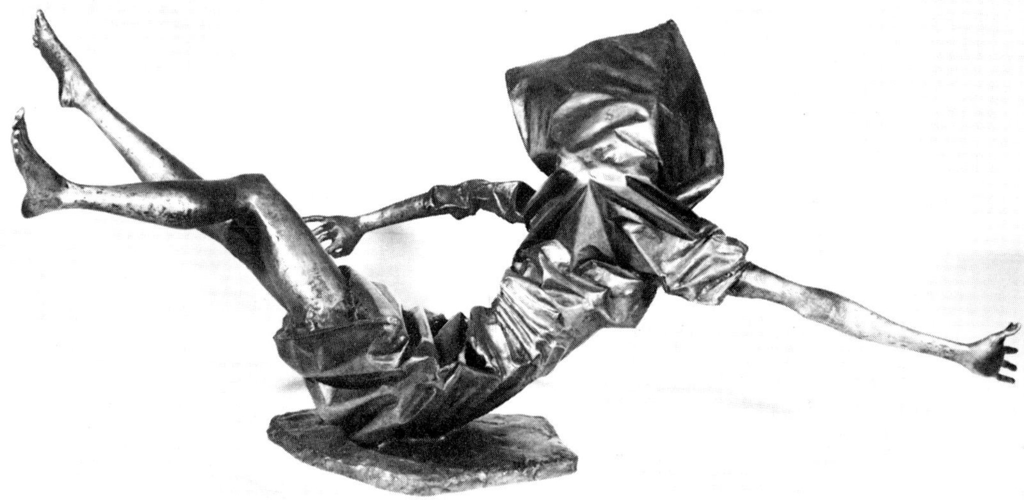

presentative example. The single strand of barbed wire seems a little too conscious a metaphor to be successful and the effect is strained. Possibly the sculptures which will be remembered longest as capturing both the actual violence and its reverberations are the works in the series *Women of Belfast* by F E McWilliam.

There are some twenty variations on this theme and closely related to them is this work *Woman in Bomb Blast* of 1974. All are concerned with women caught and frozen in the moment of the explosion. The choice of women as victims rather than men suggests that they are the biggest victims of all: they are not only the ones caught in the blast, they feel its repercussions longer since they are the mothers and wives who sustain the generations. However it should not be forgotten that the women are as capable as their men of being active participants in events good and evil. McWilliam wrote of his works,

> 'I did not choose the subject consciously, it happened I suppose because the situation in Ulster is inescapable; even at this safe remove, something that is always nagging at the back of one's mind...
>
> ... Inevitably the figures clothed themselves. The drapery used obeys the nature of drapery, but it is used schematically in the sense that it is intended to further the emotion of the experience rather than to depict actual clothing... I would like the drapery itself to be a sort of metaphor for the event.' [5]

I can only wish that McWilliam had either given up the theme after these or had become more intensely specific in his selection because the small bronzes exhibited in Belfast in 1977 completely fudged the issues he had confronted so squarely in *Women of Belfast*. The new works showed single figures and groups carrying banners of protest. The legends on the banners read 'No Words', 'Ban all Banners', 'Buy More Art', 'Don't March, Walk' and so on. The preciousness of the jokes obscured the actual technical skill of the sculptures and somewhat clouded the clarity of the impact of the earlier works. Protesting about protests is just not the same thing at all.

At the beginning of this chapter I mentioned the media coverage of events. Much has been written about the distortions of the facts created by this press coverage. It has even been suggested that some incidents such as stone throwing and rioting were not only exacerbated by the presence of cameras but were in fact instigated by press men seeking better pictures. Whether this is true or not is almost irrelevant; what is relevant is that film and video purport to offer objective truths when in fact they are the media most open to both accidental and wilful distortion. The selection of images which are further re-selected by an editor can alter the entire 'reading' of any event. Sometimes film and television aspire to the status of art and this cannot be denied them even when they produce propaganda. We know that films like Leni Riefenstahl's *Triumph of the Will* or Humphrey Jennings' *London Can Take It* are war propaganda but they also illustrate the art of the film. Inevitably the conflict here has attracted not only the news cameramen but also the documentary film makers. Films like *Ireland Behind The Wire*, *Grand Central Hotel, Belfast* and Marcel Ophuls' *A Sense of Loss* are strongly political, often perceptive, but they are outside views whether made with Ulster helpers or not. For less strident but equally committed interpretations by local workers in this medium one must look to the community video groups and to a handful of modest, low key documentaries made by the two television stations in Ulster. Of these I would single out two which sum up the sense of attrition felt here, and both these films were directed by Robin Wylie who began his career as a painter before moving into the world of television. *In The Name of God* (BBC NI 1974) uses news footage mixed with original film to present a picture of contemporary Belfast that wisely uses no commentary. There is drama, with slowed down shots of a fireman hurled backwards by blast, there is the accidental humour of the city and there is even a grim beauty in the shots of light filtering through the twisted girders and the broken glass of the bombed out York Street

80 BILL KIRK
Wedding Guests, York Road
1974; photograph

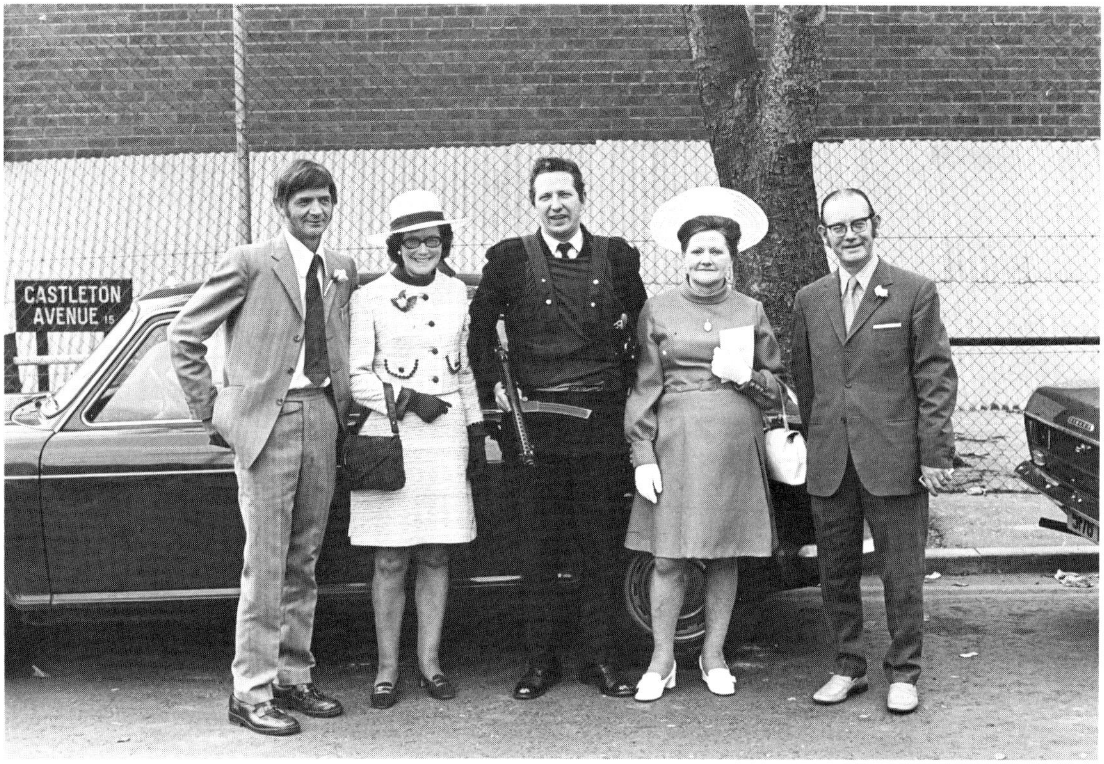

Co-op. *Sing Orange, Sing Green* (for *Man Alive* BBC 2) presented the songs, symbols and myths of the Loyalists and Republicans. By means of skilful cutting Wylie and his editor were able to point up the ironic similarities I cited on page 135.

If I was asked to choose one non-painterly image to convey the past eight or nine years I would probably look for a still photograph. It wouldn't be violent and dramatic like the shot of a Ford Anglia snapped in the very instant of exploding; an image which is on the cover of bomb disposal expert George Styles' book *Bombs Have No Pity*. It wouldn't be grainy, actuality shots of riots and suffering such as filled the pages of *The Battle of the Bogside*. Instead it would be a photograph which at first sight might seem banal. Bill Kirk (born 1937) is a local photographer who graduated two years ago from the Art and Design Centre in Belfast. Since then he has exhibited in Ulster, in Britain and in Germany and in 1977 he won a major Irish-American Foundation Grant for his compassionate images of ordinary life in Northern Ireland. The photograph of his that I have chosen is *Wedding Guests, York Road*, 1973 (no 80) because it not only re-defines the conventions of the wedding

81 DENIS McBRIDE
Northern Incident [*Peaceful*]
1977; oil on canvas; 137 x 101.6 cms; collection the artist

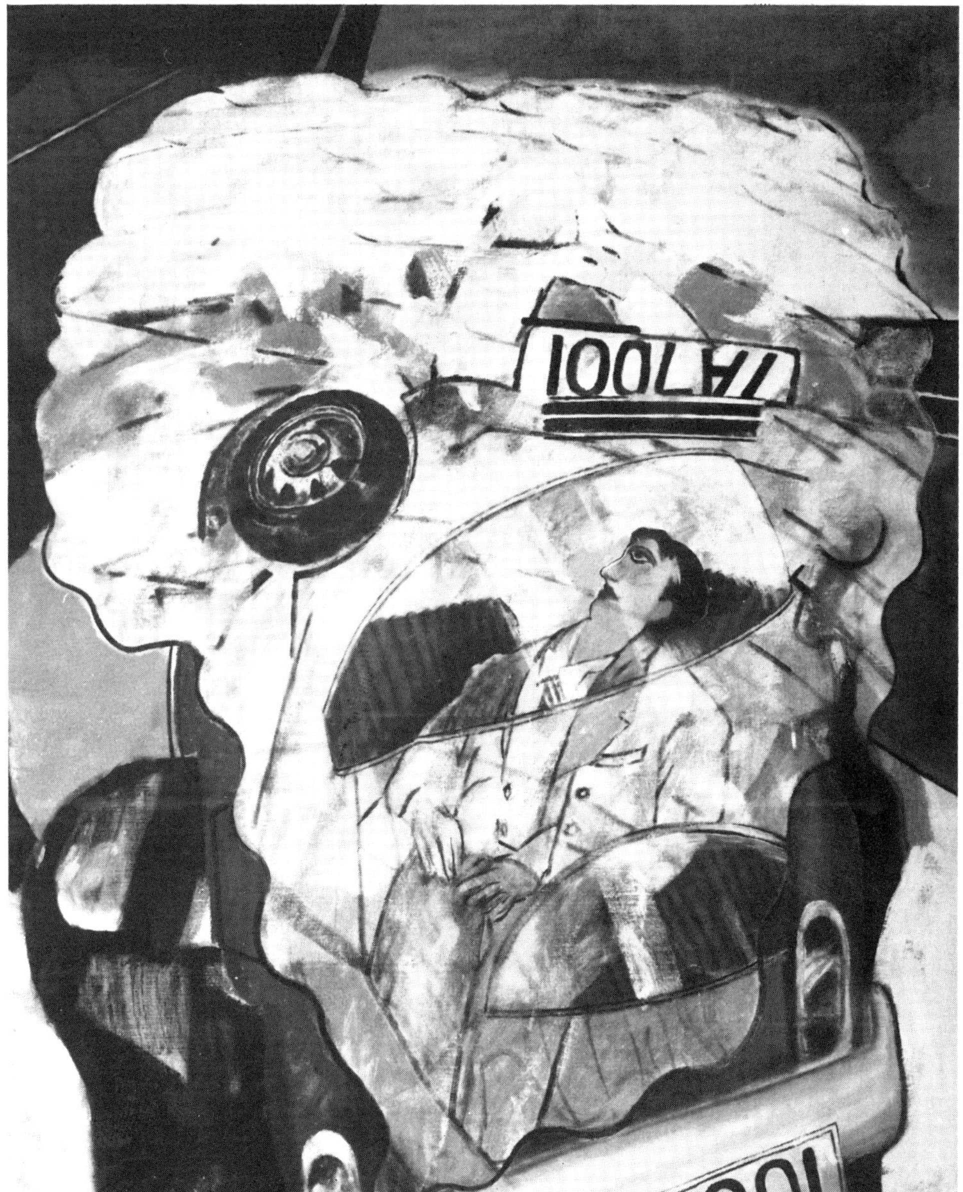

snapshot but also because it is so frighteningly *normal*. Nothing can better explain how our values have changed in only a few years than an image where an RUC man with sub-machine gun and flak jacket seems unexceptional in the midst of festivities.

A sense of perspective concerning the scale of the troubles must be noted as a conclusion to this chapter. No one here can avoid being aware that a massive cultural change has occurred in Northern Ireland, including the biggest population shift since World War Two, but with an almost defiant 'business as usual' attitude, Ulster men and women carry on with living. As Denis McBride grimly points out in this painting, *Northern Ireland* (*Peaceful*) (no 81), the final irony is that more people are killed and maimed in road accidents than have ever suffered in the terrorism.

NOTES

1. I am especialy grateful to Belinda Loftus for allowing me to see her visual researches and for discussing at length the implications of the many images of the troubles.
2. The artist gave a long reasoned argument on his attitude to art in an interview with the author in 1976.
3. *George Campbell*, with a foreword by James White, Three Candles Press, Dublin, 1966.
4. This work is discussed and reproduced in colour in *The Arts in Ireland* No. 3, Dublin, 1974.
5. Quoted in the catalogue of the exhibition *F E McWilliam: Women of Belfast*, McClelland International Galleries, Belfast, 1973.

ART AND PATRONAGE

It has already been noted that the sculptor has specific problems concerned with making and showing his creations but even if the painter can produce his work at home the majority of artists wish at some time to exhibit and, if possible, to sell their works. Patronage of one form or another has existed for many centuries but the contemporary artist cannot hope to find a Lorenzo de' Medici or even a Bishop Hervey to commission art and to provide a salary with which he can produce art on a full time basis.

Even today some international dealers do give an artist financial remuneration to paint or sculpt, in return for which the artist gives that dealer exclusive rights to exhibit and sell his work. This kind of patronage is really a form of investment rather than an act of altruism and such arrangements have been known to end in acrimony. It is more normal for a dealer or gallery owner to accept an artist's work on a continuous basis or for a one-man show. If paintings are sold from an exhibition or 'stock', commissions of one third are payable to the dealer. In these inflationary times 40% is becoming more common and some Bond Street galleries, with their large overheads, charge 50% commission. In this province there has never been a continuous tradition of big influential private dealers and galleries similar to those in London or even Dublin. The art market in Ulster was never big enough to sustain such a system although fine art dealers, small galleries and picture framers who showed a few paintings have come and gone over the years. The Piccolo, the New Gallery, the McClelland Gallery all have their place in the art history of this province, while today the main commercial galleries in

Belfast are the Tom Caldwell Gallery, the Bell Gallery and the Octagon. All have slightly different policies: Tom Caldwell (who also has a gallery in Dublin) has an established 'stable' of well known names who exhibit with him, Nelson Bell has fewer one-man exhibitions but does bring important artists' work over to this province, and the Octagon, which is run by a committee of artists and enthusiasts tends to show younger and less well known artists. While sales are the life blood of a commercial gallery all three do put on exhibitions, from time to time, of work which is worth showing but which may have a limited sales value. In addition, the Octagon has twice commissioned editions of prints from recognised Ulster artists, thus making multiple versions of their work more readily available. Outside Belfast there are several galleries, notably the Keys in Londonderry, the Grendor in Holywood and the Hillsborough in that town. Hardly surprisingly, in a small province, Belfast remains the focus for art sales and galleries outside the metropolis fulfil a vital role without receiving the publicity and recognition which more readily come to urban galleries in every country.

If an artist does get to show his work in a commercial gallery, or at the Arts Council of Northern Ireland's gallery in Belfast (and soon in the local authority gallery in Londonderry), or through a society or organisation such as the Royal Ulster Academy, he must hope to sell it. It is a fact that there are more people today buying original works of art by Ulster and Irish artists than ever before. What may begin with the tentative purchase of a print or modestly priced painting can develop over the years into an intelligent and exciting private collection. The big private collectors are often well known and their collections are admired, containing as they do some of the best representative examples of artists' *oeuvres* chosen as the result of personal taste. The collections of the late Zoltan Lewinter Frankl, W A N McGeough Bond or Gordon Lambert have been shown to the public, either as complete exhibitions or as loans to retrospective or thematic exhibitions. But there are many others in this province alone who have built up, without publicity, excellent collections of work by Irish artists. Some concentrate on the work of one artist, others on a style of painting, a genre or a particular medium (such as watercolour) while others are amazingly eclectic in their choice. All are patrons of living art.

Of course there is an element of élitism in this: a few dozen people regularly buying the work of a few score artists. To this must be added the occasional buyer and the organisations, from banks to pubs, that purchase works to show on their walls. But there are those interested in art who cannot afford to buy much, or who have not had the experience to make that first purchase. And there is also art which is not for sale: ephemeral pieces, performance art or works which already have an owner. So in this province we have both the Arts Council of Northern Ireland and the Ulster Museum to buy art, to show that art to the public and to sponsor exhibitions and works which might otherwise fail to be carried out.

The Arts Council of Northern Ireland began as the Council for the Encouragement of Music and the Arts in 1943 and was given its present title in 1962. The present gallery in Bedford Street dates from 1968 but before that CEMA/Arts Council

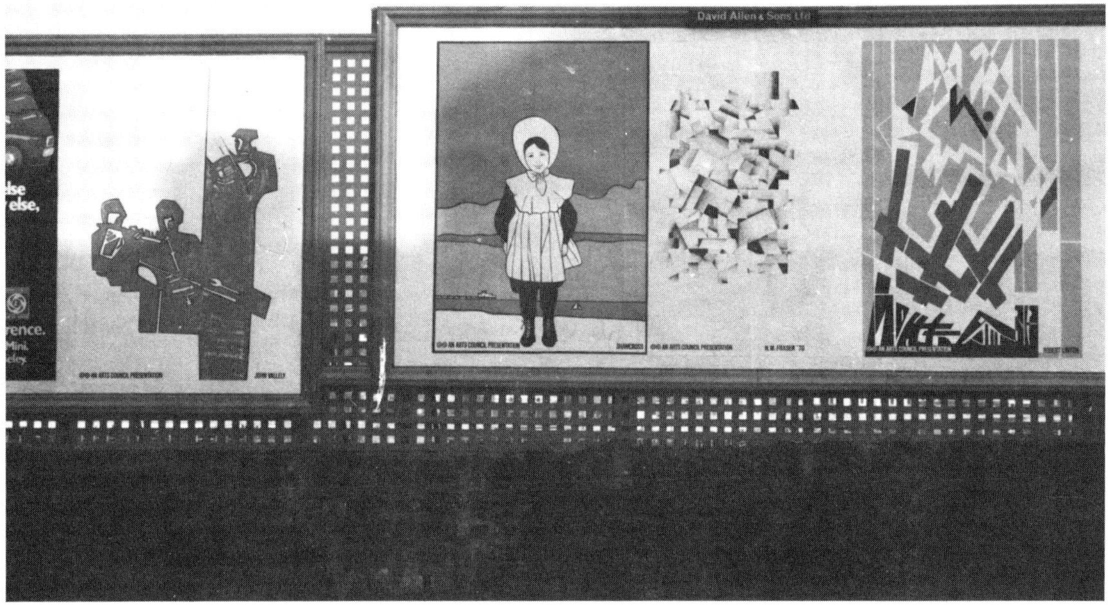

82 *Arts Council billboard posters*
Left to right; John Vallely, Neil Shawcross, Norman Fraser, Robert Linton 1970

had two previous galleries including the small but fine basement gallery in Chichester Street, Belfast. Although the Bedford Street gallery has a flexible internal wall system its proportions downstairs are a little antagonistic to some kinds of art, but for the smaller works the mezzanine floor provides an intimate atmosphere, and overall the gallery does provide a good shop window for the arts. It is highly regrettable that the shop window has had its glass broken so often in recent years, and indeed the period since its opening has coincided with the present troubles so attendances have sometimes been lower than might reasonably be expected in a city of this size. But the Arts Council of Northern Ireland's contribution to the visual arts doesn't simply lie in exhibiting works in a gallery. Recognising that work ought to be seen by as many people as possible, over the years the Council has experimented with various schemes to take art out to the province. This has involved traditional ventures like touring exhibitions but it has also meant the dissemination of reproductions: these might be very big, as in the series of billboard posters 1969 to 1970 (no 82) or smaller (76.2 cms x 50.8 cms) as with the series of posters distributed to schools and stuck on small billboards throughout the province. Padraig Murphy's *The Francis Petrarch Affair* (see page 00) was one such image; others have been as diverse as the primitive zest of Gretta Bowen's paintings, a reproductions of an old photograph by Robert Welch and a schoolchild's peace poster. There was also the attempt to bring

83 JOHN MIDDLETON and FRANK ORMSBY
Floods
1972; screenprint poster-poem; 73 x 48 cms

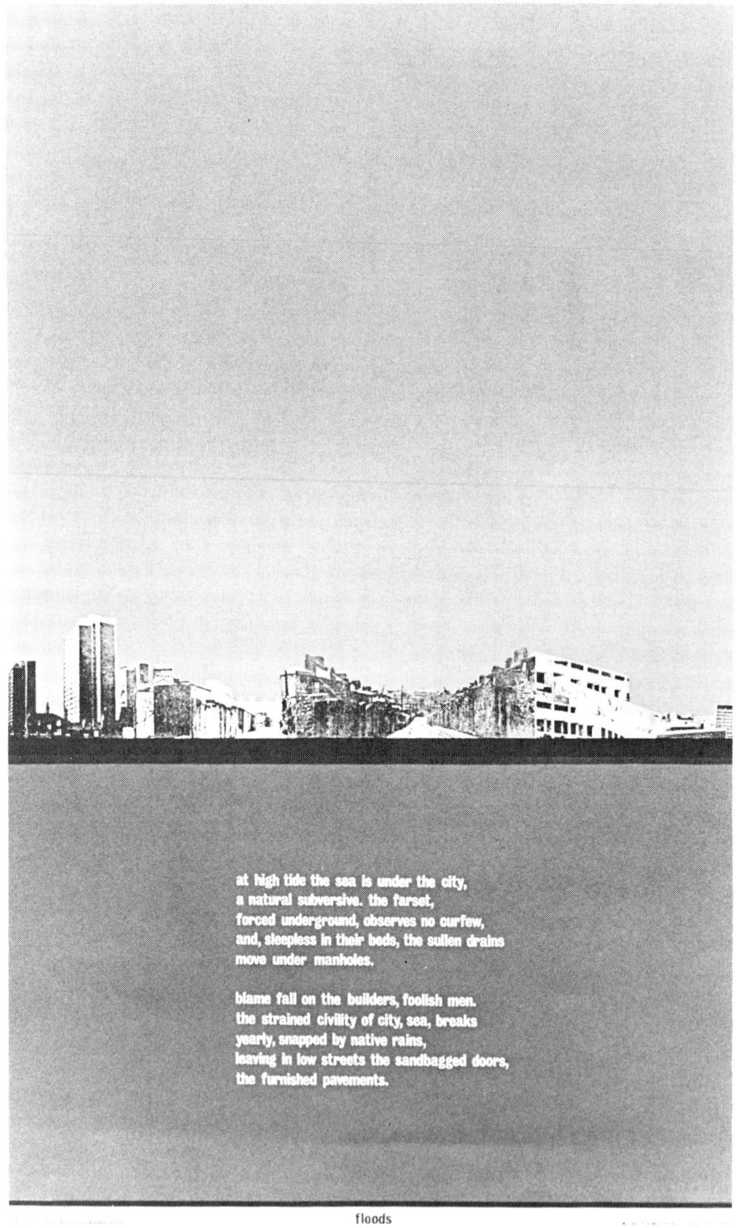

artist and poet together in a series of poster poems of which illustration no 83 is an example. The gallery-oriented Open Painting Competition which successfully ran bi-annually from 1962 to 1970 has been replaced by the Art in Context scheme whereby artworks in all permanent and some ephemeral media are judged, again every two years, and the chosen winning schemes are placed in locations around the province. The Roy Johnston panel, the Graham Gingles trees and the Arthur Armstrong play sculpture all alluded to previously have been examples of this scheme.

The Arts Council of Northern Ireland purchases work each year for its collection and most of that collection is available for loan to organisations thus ensuring that it does not lie unseen in a store-room (which is all to the good, since a large number of works were destroyed in an accidental fire in 1967). Many of the reproductions in this book come from the Council's collection. The Arts Council, *any* Arts Council is in a different position regarding allocation of funds to the arts. It will be cited as reactionary by some artists and wildly revolutionary by many members of the public. Generally speaking it successfully fulfils a difficult role. Each year it gives bursaries to artists to help with special projects: Norman Fraser's visit to computer arts centres in the USA and Bob Sloan's foundry scheme are just two of the projects helped by the Council in this way. It gives grants and guarantees to artists, publications and organisations, it helps with transport of works, it organises lectures and regional projects in conjunction with area boards and education authorities, and much more. Its patronage of the arts is widespread, including giving an additional boost to artists by means of the Partnership Purchase Scheme whereby the Council pays 50% of the cost of a work of art bought by or for an organisation big or small that can guarantee that the work will be seen by members of the public.

The Ulster Museum is also a great patron of Irish art, although, as the province's National Gallery, its scope is wider, purchasing good examples of modern art from all round the world. The Belfast City Museum and Art Gallery became the Ulster Museum in 1961, and given the impossibility of trying to compete with European and American galleries for accredited masterpieces from the Renaissance onwards, it took the decision to purchase contemporary British, European and American art. Works by Morris Louis, Kenneth Noland, Victor Vasarely are all in the collection, as are many of the works by local artists reproduced in this book. Since the opening earlier this decade of the modern extension to the old museum this province can boast of a national gallery with a very useful and expanding collection *and* the space in which to view it properly. From its permanent displays, through its large temporary exhibition space and its art department with an energetic and knowledgeable staff to the work done by its education department, the Ulster Museum is doing much to popularise art and to dispel any notions of a museum being an ivory tower. Possibly no finer (if indirect) compliment to its accessibility has been paid than that of the teacher who complained that her pupils kept playing truant to go to the museum. But education is not for children only, and several artists have told the author that they were genuinely influenced by seeing such exhibitions as those of Surrealist Art, Francis Bacon and American Art of the '60s in the old Museum and Art Gallery exhibition space.

In the past twenty years there have been several efforts at patronage by industry and commerce beyond the individual commissions cited throughout this survey. The Bass Charrington Arts Award, the Butlin Foundation for Young Irish Artists and others have all helped. A unique example of private patronage is that of the Alice Berger Hammerschlag Award, set up by Heinz Hammerschlag to continue the excellent help that his late wife had given to art and artists over the years.

Finally, a word about a form of indirect patronage. Artists would not be living and working in this province if there was not an establishment which both trained and employed artists. In this province, in addition to the training in art provided by colleges such as Stranmillis, St Mary's and St Joseph's, there is an art college which has been in existence (off and on) since 1849. For very many years the City of Belfast College of Art occupied one floor of the 'Tech'. Since the late 1960s it has been housed in a modern custom-built (albeit now full) building. Whether it is known as the Belfast College of Art, the Ulster College of Art and Design or, as it is now, the Art and Design Centre, Ulster College, the Northern Ireland Polytechnic the main point about it is that, at one time or another, over 80% of the local artists mentioned in this book have been trained or have taught in that college.

SELECTED BIOGRAPHICAL NOTES

JAMES ALLEN
b 1941 Lurgan

Education and career

1953-1960	Annadale Grammar School, Belfast.
1961-1965	Belfast College of Art.
1965-1967	Brighton College of Art.
1967-1970	Teacher of etching, Goldsmith's School of Art, London.
1971-1976	Teacher of silkscreen printing, Ravensbourne College of Art, London.
1972	Arts Council of Northern Ireland travel award, Middle-East.
1972	Arts Council of Northern Ireland portrait commission, Mrs Magennis.
1974	Arts Council of Northern Ireland, Art in Context competition prizewinner; Lyric Theatre mural, Belfast.
1975	Arts Council of Northern Ireland portrait commission, Sue Robinson.
1977	Arts Council of Northern Ireland printmaking fellowship award to organise and run print workshop at Arts Council of Northern Ireland headquarters, Belfast.

Principal Exhibitions

1965	Young Irish Artists Foundation, Belfast, Dublin, Cork.
1967	Butlin Foundation for Young Irish Artists, Belfast, Cork, Dublin, Mosney.
1967	Two man show, Arts Council of Northern Ireland Gallery.
1968	Two man show, Gallery 185, Brighton.
1968	Ulster Painting '68, Arts Council of Northern Ireland Gallery.
1968	First British International Print Biennale, Bradford.
1968	Dúchas, Queen's University, Belfast.
1971	Ulster Printmakers, Arts Council of Northern Ireland Gallery.
1971	Ulster Places, Arts Council of Northern Ireland Gallery.
1972	Prints, Serpentine Gallery, London.
1972	One man show, The Room Gallery, Greenwich, London.
1972	Prints, 'Fortresses to Follies', Oxford Gallery.

1972	Prints, Warwick Gallery, Warwick.
1972	Ulster Faces, Arts Council of Northern Ireland, touring.
1973	One man show, Burleighfield House Gallery, Loudwater, Bucks.
1973	One man show, Arts Council of Northern Ireland Gallery.
1973, 1976	Invited Artist, Biella International Print Biennale, Italy.
1973	Four Printmakers, DM Gallery, London.
1973	Belfast Schools Art Collection, Arts Council of Northern Ireland Gallery.
1974	Two man show, Upper Street Gallery, London.
1974	Barclay Gallery, Atlanta, Georgia, USA.
1974	New British Printmakers, Brooklyn Museum, New York.
1975	One man show, Queen's University, Belfast.
1975	Prints, Sunderland Arts Centre.
1975	One man show, Upper Street Gallery, London.
1975	Belfast Education and Library Board Prints, Arts Council of Northern Ireland Gallery.
1975	Women of Ulster, Arts Council of Northern Ireland, touring.
1976	30 Contemporary Printmakers, Arnolfini Gallery, Bristol.
1976	One man show, Tom Caldwell Gallery, Belfast.
1977	Five Landscape Painters, Tom Caldwell Gallery, Dublin.
1977	Eight Northern Irish Artists, Third Eye Centre, Glasgow.
1977	Oireachtas, Dublin, Belfast and Letterkenny.
1977	Realism Now, An Chomhairle Ealáion/Arts Council of Northern Ireland, touring.

Collections

Armagh County Museum, Arts Council of Northern Ireland, Belfast Education and Library Board, Lloyds Bank, Queen's University Belfast, Ulster Museum, Ulster Television.

Bibliography

'Painting and Sculpture' by Kenneth Jamison, *Causeway, the Arts in Ulster*, Arts Council of Northern Ireland and Gill and Macmillan, Belfast and Dublin, 1971.

ARTHUR ARMSTRONG
b 1924 Carrickfergus

Education and career

1939-1941	Queen's University, Belfast.
1942-1943	Belfast College of Art, evening course.
1957	CEMA travel scholarship, Spain.
	Returned to Dublin 1962 having lived and worked in London.
1967	Gibraltar International Art Exhibition prizewinner.
1968	Oireachtas exhibition winner of Douglas Hyde gold medal.
1969	Royal Hibernian Academy Associate member.
1972	Royal Hibernian Academy Member.
1973	Arts Council of Northern Ireland Art in Context prizewinner, Belmont House School, Londonderry, play sculpture.
1973	Arts Council of Northern Ireland poster-poem commission with Roy McFadden.

Principal Exhibitions

1957, 1958, 1961-1965	Irish Exhibition of Living Art, Dublin.
1961	One man show, CEMA, Belfast.
1962, 1963, 1966-1971, 1973	Oireachtas, Dublin.
1962-1973, 1975, 1977	Royal Hibernian Academy, Dublin.

1964, 1966	
1969	One man shows, Ritchie Hendriks Gallery, Dublin.
1964	Twelve Irish Artists, Ritchie Hendriks Gallery, Dublin.
1965	Paintings and Sculpture by Irish Artists, Ritchie Hendriks Gallery, Dublin.
1966	Eight North of Ireland Painters, New Charing Cross Gallery, Glasgow.
1966	One man show, Arts Council of Northern Ireland Gallery.
1967	Irish Artists, Ritchie Hendriks Gallery, Dublin.
1968	Ulster Painting '68, Arts Council of Northern Ireland Gallery.
1968	Open Painting, Arts Council of Northern Ireland Gallery.
1969	Two man show, Ulster Arts Club, Belfast.
1970, 1972	One man shows, Tom Caldwell Gallery, Belfast.
1971	David Hendriks Gallery, Dublin.
1972	Gordon Lambert Collection, Municipal Gallery of Modern Art, Dublin.
1972	One man show, Cork Arts Society Gallery, Cork.
1973	Belfast Schools Arts Collection, Arts Council of Northern Ireland Gallery.
1974	One man show, Galeria Avinon, Madrid.
1974	Watergate Gallery, Washington DC.
1976	One man show, Kenny's Art Gallery, Galway.
1977	One man show, Galeria Kreisler, Madrid.

Collections
Aer Lingus, Allied Irish Investment Bank Ltd, An Chomhairle Ealáion, Arts Council of Northern Ireland, P J Carroll & Co Ltd, Córas Iompair Éireann, Cork Municipal Art Gallery, Leicestershire Education Committee, Limerick Municipal Art Gallery, Malaga Museum of Fine Arts, Radio Telefís Éireann, Trinity College Dublin Gallery, Ulster Museum, Waterford Municipal Art Gallery.

Bibliography
A Concise History of Irish Art by Bruce Arnold, Thames and Hudson, London, 1969.
'Painting and Sculpture' by Kenneth Jamison, *Causeway: The Arts in Ulster*, Arts Council of Northern Ireland and Gill and Macmillan, Dublin, 1971.
'Harriet Cooke talks to Arthur Armstrong', *Irish Times*, 2 May 1972.
'Speaking Personally', BBC Radio Ulster, 21 June 1975.

BRIAN BALLARD
b 1943 Belfast

Education and career

1954-1961	Annadale Grammar School, Belfast.
1961-1964	Belfast College of Art.
1964-1965	Liverpool College of Art.
1968	Joined staff of Arts Council of Northern Ireland; at present Exhibitions Officer.
1970	Irish Exhibition of Living Art, Caroll prizewinner.
1973	Arts Council of Northern Ireland poster-poem commission with John Montague.

Principal Exhibitions

1967	Butlin Foundation for Young Irish Artists, Belfast, Cork, Dublin, Mosney.
1968	Dúchas, Queen's University, Belfast.
1968	Ulster Painting '68, Arts Council of Northern Ireland Gallery.
1969	Seven North of Ireland Painters, David Hendriks Gallery, Dublin.
1969	Contemporary Irish Art, Park Square Gallery, Leeds; Compass Gallery, Glasgow.
1969-1972	Irish Exhibition of Living Art, Dublin.
1970	One man show, Queen's University, Belfast.
1970	Two man show, David Hendriks Gallery, Dublin.

1971	Art Spectrum Ulster, Arts Council of Northern Ireland Gallery.
1971	ROSC Young Irish Artists, Kenny's Art Gallery, Galway, and Edinburgh.
1971	Royal Hibernian Academy, Dublin.
1972, 1976	Gordon Lambert Collection, Municipal Gallery of Modern Art, Dublin; and Wexford Festival and Ulster Museum.
1972, 1973	One man shows, Tom Caldwell Gallery, Belfast.
1973	Belfast Schools Art Collection, Arts Council of Northern Ireland Gallery.
1975	One man show, Queen's University, Belfast.
1976	Collectors' Choice, Leeds Playhouse Gallery.
1976	One man show, Bell Gallery, Belfast.
1976	Dartington College of Art Gallery, Devon.
1977	Oireachtas, Dublin, Belfast and Letterkenny.

Collections

An Chomhairle Ealáion, Arts Council of Northern Ireland, Belfast Education and Library Board, P J Carroll & Co Ltd, Cork Municipal Art Gallery, Great Southern Hotels, New University of Ulster, Coleraine; Salzburg Seminar, Ulster Museum.

Bibliography

'Painting and Sculpture' by Kenneth Jamison, *Causeway, The Arts in Ulster*, Arts Council of Northern Ireland and Gill and Macmillan, Dublin, 1971.

DAVID BARKER
b 1945 Dorchester, Dorset

Education and career

1962-1967	Goldsmith's College, University of London.
1966	Royal Society of Painter-Etchers and Engravers associate Fellow.
1967	Printmakers' Council of Great Britain Member.
1967-1968	Assistant in printmaking, Cambridge School of Art.
1968-1972	Lecturer, Foundation Studies, Ulster College of Art and Design.
1970	Arts Council of Northern Ireland commission poster design.
1972-1974	Lecturer, School of Visual Communications, Art and Design Centre, Ulster College.
1972	Alice Berger Hammerschlag Trust award, travel Scandanavia.
1974-	Senior Lecturer, School of Fine Art, Art and Design Centre, Ulster College.

Principal Exhibitions

1965, 1966	South London Artists.
1965-1968	Royal Society of Painter-Etchers and Engravers, London.
1965	Young Craftsmen, Craft Centre, London.
1966	AAA Gallery, New York.
1967	Brighton Festival.
1967	Grabowski Gallery, London.
1967	Printmakers' Council of Great Britain, London.
1967	Royal Society of Painter-Etchers and Engravers, St Louis, USA.
1968	Ulster Painting '68, Arts Council of Northern Ireland Gallery.
1968	Cambridge Festival.
1969	Contemporary Prints, Augustine Gallery, Norfolk.
1969	Two man show, Arts Council of Northern Ireland Gallery.
1971	Ulster Printmakers, Arts Council of Northern Ireland, touring.
1971	Art Spectrum Ulster, Arts Council of Northern Ireland Gallery.
1972	Octagon Gallery, Belfast.
1973, 1976	Two man show, Octagon Gallery, Belfast.
1973	Belfast Schools Art Collection, Arts Council of Northern Ireland Gallery.

1973	Octagon Editions, Octagon Gallery, Belfast.
1973	Two man show, New University of Ulster, Coleraine.
1973	One man show, Covent Garden Gallery, London.
1974	One man show, Setanta Gallery, Dublin.
1974	Alice Berger Hammerschlag Trust Award Winners, Arts Council of Northern Ireland Gallery; Municipal Gallery of Modern Art, Dublin.
1975	Belfast Education and Library Board Prints, Arts Council of Northern Ireland Gallery.
1976	One man show, Neptune Gallery, Dublin.
1976	One man show, Keys Gallery, Londonderry.
1976	Octagon Prints, Printmakers Workshop Gallery, Edinburgh; Third Eye Centre, Glasgow.

Collections

Arts Council of Northern Ireland, Belfast Education and Library Board, Calfornia College of Arts and Crafts, California, USA; New University of Ulster; Northern Bank, Northern Ireland Department of Commerce, Southwark Print Collection, London.

MALCOLM BENNETT
b 1942 Derby

Education and career

1956-1960	Technical High School, Belfast.
1962-1966	Stranmillis College, Belfast.
1966-1970	Lived in South Derry, West of Ireland, France and Switzerland.
1970-	Art Teacher, Glastry Secondary School, Co Down.
1973	Arts Council of Northern Ireland poster-poem commission with Stewart Parker.

Principal Exhibitions

1963	Eight Painters, Magee Gallery, Belfast.
1964-1971	Irish Exhibition of Living Art, Dublin.
1965	Four man show, Brooke Park Gallery, Londonderry.
1965	Six Ulster Painters, Queen's University, Belfast.
1965	Young Irish Artists Foundation, Belfast, Dublin, Cork.
1966, 1970	One man shows, Bell Gallery, Belfast.
1967	Group 63, Queen's University, Belfast.
1968	Ulster Painting '68, Arts Council of Northern Ireland Gallery.
1968	Dúchas, Queen's University, Belfast.
1969, 1972	Independent Artists, Municipal Gallery of Modern Art, Dublin.
1969	One man show, Brown Thomas Gallery, Dublin.
1969	Group 63, Ulster Museum.
1970	Group 63, Tom Caldwell Gallery, Belfast.
1971	Ulster Places, Arts Council of Northern Ireland Gallery.
1973	Belfast Schools Art Collection, Arts Council of Northern Ireland Gallery.
1970	Group 63, Ulster Office, London.
1971	Royal Hibernian Academy, Dublin.
1971	Group 63, Tom Caldwell Gallery, Belfast.
1972	One man show, Arts Council of Northern Ireland Gallery.
1972	One man show, Davis Gallery, Dublin.
1973, 1976	One man shows, Tom Caldwell Gallery, Belfast.
1974	One man show, Barrenhill Gallery, Dublin.

Collections

Allied Irish Banks, Arts Council of Northern Ireland, Belfast Education and Library Board, Córas Iompair Éireann, Government of Northern Ireland, Ministry of Finance; New University of Ulster, Coleraine; Northern Bank, Stranmillis College.

Bibliography
'Painting and Sculpture' by Kenneth Jamison, *'Causeway, The Arts in Ulster*, Arts Council of Northern Ireland and Gill and Macmillan, Dublin, 1971.

BASIL BLACKSHAW
b 1932 Glengormley, Co Antrim

Education and career

1946-1948 Methodist College, Belfast.
1948-1951 Belfast College of Art.
1951 CEMA travel scholarship, Paris.
1970 Arts Council of Northern Ireland portrait commission, Harry Thompson.
1973 Arts Council of Northern Ireland poster-poem commission with Derek Mahon.
1975 Arts Council of Northern Ireland portrait commission, Patricia Mulholland.

Principal Exhibitions

1957 CEMA Scholarship Holders.
1958 Lewinter-Frankl Collection, Belfast Museum and Art Gallery.
1958 The Religious Theme, Tate Gallery, London.
1958-1960, 1961, 1975 Irish Exhibition of Living Art, Dublin.
1960 Two man show, Ritchie Hendriks Gallery, Dublin.
1961 One man show, CEMA Gallery, Belfast.
1962 One man show, Studio 25, Belfast.
1964 One man show, Arts Council of Northern Ireland Gallery, Belfast.
1965 Aspects of the Ulster Landscape, Arts Council of Northern Ireland Gallery, Belfast.
1965 Four Ulster Painters, Arnolfini Gallery, Bristol.
1965 Paintings and Sculpture by Irish Artists, Ritchie Hendriks Gallery, Dublin.
1966 Open Painting, Arts Council of Northern Ireland; Ulster Museum.
1967 Two Ulster Painters (with T P Flanagan), Arts Council of Northern Ireland, touring.
1968 Dúchas, Queen's University, Belfast.
1968 Ulster Painting '68, Arts Council of Northern Ireland Gallery, Belfast.
1970 Ulster Faces by Ulster Artists, Arts Council of Northern Ireland, touring.
1970 Aspects of Landscape by Irish Artists, An Chomhairle Ealáion, Dublin.
1970 One man shows, Bell Gallery, Belfast.
1973, 1977 One man shows, Tom Caldwell Gallery, Belfast.
1974 Watergate Gallery, Washington DC.
1974 Retrospective Exhibition, Arts Council of Northern Ireland, Belfast.
1974 Drawings, Arts Council of Northern Ireland, touring.
1975 One man show, Tom Caldwell Gallery, Dublin.
1975 Women of Ulster, Arts Council of Northern Ireland, touring.
1977 Oireachtas, Dublin, Belfast, Letterkenny.

Collections
An Chomhairle Ealáion, Arts Council of Northern Ireland, Bank of Ireland, Herbert Art Gallery and Museum, Coventry; New University of Ulster, Coleraine; Northern Bank, Rotherham Museum and Art Gallery, Trinity College, Dublin; Ulster Museum.

Bibliography
'Portrait of a Young Man as the Artist' by John Hewitt, *Threshold*, February 1957.
A Concise History of Irish Art by Bruce Arnold, Thames and Hudson, London, 1969.
'Painting and Sculpture' by Kenneth Jamison, *Causeway: The Arts in Ulster*, Arts Council of Northern Ireland and Gill and Macmillan, Dublin, 1971.

DEBORAH BROWN
b 1927 Belfast

Education and career

1946	Belfast College of Art.
1947-1950	National College of Art, Dublin.
1950	Paris.
1965	Ferranti Ltd commission to paint a series of canvases for their offices at Hollinwood, Manchester.
1970	Arts Council of Northern Ireland Open Painting prizewinner.
1970	Irish Exhibition of Living Art, Carroll first prize, open award.
1973	Arts Council of Northern Ireland poster-poem commission with Padraic Fiacc.

Principal Exhibitions

1959, 1964	One woman shows, New Vision Centre Gallery, London.
1960-1962	Women's International Art Club, London.
1961, 1966-1968, 1970-1973, 1975, 1976	Irish Exhibition of Living Art, Dublin.
1962, 1969	One woman shows, Arts Council of Northern Ireland Gallery, Belfast and (1969) Brooke Parke Gallery, Londonderry.
1964	One woman show, New Gallery, Belfast.
1966	Open Painting, Arts Council of Northern Ireland Gallery, Belfast.
1966	Eight North of Ireland Painters, New Charing Cross Gallery, Glasgow.
1966, 1968	One woman shows, Ritchie Hendriks Gallery, Dublin.
1967	Irish Artists, Ritchie Hendriks Gallery, Dublin.
1968	Dúchas, Queen's University, Belfast.
1968, 1970	Open Painting, Arts Council of Northern Ireland Gallery.
1969	Contemporary Irish Art, Park Square Gallery Leeds; Compass Gallery, Glasgow.
1970, 1975	Oireachtas, Dublin.
1971	David Hendriks Gallery, Dublin.
1971	Art Spectrum Ulster, Arts Council of Northern Ireland Gallery, Belfast.
1972, 1976	Gordon Lambert Collection, Municipal Gallery of Modern Art, Dublin and (1976) Ulster Museum and Wexford Festival.
1973, 1977	One woman shows, David Hendriks Gallery, Dublin.
1974	Contemporary Irish Sculpture, Dublin Arts Festival, Bank of Ireland, Dublin.
1975	Creative Women, Arts Council of Northern Ireland.
1975	Cagnes sur Mer International Festival of Painting, representing Ireland with Theo McNab.

Collections

An Chomhairle Ealáion, Arts Council of Northern Ireland, Bank of Ireland, British Broadcasting Corporation, Northern Ireland; P J Carroll and Co Ltd, Ferranti Ltd, Great Southern Hotels, Hugh Lane Municipal Gallery of Modern Art, Dublin; Radio Telefís Éireann, Ulster Museum.

Bibliography

'A youthful disciple of Humbert Craig', *News Letter*, 14 December 1951.
'Artist in Abstract' by Betty Lowry, *Belfast Telegraph*, 13 May 1963.
'Why' by Deborah Brown, *Ferranti Journal*, 1966.
A Concise History of Irish Art by Bruce Arnold, Thames and Hudson, London, 1969.
'Deborah Brown: an appreciation' by T P Flanagan, *Threshold* No 22, 1969.
'Painting and Sculpture', by Kenneth Jamison, *Causeway: The Arts in Ulster*, Arts Council of Northern Ireland and Gill and Macmillan, Dublin, 1971.
'Harriet Cooke talks to the artist Deborah Brown', *Irish Times*, 13 June 1973.
'Deborah Brown' by A Crookshank, *The Arts in Ireland*, Vol 1 No 4, 1973.

R J CROFT
b 1935 London

Education and career

1951-1955	Bromley College of Art.
1957-1958	Brighton College of Art.
1963-	Head of Art Department, Annadale Grammar School, Belfast.
1966	Gallagher portrait competition commended prize.
1967	Royal Ulster Academy academician.
1970	Royal Ulster Academy Conor award.

Principal Exhibitions

1957	Young Contemporaries, London.
1961	One man show, CEMA, Belfast.
1961, 1964	One man shows, Queen's University, Belfast.
1962-1971	Irish Exhibition of Living Art, Dublin.
1962	Open Painting, CEMA; Ulster Museum.
1963	One man show, Magee Gallery, Belfast.
1963	Eight Painters, Magee Gallery, Belfast.
1964	Open Painting, Arts Council of Northern Ireland; Ulster Museum.
1964	One man show, Oxford University.
1965	Six Ulster Painters, Queen's University, Belfast.
1966, 1970	One man show, Arts Council of Northern Ireland Gallery.
1967	Group 63, Queen's University, Belfast.
1968	Dúchas, Queen's University, Belfast.
1968	Open Painting, Arts Council of Northern Ireland Gallery.
1968	Ulster Painting '68, Arts Council of Northern Ireland Gallery.
1969, 1970	Group 63, Ulster Museum and Ulster Office, London.
1970, 1971	Group 63, Tom Caldwell Gallery, Belfast.
1971	Royal Hibernian Academy, Dublin.
1971	One man show, Davis Gallery, Dublin.
1971	Art Spectrum Ulster, Arts Council of Northern Ireland Gallery.
1972, 1974, 1976	One man shows, Tom Caldwell Gallery, Belfast.
1973	Group 63, Arts Council of Northern Ireland Gallery.
1973	Belfast Schools Art Collection, Arts Council of Northern Ireland Gallery.
1974	Watergate Gallery, Washington, DC.
1976	One man show, Tom Caldwell Gallery, Dublin.
1977	One man show, Octagon Gallery, Belfast.

Collections

Arts Council of Northern Ireland, Belfast Education and Library Board, Cork Municipal Art Gallery, Government of Northern Ireland, London University, Northern Bank, Oxford University, Queen's University, Belfast.

Bibliography

'Painting and Sculpture' by Kenneth Jamison, *Causeway, The Arts in Ulster*, Arts Council of Northern Ireland and Gill and Macmillan, Dublin, 1971.

DAVID CRONE
b 1937 Belfast

Education and career

1950-1956	Annadale Grammar School, Belfast.
1956	Belfast College of Art.
1961-1963	Teacher of Art, Larkfield Secondary School, Belfast.
1962	CEMA Open Painting competition prizewinner.

1963-1975	Teacher of Art, Annadale Grammar School, Belfast.
1964	Arts Council of Northern Ireland travel scholarship, Germany, Holland and Italy.
1970	Arts Council of Northern Ireland portrait commission, Michael Baguley.
1971	Ulster '71 commission, County Armagh mural.
1972	Arts Council of Northern Ireland portrait commission, Buster McShane.
1975-	Lecturer, Foundation Studies, Ulster College, the Northern Ireland Polytechnic.

Principal Exhibitions

1962	Open Painting, CEMA; Ulster Museum.
1963	Two man show, Arts Council of Northern Ireland Gallery, Belfast.
1963	Eight Painters, Magee Gallery, Belfast.
1963, 1964, 1967	Irish Exhibition of Living Art, Dublin.
1964	Open Painting, Arts Council of Northern Ireland; Ulster Museum.
1965, 1968, 1973	One man shows, Arts Council of Northern Ireland Gallery, Belfast.
1965	Aspects of the Ulster Landscape, Arts Council of Northern Ireland Gallery.
1965	Six Ulster Painters, Queen's University, Belfast.
1965	Young Irish Artists Foundation, Belfast, Dublin, Cork.
1968	Ulster Painting '68, Arts Council of Northern Ireland Gallery.
1969	Seven North of Ireland Painters, David Hendriks Gallery, Dublin.
1970	Ulster Faces by Ulster Artists, Arts Council of Northern Ireland, touring.
1970-1971	Celtic Triangle, An Chomhairle Ealáion, Dublin and Cork; Arts Council of Northern Ireland Gallery, Belfast and Brooke Park Gallery, Londonderry; Scottish Arts Council Gallery, Edinburgh; Welsh Arts Council Gallery, Cardiff.
1972	Ulster Faces, Arts Council of Northern Ireland, touring.
1973	Group 63, Arts Council of Northern Ireland Gallery.
1973	Belfast Schools Art Collection, Arts Council of Northern Ireland Gallery.
1976	Two man show, Tom Caldwell Gallery, Belfast.
1977	Eight Northern Irish Artists, Third Eye Centre.
1977	Group Show — 14 Artists, Arts Council of Northern Ireland Gallery, Belfast.

Collections

An Chomhairle Ealáion, Arts Council of Northern Ireland, Dalriada School, Ballymoney; Ulster Museum.

Bibliography

'Painting and Sculpture' by Kenneth Jamison, *Causeway; The Arts in Ulster*, Arts Council of Northern Ireland and Gill and Macmillan, Dublin, 1971.

GERARD DILLON
b 1916 Belfast
d 1971 Dublin

Education and career

1921-1927	Raglan Street Public Elementary School, Belfast.
1927-1930	Christian Brothers School, Harding Street, Belfast.
	Lived in London from 1934 to 1939; in Ireland from 1939 to 1945; in London from 1945 to 1968 apart from one year in Ireland and trips abroad; in Dublin from 1968 to 1971.
1952	St Patrick's Day celebrations, New York, supervised large design for Macy's store.
1963	Member of Irish Trade and Culture delegations to USA.
1963	Bord Fáilte Christmas card design.
1966	UNICEF reproduced painting on Christmas card.
1968	Arts Council of Northern Ireland poster design commission.
1968	Designed set and costumes for *Juno and the Paycock*, Abbey Theatre.

1968 Radio Telefís Éireann Christmas card design.
1969 Lecturer, Municipal Gallery of Modern Art, Dublin.
1969 Lecturer, National College of Art, Dublin.
1969 Dublin Tourism wall hanging commission.

Principal Exhibitions

1942 One man show, Country Shop, Dublin.
1943, 1944
1947-1970 Irish Exhibition of Living Art, Dublin.
1943, 1952, 1958, 1959, 1965, 1966, 1968-1971 Royal Hibernian Academy, Dublin.
1946, 1950 One man shows, CEMA Gallery, Belfast.
1946 Leicester Gallery, London.
1949-1954, 1959, 1960, 1962-1964, 1967-1970 Oireachtas, Dublin.
1950, 1953 One man shows, Victor Waddington Galleries, Dublin.
1950 New Irish Painters, Institute of Contemporary Art, Boston, Mass.
1951 Five Irish Artists, Tooth Galleries, London.
1953, 1954 Piccadilly Gallery, London.
1954 Maxwell Galleries, San Francisco, California.
1957, 1959, 1960, 1962, 1963, 1965, 1966, 1967, 1968, 1969, 1971 One man shows, Dawson Gallery Dublin.
1958 Pittsburgh International Exhibition of Contemporary Art.
1958 Lewinter Collection, Belfast Museum and Art Gallery.
1958 One man show, Queen's University of Belfast.
1958, 1960 Guggenheim International, USA.
1961, 1963 Marzotto International, Rome.
1962 Festival of Modern Art, Boston, Mass.
1962 Obelisk Gallery, Washington, DC.
1962 Irish Cultural Relations, Holland, Sweden, Germany, Wales and USA.
1963 One man show, Studio 25, Belfast.
1963 Twelve Irish Artists, New School Gallery; Lord & Taylor's, New York City.
1963 Whitechapel Gallery, London.
1966 One man show, Arts Council of Northern Ireland Gallery.
1966 Eight North of Ireland Painters, New Charing Cross Gallery, Glasgow.
1967 One man show, Mercury Gallery, London.
1968 Ulster Painting '68, Arts Council of Northern Ireland Gallery.
1969 Two man show, Ulster Arts Club, Belfast.
1969 Independent Artists, Municipal Gallery of Modern Art, Dublin.
1971 One man show, Tom Caldwell Gallery, Belfast.
1972-1973 Retrospective, Ulster Museum and Arts Council of Northern Ireland Gallery; Municipal Gallery of Modern Art, Dublin.
1973 Belfast Schools Art Collection, Arts Council of Northern Ireland Gallery.

Collections

An Chomhairle Ealáion, Arts Council of Northern Ireland, Carnegie Institute, P J Carroll & Co Ltd, Cork Municipal Art Gallery, Drogheda Municipal Art Gallery, Great Southern Hotels, Hugh Lane Municipal Gallery of Modern Art, Dublin; Irish Tourist Board, Limerick County Library, National Gallery of Ireland, New University of Ulster, Coleraine; Queen's University, Belfast; Sligo County Library and Museum, Trinity College, Dublin, Gallery; Ulster Museum, Waterford Municipal Art Gallery.

Bibliography

'Painting and Sculpture in Ulster' by John Hewitt, *The Arts in Ulster,* George G Harrap & Co Ltd, London, 1951.
'Rebel in Art' by Martin Wallace, *Belfast Telegraph*, 11 November 1960.

'The Artist Talks — Gerard Dillon' by M FitzGerald, *Irish Times*, 23 September 1964.
'Dillon in Dublin' by W Boyd, *Irish Times*, 25 January 1968.
A Concise History of Irish Art by Bruce Arnold, Thames and Hudson, London, 1969.
'Painting and Sculpture' by Kenneth Jamison, *Causeway: The Arts in Ulster*, Arts Council of Northern Ireland and Gill and Macmillan, Dublin, 1971.
'Death of Mr Gerard Dillon', *Irish Times*, 15 June 1971.
'A Simple Complex Man' by G Campbell, *Irish Times*, 8 July 1971.
'In memory of Gerard Dillon' by Michael Longley, *Irish Times*, 2 September 1972.
'Reminder of a great character' by Theo Snoddy, *News Letter* 20 December 1975.

BRIAN FERRAN
b 1940 Londonderry

Education and career

1959-1962 St Joseph's College of Education, Belfast.
1962-1963 St Mary's College of Education, Belfast.
1963-1966 Taught art in St Joseph's Secondary School, Londonderry.
1965 Oireachtas Exhibition, President Hyde gold medal and An Chomhairle Ealáion supplementary award.
1966 Joined staff of Arts Council of Northern Ireland.
1967 North-West Arts Festival commission.
1968 Magee University College commission.
1969 Leverhulme European award to study aspects of communication in visual arts, Brera Academy, Milan, 1970-1971.
1972 Irish American Cultural Institute commission, reproduction in colour *Eire-Ireland* cover.
1973 Arts Council of Northern Ireland poster-poem commission with Ciarán Carson.
1974, 1975, 1977 University and college lecture tour in USA.
1977 St Columb's College, Londonderry, mural commission.
At present Arts Council of Northern Ireland Director, Art/Film.

Principal Exhibitions

1965 Young Irish Artists Foundation, Belfast, Dublin, Cork.
1966 One man show, Waterside Library Gallery, Londonderry.
1965-1967, 1969, 1974, 1975 Oireachtas, Dublin.
1965-1969, 1971-1973 Royal Hibernian Academy, Dublin.
1966 1916 Commemoration, Municipal Gallery of Modern Art, Dublin.
1967 Butlin Foundation for Young Irish Artists, Belfast, Cork, Dublin, Mosney.
1967-1974, 1976 Irish Exhibition of Living Art, Dublin.
1967 One man show, Molesworth Gallery, Dublin.
1968 Dúchas, Queen's University, Belfast.
1968 Irish Graphic Artists, Minnesota, USA.
1968 One man show, New Gallery, Belfast.
1968 Ulster Painting '68, Arts Council of Northern Ireland Gallery.
1968 Irish Graphic Artists, Minnesota, USA.
1968, 1970, 1975 One man shows, Queen's University, Belfast.
1969 Two man show, Westgate Gallery, Newcastle-upon-Tyne.
1969 Seven North of Ireland Painters, Ritchie Hendriks Gallery, Dublin.
1969 Group 63, Ulster Museum, Belfast.
1969 Independent Artists, Municipal Gallery of Modern Art, Dublin.
1970 One man show, Nat Gordon Gallery, Londonderry.

1970	Group 63, Ulster Office, London.
1970	One man show, Brown Thomas Gallery, Dublin.
1971	ROSC Young Irish Artists, Kenny's Art Gallery, Galway; and Edinburgh.
1972, 1975	One man shows, Tom Caldwell Gallery, Belfast.
1972, 1976	Gordon Lambert Collection, Municipal Gallery of Modern Art, Dublin; and Wexford Festival and Ulster Museum.
1972	Independent Artists, Dublin, invited.
1972	Young Irish Artists, Brown Thomas Gallery, Dublin.
1972	From Yeats till Ballagh, Lunds Konstall, Sweden.
1973	One man show, New University of Ulster, Coleraine.
1973	Belfast Schools Art Collection, Arts Council of Northern Ireland Gallery.
1973	Galerie des Philosophes, Geneva.
1974	One man show, David Hendriks Gallery, Dublin.
1975	One man show, Irish Tourist Board Offices, New York City.
1975	One man show, Sean Desmond Gallery, New York City.
1976	Collectors' Choice, The Playhouse Gallery, Leeds.
1976	Dartington College of Art Gallery, Devon.
1977	Oireachtas, Dublin, Belfast and Letterkenny.

Collections

An Chomhairle Ealáion, Arts Council of Northern Ireland, Belfast Education and Library Board, Córas Iompair Éireann, Córas Tráchtála, Dublin; Great Southern Hotels, Institute of Public Administration, Dublin; Kilkenny Design Centre, Gordon Lambert, Magee University College, New University of Ulster, Coleraine; North West Art Trust; Northern Bank Finance Group, Northern Ireland Department of Commerce, Queen's University, Belfast; St Columb's College, Londonderry; St John Fisher College, New York; St Joseph's College of Education, Belfast; St Mary's College of Education, Belfast; Stranmillis College, Belfast; Ulster Arts Club, Ulster College, Art and Design Centre; Ulster Museum.

Bibliography

'Painting and Sculpture' by Kenneth Jamison, *Causeway, The Arts in Ulster*, Arts Council of Northern Ireland and Gill and Macmillan Dublin, 1971.

T P FLANAGAN

b 1929 Enniskillen

Education and career

1943-1949	St Michael's Presentation Brothers Grammar School, Enniskillen.
1943-1949	Enniskillen Technical College, evening.
1949-1953	Belfast College of Art.
1953-1954	Teacher of Art, Convent of the Sacred Heart of Mary, Lisburn; Assumption Convent, Ballynahinch; Belfast College of Art.
1954-1956	Lecturer in art, St Mary's College of Education, Belfast.
1963-1968	Visiting teacher in life drawing, Belfast College of Art.
1964	Royal Ulster Academy Academician.
1965-	Head of Art Department, St Mary's College of Education, Belfast.
1970	Ulster '71 commission, postage stamp.
1971	Ulster '71 commission, County Fermanagh mural.
1971	Trustee of Lyric Theatre and designer of costumes and decor.
1972	Arts Council of Northern Ireland poster-poem commission with Seamus Heaney.
1972	Arts Council of Northern Ireland portrait commission, John D Stewart.
1973-1974	Sabbatical, USA.
1974	Oireachtas painting prize.
1975	Arts Council of Northern Ireland portrait commission, Sadie Patterson.
1976	USA lecture tour.

1976	Royal Ulster Academy gold medal award.
1977	Gael-Linn portrait commission of John Doherty for record sleeve.

Principal Exhibitions

1958	Lewinter-Frankl Collection, Belfast Museum and Art Gallery.
1958	Royal Academy, London.
1960, 1962-1968, 1970, 1971, 1973, 1974, 1976	Irish Exhibition of Living Art, Dublin.
1960	Painting and Sculpture by Ulster Artists, CEMA Gallery, Belfast.
1961	One man show, CEMA Gallery, Belfast.
1962	Open Painting, CEMA; Ulster Museum.
1963, 1965, 1967	One man shows, Ritchie Hendriks Gallery, Dublin.
1964-1966	One man shows, Queen's University, Belfast.
1964	Graphic Art, An Chomhairle Ealáion; Municipal Gallery of Modern Art, Dublin.
1964	Twelve Irish Artists, Ritchie Hendriks Gallery, Dublin.
1964, 1966	Open Painting, Arts Council of Northern Ireland; Ulster Museum, Belfast.
1965	Paintings and Sculpture by Irish Artists, Ritchie Hendriks Gallery, Dublin.
1965	Aspects of the Ulster Landscape, Arts Council of Northern Ireland Gallery.
1965, 1968, 1969, 1971, 1972	Royal Hibernian Academy, Dublin.
1966, 1969	One man shows, Arts Council of Northern Ireland Gallery.
1966	Eight North of Ireland Painters, New Charing Cross Gallery, Glasgow.
1967	2 Ulster Painters, with Basil Blackshaw, Arts Council of Northern Ireland, touring.
1967	Irish Artists, Ritchie Hendriks Gallery, Dublin.
1968	Dúchas, Queen's University, Belfast.
1968	Ulster Painting '68, Arts Council of Northern Ireland Gallery.
1968, 1970	Open Painting, Arts Council of Northern Ireland Gallery.
1968	Two Irish Painters, with Colin Middleton, Herbert Art Gallery and Museum, Coventry.
1969, 1971-1976	Oireachtas, Dublin.
1969, 1971, 1973, 1975	One man shows, David Hendriks Gallery, Dublin.
1969	Contemporary Irish Art, Park Square Gallery, Leeds; Compass Gallery, Glasgow.
1969	Contemporary Irish Painting, An Chomhairle Ealáion; Wexford Festival.
1969, 1970, 1971, 1974	David Hendriks Gallery, Dublin.
1970, 1973, 1975	One man shows, Tom Caldwell Gallery, Belfast.
1971	One man show, A Lissadell Theme, Municipal Gallery of Modern Art, Dublin.
1971	Art Spectrum Ulster, Arts Council of Northern Ireland Gallery.
1971	ROSC The Irish Imagination, Municipal Gallery of Modern Art, Dublin.
1972, 1976	Gordon Lambert Collection, Municipal Gallery of Modern Art, Dublin; and Wexford Festival and Ulster Museum, Belfast.
1972	Ulster Faces, Arts Council of Northern Ireland, touring.
1972, 1973	Tom Caldwell Gallery, Belfast.
1973	Kathleen Bridle, William Scott, T P Flanagan Arts Council of Northern Ireland Gallery, Belfast; Enniskillen Collegiate School and touring.
1973	One man show, Cork Art Society Gallery, Cork.
1973	Belfast Schools Art Collection, Arts Council of Northern Ireland Gallery.
1975	Women of Ulster, Arts Council of Northern Ireland, touring.
1975	Wexford Festival.
1976	Dartington College of Art Gallery, Devon.

1976	Listowel Graphics.
1977	One man show, Keys Gallery, Londonderry.
1977	Mid-Career Assessment, Arts Council of Northern Ireland Gallery, Belfast.

Collections
Aer Lingus, An Chomhairle Ealáion, Arts Council of Northern Ireland, Bank of Ireland P J Carroll & Co, Ltd, Herbert Art Gallery and Museum, Coventry; Irish Hotels Federation, Irish Institute, New York City; Gordon Lambert Collection, Hugh Lane Municipal Gallery of Modern Art, Dublin; New University of Ulster, Coleraine; Queen's University, Belfast; Ulster Museum; Usher Gallery, Lincoln; Waterford Municipal Art Gallery.

Bibliography
Cúchulainn by J J Campbell, with drawings by T P Flanagan, C J Fallon (London) Ltd, Belfast, 1957.
Gallery, BBC TV NI, 1966.
Contrasts, Ulster Television, 1966.
'Sligo inspired his landscapes' by Theo Snoddy, *News Letter*, 26 May 1966.
'Talking to T P Flanagan' by Seamus Heaney, *Irish Times* 21 September 1967.
A Concise History of Irish Art by Bruce Arnold, Thames and Hudson, London, 1969.
'Talking to Ulster Artists', Ulster College of Art and Design taped and illustrated project, 1971.
'The Other Belfast', *Aquarius*, London Weekend Television, 1971.
'Painting and Sculpture' by Kenneth Jamison, *Causeway: The Arts in Ulster*, Arts Council of Northern Ireland and Gill and Macmillan, Dublin, 1971.
'The Artists in Northern Ireland' *The Arts in Ireland*, Vol 1 No 1, Autumn, 1972.
'Drawings of William Scott' by T P Flanagan, *The Arts in Ireland* Vol 1 No 3, Spring 1973.
'Painter — T P Flanagan', *Gallery*, BBC TV NI, 1 May 1973.
Speaking Personally, BBC Radio 4, Northern Ireland, 2 February 1974. Interview on Radio Telefis Eireann (radio) October 1975.
'To Speak of Drawing' by T P Flanagan, *Introspect* No 1, December 1975.
'Caroline Walsh talks to the painter T P Flanagan', *Irish Times*, 14 August 1976.

NORMAN FRASER
b 1943 Belfast

Education and career

1955-1960	Annadale Grammar School, Belfast.
1960-1965	Belfast College of Art.
1965-1968	Hornsey College of Art, London.
1966-1967	Art Teacher, Orangefield Boys Secondary School, Belfast.
1967-	Lecturer, Department of Foundation Studies, Ulster College.
1974	Arts Council of Northern Ireland travel bursary, USA, and Canada researching developments in Computer Art.

Principal Exhibitions

1967	Butlin Foundation for Young Irish Artists, Belfast, Cork, Dublin, Mosney.
1968	Ulster Painting '68, Arts Council of Northern Ireland Gallery.
1971	Art Spectrum Ulster, Arts Council of Northern Ireland Gallery.
1973	Belfast Schools Art Collection, Arts Council of Northern Ireland Gallery.
1974	Octagon Gallery, Belfast.
1974	Irish Exhibition of Living Art, Dublin.
1975	Annadale Group Show, Arts Council of Northern Ireland Gallery.
1977	Eight Northern Irish Artists, Third Eye Centre, Glasgow.
1977	Group Show, Arts Council of Northern Ireland Gallery.

Collections
Arts Council of Northern Ireland, Belfast Education and Library Board.

ADRIAN HALL
b 1943 Cornwall

Education and career

1959-1963	Plymouth College of Art.
1964-1967	Royal College of Art, London.
1967	Young Contemporaries prizewinner.
1967	Royal College of Art travel scholarship, USA.
1967	Yale University, USA, scholarship.
1967-1969	Yale University, USA.
1969-1970	Lecturer, University of California, Los Angeles.
1971-1972	Senior Visiting Lecturer, University of Auckland, New Zealand.
1972	Hansell's award for environmental sculpture, New Zealand.
1973	Festival of Progress award of merit, City of Liverpool, Australia.
1973-	Principal Lecturer (Sculpture), School of Fine Art, Art and Design Centre, Ulster College.
1975	Arts Council of Northern Ireland Art in Context commission, land sculpture, Northern Ireland Housing Executive, Kilcooley Estate, Bangor.
1975	Irish Exhibition of Living Art, Carroll award for sculpture.

Principal Exhibitions

1961	Arnolfini Gallery, Bristol.
1965	Plymouth City Art Gallery.
1965	Camberwell Art Gallery, London.
1965	London Group, FBA Galleries, London.
1966	Young Contemporaries, FBA Galleries, London.
1967	Young Contemporaries, Tate Gallery, London.
1967	One man show, Sheffield Arts Festival.
1968	Young Artists Fall Exhibition, New Haven, Connecticut, USA.
1971, 1977	One man shows, Barry Lett Galleries, Auckland, New Zealand.
1971	Young Contemporaries, City Museum, Auckland, New Zealand, touring.
1972	New Zealand Sculpture, Barry Lett Galleries, Auckland, New Zealand.
1972	New Zealand Drawings, Barry Lett Galleries, Auckland, New Zealand.
1972	Wairarapa Contemporary Sculpture, New Zealand.
1972	North Shore Sculpture, Auckland, New Zealand.
1973	Documentation from New Zealand, Paris Biennale.
1975	Cleveland, UK International Drawing Biennale.
1975	Oasis Outdoor Sculpture, Dublin.
1975, 1976	Irish Exhibition of Living Art, Dublin.
1975, 1977	Project Gallery, Dublin.
1976	One man show, Watters Gallery, Sydney, Australia.
1976	One man show, Nigel Greenwood Inc Ltd, London.
1976	Arts Council of Great Britain International Drawing, touring.
1976	One man show, David Hendriks Gallery, Dublin.
1976	Gordon Lambert Collection, Wexford Festival and Ulster Museum.
1976	Pan-Pacific Biennale, City Museum, Auckland, New Zealand.
1977	Sets, Series, Sequences, Watters Gallery, Sydney, Australia.
1977	Watters at Pinacotheca, Pinacotheca, Melbourne, Australia.
1977	Oireachtas, Dublin, Belfast and Letterkenny.

Collections

University of Auckland, New Zealand; Gordon Lambert, New University of Ulster, Coleraine.

ALICE BERGER HAMMERSCHLAG
b 1917 Vienna
d 1969 Belfast

Education and career

1929-1938	Professor Cizek, The Kunstgewerbeschule and Vienna Academy of Arts.
1938	Came to Northern Ireland. Designed for publishers and executed stage sets in Belfast and Dublin.

Principal Exhibitions

1956, 1958, 1960, 1964, 1968 One woman shows, Queen's University, Belfast.

1959	One woman show, New Vision Centre Gallery, London.
1959, 1962	One woman shows, CEMA Gallery, Belfast.
1960	One woman show, Avgarde Gallery, Manchester.
1961, 1964-1967	Irish Exhibition of Living Art, Dublin.
1962	One woman show, Arnolfini Gallery, Bristol.
1963	9 Irish Artists, Arts Council of Northern Ireland; Edinburgh.
1963	9 Artists from Ireland, Arts Council of Northern Ireland; Glasgow.
1963	Lord and Taylor, New York.
1963	United Nations Building, Rome.
1964, 1966	Open Painting, Arts Council of Northern Ireland; Ulster Museum.
1965, 1968	One woman shows, Dawson Gallery, Dublin.
1965	Aspects of the Ulster Landscape, Arts Council of Northern Ireland Gallery.
1966, 1970	One woman shows, Arts Council of Northern Ireland Cross Gallery; 1970, memorial, also Brooke Park Gallery, Londonderry.
1966	One woman show, Ulster Office, London.
1966	Eight North of Ireland Painters, New Charing Cross Gallery, Glasgow.
1967	12 British Artists, Lauderdale Museum, Miami, Florida.
1967	Galerie Creuze, Paris.
1968	Open Painting, Arts Council of Northern Ireland Gallery.
1968	Dúchas, Queen's University, Belfast.
1968, 1969	Salon International Cannes, France.
1968	Ulster Painting '68, Arts Council of Northern Ireland Gallery.
1969	Scottish Society of Women Artists, invited; Royal Scottish Academy Galleries, Edinburgh.

Collections

An Chomhairle Ealáion, Arts Council of Northern Ireland, Great Southern Hotels, North West Art Trust, Oxfam Building, Oxford; Queen's University, Belfast; Ulster Museum, Ulster Television.

Bibliography

'A Study of Four Painters', *Contrast*, Ulster Television, 1966.
'Painting and Sculpture' by Kenneth Jamison, *Causeway, The Arts in Ulster*, Arts Council of Northern Ireland and Gill and Macmillan, Dublin, 1971.

COLIN HARRISON
b 1939 Boston, Lincolnshire

Education and career

1957-1961	Leicester College of Art.
1961-1964	Royal College of Art, London.
1961	Royal Academy Schools David Murray scholarship.
1964	Royal College of Art silver medal award.
1964-1973	Lecturer in Fine Art Department, Ulster College of Art and Design.
1966	Arts Council of Northern Ireland travel award, London.
1969	Irish Exhibition of Living Art prizewinner.
1970	Arts Council of Northern Ireland portrait commission, Ruby Murray.
1970	Arts Council of Northern Ireland project award for film making with William Bogle.

1973	Visiting lecturer in Fine Art, Wolverhampton Polytechnic.

Principal Exhibitions

1966	Three man show, Arts Council of Northern Ireland Gallery.
1967	New '57 Gallery, Edinburgh.
1968	Open Painting, Arts Council of Northern Ireland Gallery.
1968-1971, 1976	Irish Exhibition of Living Art, Dublin.
1968	Ulster Painting '68, Arts Council of Northern Ireland Gallery.
1969	One man show, Brown Thomas Gallery, Dublin.
1969	Contemporary Irish Art, Park Square Gallery, Leeds; Compass Gallery, Glasgow.
1970	Ulster Faces by Ulster Artists, Arts Council of Northern Ireland, touring.
1971	Art Spectrum Ulster, Arts Council of Northern Ireland Gallery.
1971	'Corsica', with William Bogle, Arts Council of Northern Ireland Gallery.
1971	ROSC Young Irish Artists, Kenny's Art Gallery, Galway; and Edinburgh.
1973-1977	Oireachtas, Dublin.
1973	Two man show, Richard Demarco Gallery, Edinburgh.
1973, 1975	British Drawing Biennale.
1973	Two man show, Tom Caldwell Gallery, Belfast.
1974, 1976	One man shows, Dawson Gallery, Dublin.
1975	Three man show, Tom Caldwell Gallery, Belfast.
1976	Gordon Lambert Collection, Wexford Festival and Ulster Museum.
1977	4 Glass Case Jobs, Wolverhampton Polytechnic.

Collections

An Chomhairle Ealáion, Arts Council of Northern Ireland, Bank of Ireland, Gordon Lambert, Hugh Lane Municipal Gallery of Modern Art, Dublin; New University of Ulster, Coleraine; Ulster Museum.

Bibliography

'Painting and Sculpture' by Kenneth Jamison, *'Causeway, The Arts in Ulster*, Arts Council of Northern Ireland and Gill and Macmillan, Dublin, 1971.

DERRICK HAWKER
b 1936 Seaton, Devon

Education and career

1946-1953	Allhallows School, Devon.
1953-1959	South Devon College of Art and Cardiff College of Art.
1959-1960	Lecturer, South Devon College of Art.
1960-1965	Lecturer, Shrewsbury School of Art.
1965-1973	Director of Foundation Studies, Ulster College of Art and Design.
1973-	Principal, Teesside College of Art, Middlesborough.

Principal Exhibitions

1963	One man show, New Vision Centre, London.
1964	One man show, Woodstock Gallery, London.
1965	Three man show, Shrewsbury Civic Gallery.
1966	Three man show, Arts Council of Northern Ireland Gallery.
1967	One man show, New Gallery, Belfast.
1967, 1968, 1971	Irish Exhibition of Living Art, Dublin.
1968	Ulster Painting '68, Arts Council of Northern Ireland Gallery.
1970	One man show, Arts Council of Northern Ireland Gallery.

1971	Art Spectrum Ulster, Arts Council of Northern Ireland Gallery.
1971, 1976	One man shows, Barrenhill Gallery, Dublin.
1973	Belfast Schools Art Collection, Arts Council of Northern Ireland Gallery.
1975	One man show, Octagon Gallery, Belfast.

Collections
An Chomhairle Ealáion, Arts Council of Northern Ireland, Belfast Education and Library Board.

ROY JOHNSTON
b 1936 Pomeroy

Education and career

1947-1953	Dungannon Royal School.
1957-1959	Stranmillis College, Belfast.
1959-1962	Teacher of Art, Ballygomartin Secondary School, Belfast.
1962-1966	Belfast College of Art.
1964-1968	Lecturer in Art, Rupert Stanley College of Further Education, Belfast.
1964-1966	Lecturer in Art, Belfast College of Art.
1966	Arts Council of Northern Ireland travel scholarship, Greece.
1968-1969	Cardiff College of Art.
1969-1972	Senior Lecturer, Art Education, School of Education Studies, Ulster College.
1970	Arts Council of Northern Ireland Open Painting supplementary prize.
1972-1974	Senior Lecturer, School of Fine Art, Art and Design Centre, Ulster College.
1973	Irish Exhibition of Living Art Carroll prize.
1973	University College, Galway, tapestry wall hanging commission.
1974-	Principal Lecturer, School of Fine Art, Art and Design Centre, Ulster College.
1975, 1976	USA lecture tour.
1975	Arts Council of Northern Ireland Art in Context commission, Cross and Passion Secondary School, Belfast, exterior modular relief mural.
1976	International Festival of Painting at Cagnes-sur-Mer, France, selected; not represented.
1977	Organiser 'All His Own Work, Newton Penprase' exhibition, Arts Council of Northern Ireland Gallery.
1977-1978	USA exchange visit, Barat College, Illinois.

Principal Exhibitions

1964	Painters of Promise, Arts Council of Northern Ireland Gallery.
1966-1976	Irish Exhibition of Living Art, Dublin.
1967	Two man show, Arts Council of Northern Ireland Gallery.
1968	Ulster Painting '68, Arts Council of Northern Ireland Gallery.
1968	Dúchas, Queen's University, Belfast.
1970	Open Painting, Arts Council of Northern Ireland Gallery.
1971	One man show, Arts Council of Northern Ireland Gallery.
1971	Art Spectrum Ulster, Arts Council of Northern Ireland Gallery.
1971	ROSC Young Irish Artists, Kenny's Art Gallery, Galway; and Edinburgh.
1972	One man show, Richard Demarco Gallery, Edinburgh.
1972, 1976	Gordon Lambert Collection, Municipal Gallery of Modern Art, Dublin; and Wexford Festival, Ulster Museum.
1972	One man show, Davis Gallery, Dublin.
1972	The Irish Imagination, Municipal Gallery of Modern Art, Dublin; Boston, Philadelphia, Washington, DC.
1972	Young Irish Artists, Richard Demarco Gallery, Edinburgh.
1973	'Aos Og', Musée d'art Moderne de la Ville de Paris; Municipal Gallery of Modern Art, Dublin.
1973	Belfast Schools Art Collection, Arts Council of Northern Ireland Gallery.
1974-75	Irish Directions of '70s, Ulster Museum, Belfast; Municipal Gallery of Modern Art, Dublin; USA tour: New England and New York City.
1975	One man show, David Hendriks Gallery, Dublin.

1975	5 + 1 Exhibition, Project Art Centre, Dublin.
1975-1976	Listowel Graphics, touring.
1976	Dartington College of Art Gallery, Devon.
1976	Octagon Prints, Glasgow and Edinburgh.
1977	Eight Northern Irish Artists, Third Eye Centre, Glasgow.
1977	Oireachtas, Dublin, Belfast and Letterkenny.

Collections

An Chomhairle Ealáion, Arts Council of Northern Ireland, Bank of Ireland, Belfast Education and Library Board, Hugh Lane Municipal Gallery of Modern Art, Northern Ireland Government, Ministry of Finance; New University of Ulster, Coleraine; Ulster Museum.

Bibliography

'Painting and Sculpture' by Kenneth Jamison, *Causeway, The Arts in Ulster*, Arts Council of Northern Ireland and Gill and Macmillan, Dublin, 1971.

'System and Art' by Roy Johnston, *Introspect* No 1, Dublin, 1975.

'The House that Pen Built', script by Roy Johnston, *Gallery*, BBC TV, NI, 21 January 1977.

'Pomeroy and Permutations', by Theo Snoddy, *News Letter*, 3 August 1977.

DENIS McBRIDE
b 1939 Belfast

Education and career

1958-1963	Belfast College of Art.
1963	Northern Ireland Disabled Ex-Servicemen's Association mural commission.
1964	Hornsey College of Art, London.
1964-1974	Lecturer, Ulster College of Art and Design.
1968	Arts Council of Northern Ireland travel award, Switzerland, France and Spain.
1968	Arts Council of Northern Ireland poster design commission.
1971	Ulster '71 commission, County Tyrone mural.
1972	Arts Council of Northern Ireland portait commission, John McBride.
1974	Senior Lecturer, Foundation Studies, Ulster College, Northern Ireland Polytechnic.
1975	Arts Council of Northern Ireland Art in Context commission, Strabane County Secondary School, two dimensional assemblage.

Principal Exhibitions

1963	Painters of Promise, Arts Council of Northern Ireland Gallery.
1964	Four Young Painters, Arts Council of Northern Ireland Gallery.
1964	Open Painting, Arts Council of Northern Ireland; Ulster Museum.
1965	Four man show, Brooke Park Gallery, Londonderry.
1965	Young Irish Artists Foundation, Belfast, Dublin, Cork.
1966	Eight North of Ireland Painters, New Charing Cross Gallery, Glasgow.
1966, 1967	Irish Exhibition of Living Art, Dublin.
1967	Two man show, Arts Council of Northern Ireland Gallery.
1968	Ulster Painters, Ritchie Hendriks Gallery, Dublin.
1968	Ulster Painting '68, Arts Council of Northern Ireland Gallery.
1970-1971	Celtic Triangle, Welsh Arts Council; Scottish Arts Council; Arts Council of Northern Ireland Gallery; Brooke Park Gallery, Londonderry; An Chomhairle Ealáion, Dublin, Cork.
1971	Art Spectrum Ulster, Arts Council of Northern Ireland Gallery.
1972	Ulster Faces, Arts Council of Northern Ireland, touring.
1972	One man show, Arts Council of Northern Ireland Gallery.
1973	Belfast Schools Art Collection, Arts Council of Northern Ireland Gallery.
1976	Two man show, Tom Caldwell Gallery, Belfast.

1977	Eight North Irish Artists, Third Eye Centre, Glasgow.
1977	Oireachtas, Dublin, Belfast and Letterkenny.
1977	Group show, Arts Council of Northern Ireland Gallery.

Collections
An Chomhairle Ealáion, Arts Council of Northern Ireland, Belfast Education and Library Board, New University of Ulster, Coleraine; Ulster Museum.

Bibliography
'Painting and Sculpture' by Kenneth Jamison, *Causeway, The Arts in Ulster*, Arts Council of Northern Ireland and Gill and Macmillan, Dublin, 1971.

CHERITH McKINSTRY
b 1928 Powick,
Worcestershire

Education and career

1945-1947, 1950-1953	Belfast College of Art.
1954	CEMA travel scholarship, France and Italy.
1963	Presbyterian Students' Centre, Queen's University, sculpture commission.
1968	Church of St MacNissi, Magherahoney, Co Antrim, commission, Stations of the Cross.
1973	Christ Crucified, commission for private house in Wales.
1975	Arts Council of Northern Ireland, commission, Mary Peters.

Principal Exhibitions

1961, 1963	Irish Exhibition of Living Art, Dublin.
1962	One woman show, CEMA Gallery, Belfast.
1962	Open Painting; CEMA, Ulster Museum.
1967	One woman show, New Gallery, Belfast.
1968	One woman show, Bell Gallery, Belfast.
1968	Ulster Painting '68, Arts Council of Northern Ireland Gallery.
1968, 1969	Art in Worship Today, Ulster Museum; Building Centre, Dublin.
1974	One woman show, Octagon Gallery, Belfast.
1974	Figurative Image, Wexford Festival; Trinity College, Dublin.
1975	Women of Ulster, Arts Council of Northern Ireland, touring.
1977	One woman show, Keys Gallery, Londonderry.

Collections
Arts Council of Northern Ireland, Bank of Ireland, Ulster Museum.

Bibliography
'Painting and Sculpture' by Kenneth Jamison, *Causeway, The Arts in Ulster*, Arts Council of Northern Ireland and Gill and Macmillan, Dublin, 1971.

F E McWILLIAM
b 1909 Banbridge

Education and career

1922-1926	Campbell College, Belfast.
1926-1928	Belfast College of Art.
1928-1931	Slade School, London.
1931	Slade School, Robert Ross scholarship, Paris, 1931-1932.
1946-1947	Teacher, Chelsea School of Art.
1946-1968	Lecturer, Slade School.
1956	Harlow, New Town, commission, Elizabeth Frink.

1956	Shrewsbury Technical College, commission, Archimedes.
1957	Altnagelvin Hospital, Londonderry, commission, Princess Macha.
1958	Bumpus' Bookshop, London, commission, Man and Bird.
1958	Basildon New Town commission, Man and Bird.
1959	Royal Academy Associate (resigned 1962).
1959	Teacher's Training College, Avery Hill, London, commission, Witch of Agnesi.
1960	Kent University, Canterbury, commission, Father Courage.
1962-1968	Arts Council of Great Britain arts panel member.
1962	Southampton University commission, Puy de Dome figure.
1964	Honorary Doctor of Literature, Queen's University, Belfast.
1964	Swiss Cottage, London, commission, Hampstead figure.
1966	Commander of the British Empire.
1971	Oireachtas prize, Dublin.
1971	University College, London, Fellow.
1977	Harlow New Town, commission, Help.

Principal Exhibitions

1957	Sao Paulo.
1957	Open Air Sculpture, Holland Park.
1958	Retrospective, West of England Academy, Bristol.
1958	Bildhauer-Zeichnungen des 20 Jahrhunderts Duisberg.
1959	Biennale, Open Air Museum, Middleheim, Antwerp.
1959	International Exhibition of Sculpture, Municipal Gallery of Modern Art, Dublin.
1959-1960	British Artist Craftsmen; Smithsonian Institute, USA, touring.
1960	Irish Exhibition of Living Art, Dublin.
1960	One man show, Queen's University, Belfast.
1960	International Museum of Sculpture, Belfast Museum and Art Gallery.
1961, 1963, 1966, 1968, 1971 and 1973	One man shows, Waddington Galleries, London.
1962	International Open Air Sculpture Exhibition, Keukenhof, Lisse, Holland.
1963	7th International Sculpture Exhibition, Japan.
1963	International Open Air Sculpture Exhibition, Battersea Park, London.
1963	One man show, Felix Landau Gallery, Los Angeles, USA.
1964	Painting and Sculpture of a Decade, Tate Gallery.
1969	One man show, Travers Gallery, London.
1970	One man show, Waddington Gallery, Montreal.
1971	Surrealist Group Exhibition, Hamet Gallery, London.
1971	One man show, Hillsborough Art Centre, Co Down.
1971, 1975	Oireachtas, Dublin.
1972, 1976	Gordon Lambert Collection, Municipal Gallery of Modern Art, Dublin; Wexford Festival; Ulster Museum.
1973	One man show, Dawson Gallery, Dublin.
1973	One man show, McClelland Galleries International, Belfast.
1976	One man show, Waddington & Tooth Galleries, London.
1977	One man show, Bell Gallery, Belfast.
1977	Oireachtas, Dublin, Belfast and Letterkenny.

Collections

Art Gallery of South Australia, Adelaide; Arts Council of Great Britain, Arts Council of Northern Ireland, Chicago Art Institute, Herbert Art Gallery & Museum, Coventry; Leeds City Art Gallery, Leicester Museum and Art Gallery, Middleheim Open Air Museum, Antwerp; Natural Gallery of Canada, Ottawa; National Portrait Gallery, Museum of Modern Art, New York; Oldham Art Gallery & Museum, Queen's University, Belfast; Tate Gallery, Ulster Museum, Victoria and Albert Museum, Western Australian Art Gallery, Perth.

Bibliography
'F E McWilliam' by Paul Nash, *London Bulletin*, 1939.
Sculpture Today by A T Broadbent, John Tiranti, London, 1944.
British Sculpture by Eric Newton, John Tiranti, London, 1947.
'The Sculpture of F E McWilliam' by Bryan Robertson, *Nimbus*, Vol 2 No 3, 1954.
'The Sculpture of F E McWilliam' by Albert Garrett, *The Studio*, November, 1954.
'Portrait of the Artist' by Albert Garrett, *Art News and Review*, 1956.
Architectural Design, Vol XXVIII, September 1958.
'F E McWilliam, ARA' by J Wood Palmer, *Motif*, September 1959.
'F E McWilliam', *The Times*, 17 March 1960.
'Sculptor at Work' by Martin Wallace, *Belfast Telegraph*, 10 February 1961.
McWilliam: Sculptor by Roland Penrose, Alec Tiranti, London, 1964.
'Banbridge's Man at the Tate' by Theo Snoddy, *News Letter*, 18 August 1966.
A Concise History of Irish Art by Bruce Arnold, Thames and Hudson, London, 1969.
'Painting and Sculpture' by Kenneth Jamison, *Causeway: The Arts in Ulster*, Arts Council of Northern Ireland and Gill and Macmillan, Dublin, 1971.
'Harriet Cooke talks to the sculptor F E McWilliam', *Irish Times*, 31 October 1973.
'Women of Belfast', *Aquarius*, London Weekend Television, 4 November 1973.
'The Sculptor and his Drawings' by W J Strachan, *The Connoisseur*, May 1974.
Talk with Derek Bailey, BBC Radio Ulster, November 1976.

JOE McWILLIAMS
b 1938 Belfast

Education and career

1952-1958 St Malachy's College, Belfast.
1958-1964 Belfast College of Art.
1964 Church of St Mary, Aghagallon, Co Antrim, mural commission.
1973 Troubled Image Group, co-founder.
1973 Lecturer in Art Education, Ulster College.
1973-1976 Open University.
1977 Kassel Documenta 6 participant, Free University, Northern Ireland Workshop.

Principal Exhibitions

1966 1916 Commemoration, Municipal Gallery of Modern Art, Dublin.
1969 Irish Exhibition of Living Art, Dublin.
1970 Two man show, Queen's University, Belfast.
1971-1973 Two man shows, Ulster Arts Club.
1972 Two man show, Tom Caldwell Gallery, Belfast.
1974, 1977 One man show, Tom Caldwell Gallery, Belfast.
1976 Collectors' Choice, Playhouse Gallery, Leeds.

Collections

Córas Iompair Éireann, New University of Ulster, Coleraine; Queen's University, Belfast; Ulster Arts Club.

COLIN MIDDLETON
b 1910 Belfast

Education and career

1918-1927 Belfast Royal Academy
1927-1947 Damask designer, Belfast.
1932 Royal Dublin Society Taylor Scholarship winner, attending Belfast College of Art.
1947-1948 Middleton Murry community, East Anglia
1948 Returned to Northern Ireland.
1954-1955 Part-time teacher of Art, Belfast College of Art.

1955-1961 Teacher of Art, Coleraine Technical School.

1955, 1956 Tutor, Mourne Holiday School of Art, Newcastle, Co Down.

1961-1970 Head of Art department, Friends' School, Lisburn.

1968 Arts Council of Northern Ireland poster design commission.

1968 Arts Council of Northern Ireland Open Painting prizewinner.

1969 Royal Hibernian Academy Associate.

1969 Member of the British Empire.

1970 Arts Council of Northern Ireland portrait commission, J Kenneth Jamison.

1970 Royal Hibernian Academy Member.

1970 Arts Council of Northern Ireland major subsistence award.

1971 Ulster '71 commissions, postage stamp and County Down mural.

1972 Visit to Australia.

1972 Honorary Master of Arts, Queen's University, Belfast.

1975 Visit to Spain.

Principal Exhibitions

1941, 1943, 1949, 1950, 1952-1954, 1968-1973, 1975, 1977: Royal Hibernian Academy, Dublin.

1943 One man show, Belfast Museum and Art Gallery.

1944 One man show, Grafton Gallery, Dublin.

1945, 1954, 1961 One man shows, Tyrone House, Belfast; Belfast Museum and Art Gallery and CEMA galleries.

1945, 1949-1954, 1963-1967, 1969, 1970; Irish Exhibition of Living Art, Dublin.

1949, 1951-54, 1972, 1973, 1977; Oireachtas, Dublin; 1977, also Arts Council of Northern Ireland Gallery and Letterkenny.

1949-1951, 1953, 1955 One man shows, Victor Waddington Galleries, Dublin.

1950 New Irish Painters, Institute of Contemporary Art, Boston, Mass; and touring.

1951 Five Irish Painters, Tooth Galleries, London.

1952 One man show, Tooth Galleries, London.

1952 Contemporary Irish Art, Gothenburg, Sweden.

1953 Victor Waddington Galleries, Dublin.

1954 Two man show, Tooth Galleries, London.

1955 Royal Academy, London.

1955 One man show, Hynes Gallery, Central Avenue, Bangor.

1956 Some Important Contemporaries, Tooth Galleries, London.

1956 Lewinter-Frankl Collection of Contemporary Irish Drawings, Belfast Museum and Art Gallery.

1958, 1965, 1968 One man shows, Ritchie Hendriks Gallery, Dublin.

1958 Lewinter-Frankl Collection, Belfast Museum and Art Gallery.

1962 Open Painting, CEMA; Ulster Museum.

1962 One man show, Studio 25, Belfast.

1962, 1963 One man shows, Magee Gallery, Belfast.

1964 One man show, Arts Council of Northern Ireland; Armagh County Museum, Armagh.

1965 One man show, Bell Gallery, Belfast.

1965, 1967, 1970, 1972 One man shows, Arts Council of Northern Ireland Gallery.

1970 Retrospective 1960-1970, also Brooke Park, Londonderry, Edinburgh and Glasgow.

1966 One man show, New Gallery, Belfast.

1966 Open Painting, Arts Council of Northern Ireland; Ulster Museum.

1966 Eight North of Ireland Painters, New Charing Cross Gallery, Glasgow.

1967, 1969 Ritchie Hendriks Gallery, Dublin.

1968 Two Irish Painters, (with T P Flanagan) Herbert Art Gallery and Museum, Coventry.

1968	Ulster Painting '68, Arts Council of Northern Ireland Gallery.
1968	Dúchas, Queen's University, Belfast.
1968, 1970	Open Painting, Arts Council of Northern Ireland Gallery.
1970, 1973, 1976	One man shows, David Hendriks Gallery, Dublin.
1970, 1971	David Hendriks Gallery, Dublin.
1970-1972, 1974	One man shows, Tom Caldwell Gallery, Belfast.
1970	Ulster Faces by Ulster Artists, Arts Council of Northern Ireland, touring.
1971	ROSC '71 The Irish Imagination, Municipal Gallery of Modern Art, Dublin.
1971	Art Spectrum Ulster, Arts Council of Northern Ireland Gallery.
1972, 1976	Gordon Lambert Collection, Municipal Gallery of Modern Art, Dublin; Wexford Festival; Ulster Museum.
1973	One man show, McClelland Galleries International, Belfast.
1973	One man show, Cork Arts Society, Cork.
1974	One man show, Tom Caldwell Gallery, Dublin.
1974	Drawings, Arts Council of Northern Ireland, touring.
1976	Retrospective, Ulster Museum and Hugh Lane Municipal Gallery of Modern Art, Dublin; Arts Council of Northern Ireland/An Chomhairle Ealáion.

Collections

Aer Lingus, An Chomhairle Ealáion, Arts Council of Northern Ireland, Bank of Ireland, Belfast Education and Library Board, British Broadcasting Corporation, Northern Ireland; Cambridge University, P J Carroll & Co Ltd, Cork Municipal Art Gallery, Ferens Art Gallery, Hull; Arthur Guinness, Son & Co Ltd, Herbert Art Gallery & Museum, Coventry; Hugh Lane Municipal Gallery of Modern Art, Dublin; Hull Education Committee, Meath County Library, National Gallery of Victoria, Melbourne; New University of Ulster, Coleraine; Oxford University, Queen's University, Belfast; Trinity College, Dublin, Gallery; Ulster Arts Club, Ulster Museum.

Bibliography

'Colin Middleton' by Edward Sheehy, *Envoy*, April 1950.
'Painting and Sculpture in Ulster' by John Hewitt, *The Arts in Ulster*, George G Harrap & Co Ltd, London, 1951.
'Moving Artist' by Martin Wallace, *Belfast Telegraph*, 4 January 1957.
'Art Forum' by John FitzMaurice Mills, *Irish Times*, 18 January 1966.
'Talking to Colin Middleton', by Michael Longley, *Irish Times*, 7 April 1967.
'Colin Middleton' by Michael Longley, *The Dublin Magazine*, Autumn/Winter, 1967.
'Colin Middleton' by Anne Davey, *Irish Times*, 14 August 1968.
A Concise History of Irish Art by Bruce Arnold, Thames & Hudson, London, 1969.
'Colin Middleton' by Dorothy Walker, *Hibernia*, 13 December 1968-2January 1969.
'Speaking Personally', BBC Radio 4, Northern Ireland, 5 June 1971.
'Painting and Sculpture' by Kenneth Jamison, *Causeway, The Arts in Ulster*, Arts Council of Northern Ireland and Gill and Macmillan, Dublin, 1971.
'What's the point of painting?' by Elgy Gillespie, *Irish Times*, 11 May 1972.
'Harriet Cooke talks to Colin Middleton', *Irish Times*, 25 January 1973.
'Colin Middleton' by Michael Longley, *Introspect*, No 1, December 1975.
Colin Middleton by John Hewitt, Arts Council of Northern Ireland and An Chomhairle Ealáion, 1976.
Gallery, BBC TV NI, 20 February 1976.
'The artist who never looked back' by Michael McDowell, *Belfast Telegraph*, 17 June 1977.

JOHN MIDDLETON
b 1945 Belfast

Education and career

1963-1966	Belfast College of Art.
1966-1969	Royal College of Art, London.

1969-1971	Lecturer in Printmaking, Byam Shaw School of Art, London.
1971-1973	Teacher of Art, Kelvin Secondary School, Belfast.
1972	Arts Council of Northern Ireland portrait commission, William John McBride.
1972	Arts Council of Northern Ireland poster-poem commission with Frank Ormsby.
1974-	Working as graphic/exhibition designer.
1975	Arts Council of Northern Ireland portrait commission, Mary Fearon.

Principal Exhibitions

1965	One man show, Botanic Inn, Belfast.
1965	Young Irish Artists Foundation, Belfast, Dublin, Cork.
1968	One man show, New Gallery, Belfast.
1969	Royal College of Art Printmakers, Pratt Art Centre, New York; Florida University, USA.
1971	Ulster Printmakers, Arts Council of Northern Ireland, touring.
1972	One man show, Arts Council of Northern Ireland Gallery.
1972	Ulster Faces, Arts Council of Northern Ireland, touring.
1973	Belfast Schools Art Collection, Arts Council of Northern Ireland Gallery.
1974	Irish Artists 1974, David Hendriks Gallery, Dublin.
1975	One man show, Tom Caldwell Gallery, Belfast.
1975	Irish Exhibition of Living Art, Dublin.
1975	Women of Ulster, Arts Council of Northern Ireland, touring.
1977	Eight Northern Irish Artists, Third Eye Centre, Glasgow.

Collections

Arts Council of Northern Ireland, Belfast Education and Library Board.

CAROLYN MULHOLLAND
b 1944 Lurgan

Education and career

1962-1966	Belfast College of Art.
1965	Ulster Arts Club prize for sculpture.
1966	St MacNissi Church, Magherahoney commission, panel.
1970	Arts Council of Northern Ireland portrait commission, R H McCandless.
1970	Mary Peters life-size portrait commission.
1971	Local Enterprise Development Unit commission, trophy.
1971	Arts Council of Northern Ireland travel award, Paris.
1972	Arts Council of Northern Ireland portrait commissions, Mercy Hunter and Patrick Shea.
1973	Royal Ulster Academy silver medal award.
1974	Allied Irish Banks commission, two community service trophies.
1975	Arts Council of Northern Ireland Art in Context commission, group of three freestanding figures, Antrim Forum.
1975	Arts Council of Northern Ireland portrait commission, Betty Lowry.
1977	Arts Council of Northern Ireland bursary award for work in bronze.

Principal Exhibitions

1967	Butlin Foundation for Young Irish Artists, Belfast, Cork, Dublin, Mosney.
1968	Two person show, Kenny's Art Gallery, Galway.
1968	One woman show, Ulster Arts Club, Belfast.
1969	One woman show, New Gallery, Belfast.
1969	Tom Caldwell Gallery, Belfast.
1970	Ulster Faces by Ulster Artists, Arts Council of Northern Ireland, touring.
1971	Three sculptors, Arts Council of Northern Ireland Gallery.
1972	Ulster Faces, Arts Council of Northern Ireland, touring.

1973, 1975, 1977	Independent Artists, Dublin.
1975	Women of Ulster, Arts Council of Northern Ireland, touring.
1975	Octagon Gallery, Belfast.
1975	Creative Women, Arts Council of Northern Ireland Gallery.
1977	Oireachtas, Dublin, Belfast and Letterkenny.

Collections
Arts Council of Northern Ireland.

Bibliography
Sunday Gallery, BBC-TV NI, 28 February 1971.
Profile, BBC-TV, 15 June 1971.
'Painting and Sculpture' by Kenneth Jamison, *Causeway, The Arts in Ulster*, Arts Council of Northern Ireland and Gill and Macmillan, Dublin, 1971.
Speaking Personally, BBC Radio 4, Northern Ireland, 26 October 1974.
'Dedicated to Art', by Dorothy Gharbaoui, *Ulster Tatler*, August 1975.
'Lonely, creative life of the sculptress', *Lurgan Mail*, 21 October 1976.
'Carolyn is tops with heads' by Theo Snoddy, *News Letter*, 20 July 1977.
Summer Scene BBC Radio Ulster, August 1977.

CHARLES OAKLEY
b 1925 Manchester

Education and career

1937-1943	Manchester Grammar School.
1943-1944	Queen's University, Belfast.
1948-1952	Slade School of Fine Art, London; 1951 Wilson Steer medal.
1950	British School in Florence.
1953-1956	Art master, Eden School, Cumberland.
1962-1974	Senior Lecturer in Painting, Ulster College of Art and Design.
1972	Arts Council of Northern Ireland portrait commission, James Young.
1974-	Principal Lecturer in Fine Art, Newcastle-upon-Tyne Polytechnic.

Principal Exhibitions

1957	One man show, Crane Gallery, Manchester.
1964	One man show, Tom Caldwell Gallery, Belfast.
1965, 1970	One man shows, Bondgate Gallery, Alnwick, Northumberland.
1966, 1970	Irish Exhibition of Living Art, Dublin.
1968	Open Painting, Arts Council of Northern Ireland Gallery.
1968	Ulster Painting '68 Arts Council of Northern Ireland Gallery.
1970	One man show, Arts Council of Northern Ireland Gallery; Brooke Park Gallery, Londonderry.
1971	One man show, Carlisle Art Gallery.
1971	Royal Hibernian Academy, Dublin.
1971	Art Spectrum Ulster, Arts Council of Northern Ireland Gallery.
1971, 1973	Two man shows, Tom Caldwell Gallery, Belfast.
1972	Ulster Faces, Arts Council of Northern Ireland, touring.
1974	One man show, Tom Caldwell Gallery, Dublin.
1974	Watergate Gallery, Washington, DC.
1975	Three man show, Tom Caldwell Gallery, Belfast.
1976	One man show, Polytechnic Gallery, Newcastle-upon-Tyne.
1976	One man show, University Theatre, Newcastle-upon-Tyne.

Collections
Arts Council of Northern Ireland, Belfast Education and Library Board, Brighton Art Gallery, Carlisle Art Gallery, London County Council, Manchester Education Committee, New University of Ulster, Coleraine; Royal Society of Scottish Architects, Salford Art Gallery, Shell and BP Ltd, Ulster Museum, Wadham College, Oxford.

Bibliography
'Painting and Sculpture' by Kenneth Jamison, *Causeway, The Arts in Ulster*, Arts Council of Northern Ireland and Gill and Macmillan, Dublin, 1971.
Caret, poetry magazine, cover and drawings by Charles Oakley, No 5/6, Summer/Autumn, 1974.

CLIFFORD RAINEY
b 1948 Whitehead

Education and career

1965-1968	Linen damask designer, William Ewart & Son, Ltd, Belfast.
1968-1969	Hornsey College of Art, London.
1969	Toured United States of America and Canada.
1969-1971	North East London Polytechnic.
1970	Toured Norway with circus.
1971	Worked Kastrup and Holmegaards Glassworks, Nestved, Denmark.
1971-1973	Royal College of Art, London.
1972	Royal College of Art travelling scholarship, iiallia Glassworks, Finland.
1973	London studio.
1974	Arts Council of Northern Ireland subsistence award: travel to Greece and Turkey; completion of sculptures.
1975	Toured Kenya, Tanzania, Zambia, Malawi, Botswana, Rhodesia, South Africa.
1976	Victoria and Albert Museum, London, commission of small sculpture to celebrate Silver Jubilee of Queen Elizabeth II.
1977	Sun Life Assurance commission for large sculpture in glass, Bristol.
1977	Visiting lecturer, Royal College of Art, London.

Principal Exhibitions

1973	Contemporary Studio Glass, Ulster Museum.
1973	Scottish Arts Council Gallery, Edinburgh.
1973	Aberdeen Art Gallery.
1973	Seilby, Tokyo, Japan.
1974, 1975	Royal Academy, London.
1974	Two man show, Arnolfini Gallery, Bristol.
1975	Two man show, Asset Gallery, London.
1975, 1976	Irish Exhibition of Living Art, Dublin.
1975, 1977	One man shows, David Hendriks Gallery, Dublin.
1976	Two man show, Piccadilly Gallery, London.
1976, 1977	Basle Fine Art Fair, Switzerland.
1976	Gordon Lambert Collection, Wexford Festival and Ulster Museum.
1977	One man show, Arts Council of Northern Ireland Gallery.

Collections
An Chomhairle Ealáion, Arts Council of Northern Ireland, Ulster Museum.

WILLIAM SCOTT
b 1913 Greenock, Scotland

Education and career

1926-1928	Enniskillen Technical School, evening.
1928-1931	Belfast College of Art.
1931-1935	Royal Academy Schools, London.

1936	Worked in Cornwall.
1937-1939	Worked in Italy and France.
1938	Elected Sociétaire de Salon d'Automne, Paris.
1942-1946	Royal Engineers.
1946-1956	Senior painting master, Bath Academy of Art.
1963-1964	Ford Foundation resident, Berlin.
1966	Commander of the British Empire.
1975	Honorary Doctor, Royal College of Art, London.
1976	Honorary Doctor of Literature, Queen's University, Belfast.
1977	Honorary Doctor of Literature, Trinity College, Dublin.

Principal Exhibitions

One man shows except where stated.

1942 Lager Gallery, London.

1945, 1947, 1950, 1960, 1976 Irish Exhibition of Living Art, Dublin, group.

1948, 1951 Leicester Galleries, London.

1951 Royal Hibernian Academy, Dublin, group.

1953, 1956, 1961, 1962, 1963, 1965, 1967, 1969, 1971 Hanover Gallery, London.

1953, 1961 Bienal, Sao Paulo, Brazil; 1961 also shown Rio de Janeiro and Buenos Aires.

1954, 1956, 1959, 1962, 1973, 1975 Martha Jackson Gallery, New York.

1958 XXIX Biennale, Venice; also shown Paris, Cologne, Brussels, Zurich and Rotterdam.

1959 Galleria Galatea, Turin; also Milan.

1959 Galerie Charles Lienhard, Zurich.

1960 Kestner Gaesellschaft, Hanover; also shown Freiburg, Dortmund and Munich.

1961 Esther Robles Gallery, Los Angeles.

1961 Galerie Schmela, Dusseldorf.

1963 Ulster Museum.

1963 Kunsthalle, Berne.

1963 Galerie Anderson-Mayer, Paris.

1964 Haus Am Valsee, Berlin.

1966 Gimpel and Hanover Gallery, Zurich.

1967, 1977 Dawson Gallery, Dublin.

1969 Richard Demarco Gallery, Edinburgh.

1971 Scottish National Gallery of Modern Art, Edinburgh.

1972 Tate Gallery, London, retrospective 1938-1971.

1972, 1976 Gordon Lambert Collection, Municipal Gallery of Modern Art, Dublin; Wexford Festival; Ulster Museum.

1972 Galleria Falchi, Milan.

1973, 1975 Moos Gallery, Toronto.

1973 Lister Gallery, Perth, Western Australia.

1973 Kathleen Bridle, William Scott, T P Flanagan, Arts Council of Northern Ireland Gallery; Enniskillen Collegiate School; and touring.

1973, 1975, 1976 Oireachtas, Dublin, group.

1974 Gimpel, Hanover, Zurich.

1974, 1976 Gimpel Fils Gallery, London.

1975 Albright-Knox Art Gallery, Buffalo.

1975 Santa Barbara Museum, Los Angeles.

1975 Belfast Education and Library Board, Arts Council of Northern Ireland Gallery, group.

1976 A + O Gallery, Munich.

1976 Gallery Kasahara, Osaka.

Collections

Great Britain and Ireland

An Chomhairle Ealáion, Arts Council of Great Britain, Arts Council of Northern Ireland, Belfast Education and Library Board, Birmingham City Museum and Art Gallery, Bishop Otter College, Chichester; Brighton Art Gallery, Bristol Art Gallery, British Council, London; Fizwilliam Museum, Cambridge; Hugh Lane Municipal Gallery of Modern Art, Dublin; Leeds City Art Galleries, London Contemporary Art Society, National Museum of Wales, Cardiff; Nottingham Castle Museum and Art Gallery, Scottish National Gallery of Modern Art, Edinburgh; Sheffield City Art Galleries, Southampton Art Gallery, Tate Gallery, London; Trinity College, Dublin, Gallery; Ulster Museum, Victoria and Albert Museum, London; Wakefield Art Gallery, Yorkshire; Walker Art Gallery, Liverpool; Whitworth Art Gallery, Manchester.

Elsewhere

Albright Art Gallery, Buffalo; Art Gallery of New South Wales, Sydney; Art Gallery of Toronto; Brooklyn Museum, New York; Carnegie Institute, Pittsburgh; Galleria d'Arte Moderna, Genoa; Galleria Nazionale d'Arte Moderna, Rome; Gothenburg Museum; Solomon R Guggenheim Museum, New York; Kunsthalle, Hamburg; Musée National d'art Moderne, Paris; Museo Civico, Turin; Museu de Arte Moderna de Sao Paolo; Museum Des 20 Jahrhunderts, Vienna; Museum of Modern Art, New York; National Gallery of Canada, Ottawa; National Gallery of South Australia, Adelaide; National Gallery of Victoria, Melbourne; Toledo Museum of Art; Western Australia Art Gallery, Perth; Western Institute of Technology, Perth.

Bibliography

Soldiers' Verse chosen by Patric Dickinson, with lithographs by William Scott, 1945.
Contemporary British Art by Herbert Read, Penguin Books, 1951.
Nine Abstract Artists by Lawrence Alloway, Tiranti, London, 1954.
The Changing Forms of Art by Patrick Heron, Routledge, London, 1955.
'William Scott — his art belongs to an older world' by Sheila Steen, *Belfast Telegraph*, 14 January 1955.
Great Britain in Art since 1945 by Herbert Read, Thames and Hudson, London, 1959.
A Concise History of Modern Painting by Herbert Read, Thames and Hudson, London, 1959.
Painting in the Twentieth Century by Werner Haftmann, Lund Humphries, London, 1960.
'A Mural to match Macha', An Ulsterman's Diary by 'Chichester', *Belfast Telegraph*, 28 November 1961.
William Scott by Ronald Alleyn, Methuen, London, 1963.
Naissance d'un art nouveau by Michel Ragon, Albin Michel, Paris, 1963.
William Scott: Paintings, by Alan Bowness, Lund Humphries, London, 1964.
'Ulster Painter at work in Berlin' by Theo Snoddy, *News Letter*, 7 October 1965.
'No more pots and pans' by Theo Snoddy, *Sunday News*, 24 October 1965.
A Concise History of Irish Art by Bruce Arnold, Thames and Hudson, London, 1969.
'Painting and Sculpture' by Kenneth Jamison, *Causeway: The Arts in Ulster*, Arts Council of Northern Ireland and Gill and Macmillan, Dublin, 1971.
'Ulster artist at the Tate' by Theo Snoddy, *News Letter*, 18 September 1971.
'Man from the North' by Brian Fallon, *Irish Times*, 3 May 1972.

NEIL SHAWCROSS
b 1940 Kearsely, Lancashire

Education and career

1953-1955	Bolton Junior Art School, Lancashire.
1955-1958	Bolton College of Art.
1958-1960	Lancaster College of Art.
1960-1962	Lecturer part-time, Lancaster College of Art, Lancaster Technical School and Morecombe Grammar School.
1962-1968	Lecturer part-time, Belfast College of Art.
1966	Gallaher portrait competition, first prize.
1968-	Lecturer, Ulster College of Art and Design.
1970	Arts Council of Northern Ireland portrait commission, Colin Middleton.
1972	Arts Council of Northern Ireland portrait commission, Derek Dougan.
1975	Royal Ulster Academy Conor award.

1976	Royal Ulster Academy Associate.

Principal Exhibitions

1962	Two man show, Arts Council of Northern Ireland Gallery.
1962, 1964	One man shows, Queen's University, Belfast.
1963	One man show, Tib Lane Gallery, Manchester.
1964	Human Image, RWS Gallery, London.
1964	New Gallery, Belfast.
1965, 1968	One man shows, New Gallery, Belfast.
1968	Open Painting, Arts Council of Northern Ireland Gallery.
1968, 1969	Art in Worship Today, Ulster Museum; Building Centre, Dublin.
1970	Ulster Faces by Ulster Artists, Arts Council of Northern Ireland, touring.
1970	One man show, Octagon Theatre, Bolton.
1970, 1974	One man shows, Tom Caldwell Gallery, Belfast.
1971	Art Spectrum Ulster, Arts Council of Northern Ireland Gallery.
1972	Ulster Faces, Arts Council of Northern Ireland, touring.
1972, 1975	Octagon Gallery, Belfast.
1974	One man show, Neptune Gallery, Dublin.
1974	Royal Hibernian Academy, Dublin.
1975	Oireachtas, Dublin.
1977	One man show, Bell Gallery, Belfast.

Collections

Arts Council of Northern Ireland, New University of Ulster, Coleraine; Ulster Museum.

Bibliography

'Painting and Sculpture' by Kenneth Jamison, *Causeway, The Arts in Ulster*, Arts Council of Northern Ireland and Gill and Macmillan, Dublin, 1971.

JOHN VALLELY
b 1941 Armagh

Education and career

1958	Armagh Technical School, evening.
1959-1961	Belfast College of Art.
1961	Royal Dublin Society, Taylor scholarship.
1961-1964	Edinburgh College of Art.
1964	Edinburgh College of Art minor travel scholarship, Italy; travel scholarship, Paris and Florence.
1964	Loughmacrory Chapel, Co Tyrone, commission baptistry mural.
1964-1965	Edinburgh College of Art, major travel scholarship, Spain and Morocco.
1966	Arts Council of Northern Ireland short visit award, Paris.
1968-1969	Arts Council of Northern Ireland subsistence award, Spain, Morocco and Algeria.
1970	Arts Council of Northern Ireland commission poster design.
1970	Arts Council of Northern Ireland portrait commission, J.G. Devlin.

Principal Exhibitions

1962	Open Painting, CEMA; Ulster Museum.
1963, 1964	One man shows, Studio 25, Belfast.
1963	Eight Painters, Magee Gallery, Belfast.
1964	Young Scottish Painters, Midland Gallery, Nottingham.
1964	Two man show, Studio 25, Belfast.
1965	Commonwealth Exhibition, Glasgow.
1965	Young Irish Artists Foundation, Belfast, Dublin, Cork.

1966, 1967	One man shows, Molesworth Gallery, Dublin.
1966	1916 Commemoration, Municipal Gallery of Modern Art, Dublin.
1967	Butlin Foundation for Young Irish Artists, Belfast, Dublin, Cork, Mosney.
1967	One man show, Arts Council of Northern Ireland Gallery, and Brooke Park Gallery, Londonderry.
1968, 1969	Art in Worship Today, Ulster Museum; Building Centre, Dublin.
1968	One man show, Bell Gallery, Belfast.
1968	Ulster Painting '68, Arts Council of Northern Ireland Gallery.
1969	Seven North of Ireland Painters, David Hendriks Gallery, Dublin.
1969	Oireachtas, Dublin.
1970	One man show, Ulster Arts Club, Belfast.
1970	Two man show, David Hendriks Gallery, Dublin.
1970, 1971	David Hendriks Gallery, Dublin.
1970	Ulster Faces by Ulster Artists, Arts Council of Northern Ireland, touring.
1971	Art Spectrum Ulster, Arts Council of Northern Ireland Gallery.
1971	One man show, Arts Council of Northern Ireland Gallery, and Armagh County Museum.
1972	Work in Progress, Arts Council of Northern Ireland Gallery.
1972, 1975	One man shows, Tom Caldwell Gallery, Belfast.
1973	Belfast Schools Art Collection, Arts Council of Northern Ireland Gallery.
1974	One man show, Tom Caldwell Gallery, Dublin.
1974	Watergate Gallery, Washington DC.

Collections
An Chomhairle Ealáion, Arts Council of Northern Ireland, Belfast Education and Library Board, Benburb Priory, Co Tyrone; Ministry of Finance, Northern Ireland; North West Art Trust, St Patrick's College, Armagh; Ulster Museum.

Bibliography
'New School on View' by Sydney Goodsir Smith, *The Scotsman*, 20 June 1964.
'Outside Celtic Imagery' by Theo Snoddy, *News Letter*, 15 June 1967.
'Painter who is being listened to in Dublin', by 'Chichester' *Belfast Telegraph*, 17 October 1968.
'Painting and Sculpture' by Kenneth Jamison, *Causeway, The Arts in Ulster*, Arts Council of Northern Ireland and Gill and Macmillan, Dublin, 1971.
'Dressing up when going forth to battle?' by Ann Young, *Sunday News*, 27 June 1971.
Sunday Gallery, BBC-TV NI, 5 December 1971.

DAVID WINTERS
b 1942 Belfast

Education and career

1961-1965	Belfast College of Art.
1965	Royal Dublin Society, Taylor scholarship award for modelling.
1966	Royal Dublin Society Henry Higgins travelling scholarship France, Italy and Greece.
1965-1966	Art Master, Lurgan College.
1966-1969	Royal College of Art, London.
1969-	Senior Lecturer in Sculpture, School of Fine Art, Art and Design Centre, Ulster College.
1972	Arts Council of Northern Ireland major subsistence grant, USA, Canada and Mexico.
1976	Seconded to the Tunku Abdul Rahman College, Kuala Lumpur, Malaysia, to run experimental course in sculpture and investigate possibilities for fine art education in Malay Peninsula. Visited Australia.

Principal Exhibitions

1965	Young Irish Foundation, Belfast, Dublin, Cork.
1966	The MacGeough Bond Collection, Ulster Museum.
1967	Butlin Foundation for Young Irish Artists, Belfast, Cork, Dublin, Mosney.
1969	A Metamorphosis through Fire, Whitechapel Art Gallery, London.

1971	Three Sculptors, Arts Council of Northern Ireland Gallery.
1971	Art Spectrum Ulster, Arts Council of Northern Ireland Gallery.
1974	One man show, Arts Council of Northern Ireland Gallery.
1975	Irish Sculpture, Bank of Ireland, Dublin.
1975	Irish Exhibition of Living Art, Dublin.
1976	Irish Printmakers, Edinburgh, Glasgow, Newcastle.
1977	Oireachtas, Dublin, Belfast and Letterkenny.
1977	Project Gallery, Dublin.

Collections
Arts Council of Northern Ireland, Hugh Lane Municipal Gallery of Modern Art, Dublin.

Bibliography
'Painting and Sculpture' by Kenneth Jamison, *Causeway, The Arts in Ulster*, Arts Council of Northern Ireland and Gill and Macmillan, Dublin, 1971.

BIBLIOGRAPHY

BOOKS

[*a*] *Ulster and Irish Material*

ALLEY, R. *William Scott*, Methuen, 1963.

ARNOLD, B. *A Concise History of Irish Art*, Thames and Hudson, 1969, 1977.

BELL, S H; ROBB, N A; HEWITT, J (eds). *The Arts in Ulster*, Harrap, 1951.

BOWNESS, A. *William Scott: Paintings*, Lund Humphries, 1964.

BROWN, T. *Northern Voices*, Gill and Macmillan, 1975.

CLUTTERBUCK, R. *Protest and the Urban Guerilla*, Cassell, 1973.

DEUTSCH, R and MAGOWAN, V. *Northern Ireland 1968-74: A Chronology of Events*, Vols 1, 2 and 3, Blackstaff Press, 1973-75.

FIACC, P. *The Wearing of the Black*, Blackstaff Press, 1976.

FRIERS, R. *Riotous Living*, Blackstaff Press, 1971.

______ Pig in the Parlour, Blackstaff Press, 1972.

______ *The Book of Friers*, Blackstaff Press, 1973.

______ *The Revolting Irish*, Blackstaff Press, 1974.

HEANEY, S. *Death of a Naturalist*, Faber and Faber, 1966.

______ *Door into the Dark*, Faber and Faber, 1969.

______ *North*, Faber and Faber, 1975.

HEWITT, J. *Colin Middleton*, Arts Council of Northern Ireland/An Chomhairle Ealáoin, 1976.

HEWITT, J and MONTAGUE, J. *The Planter and the Gael*, Arts Council of Northern Ireland, 1970.

INDEPENDENT TELEVISION AUTHORITY. *Religion in Britain and Northern Ireland: A Survey of Popular Attitudes*, ITA Publications, 1970.

LIMPKIN, C. *The Battle of the Bogside*, Penguin, 1972.

LONGLEY, M (ed). *Causeway: The Arts in Ulster*, Arts Council of Northern Ireland/Gill and Macmillan, 1971.

MIERS, C. *Northern Ireland: A Soldier's View*, Denovo Press, 1973.

PENROSE, R. *F E McWilliam: Sculptor*, Tiranti, 1964.
ROSE, R. *Governing Without Consensus*, Faber and Faber, 1971.
SIMMONS, J. *The Long Summer Still to Come*, Blackstaff Press, 1973.

[*b*] *Other Material*
BANN, S. *Experimental Painting*, Studio Vista, 1970.
BERGER, J. *Ways of Seeing*, BBC/Penguin, 1972.
COHEN, S and YOUNG, J. *The Manufacture of News*, Constable, 1973.
GELDZAHLER, H. *The New York School 1940-1970*, Pall Mall, 1969.
MULLER, G. *The New Avant Garde*, Pall Mall, 1972.
WADDINGTON, C H. *Behind Appearance*, Edinburgh University Press, 1969.

SELECTED ARTICLES AND REVIEWS

ANON. 'Art College Head dislikes "ultra modern" ', *Belfast Telegraph*, 13 December 1949.
______ 'Boiling up old boots for his next picture', *Northern Whig*, 22 February 1961.
ARNOLD, 'Painter of tears and laughter', *Sunday Independent*, 23 June 1968.
BOYD, W. 'Dillon in Dublin', *The Irish Times*, 28 January 1968.
______ 'The First Group', *The Guardian*, 16 August 1962.
BROWN, D. 'Why', *Ferranti Journal*, 1966.
BUTLER, A. 'Banners and Symbols', *Evening Press*, 13 June 1968.
CAMPBELL, G. 'A Simple Complex Man', *Irish Times*, 8 July 1971.
COOKE, H. 'Harriet Cooke talks to Colin Middleton', *Irish Times*, 25 January 1973.
______ 'Harriet Cooke talks to the sculptor F E McWilliam', *Irish Times*, 31 October 1973.
DILLON, G. 'Connemara is Ireland to me', *Ireland of the Welcomes* Vol 13 No 2, July/August 1964.
FALLON, B. 'Artist with a sense of humour', *Irish Times*, 2 April 1965.
______ 'The Man from the North', *Irish Times* 3 May 1972.
______ 'Gerard Dillon Retrospective', *Irish Times* 5 Janaury 1973.
FLANAGAN, T P. 'The Artists in Northern Ireland', *The Arts in Ireland* Vol 1 No 1, 1972.
______ 'To Speak of Drawing', *Introspect* No 1, 1975.
______ '66 Drawings of William Scott', *The Arts in Ireland* Vol 1 No 3, 1973.
______ 'Deborah Brown', *Threshold* No 22, Summer 1969.
FORD-SMITH, J. 'Acquisitions of Modern Art by Museums', *Burlington Magazine* Vol CXIII No 821, August 1971.
HEANEY, S. 'Talking to T P Flanagan', *Irish Times* 21 September 1967.
HEWITT, J. 'Portrait of a Young Man as the Artist', *Threshold*, February 1957.
HICKEY, P. 'Living Art Exhibition', *Hibernia*, September 1961.
LONGLEY, M. 'Talking to Colin Middleton', *Irish Times*, 7 April 1967.
______ 'Colin Middleton', *Introspect* No 1, 1975.
MacGREEVY, T. 'L'art contemporain en Irlande', *Prisme des Arts* No 18, September 1958.
O'DOHERTY, B. 'Abstracts in a Steel Town', *Irish Times*, 3 June 1959.
PYLE, H. 'For Harlequin, a Final Curtain', *Sunday Independent*, 18 July 1971.
STRAHAN, W J. 'The Sculptor and his Drawings', *Connoisseur*, May 1974.
WALSH, C. 'Caroline Walsh talks to T P Flanagan', *Irish Times*, 14 August 1976.
WHITE, J. 'This art lives above reality', *Irish Times*, 17 August 1957.

SELECTED EXHIBITION CATALOGUES (excluding those artists listed in the Biography section)

[*a*] *One Man Shows*
ANTRIM, A. Hamet Gallery (introduction by Cyril Connolly), 1972.

ATKINSON, C. *A shade of green, an orange edge* (introduction by Brian Ferran and David Wylie; text by Caroline Tisdall, John Hewitt and Conrad Atkinson), Arts Council of Northern Ireland, 1975.
BAIRD, M. Arts Council of Northern Ireland (introduction by Kenneth Jamison), 1965.
BOWEN, G. CEMA, 1955.
_____ Tom Caldwell Gallery, 1976.
BURCH, L. Tom Caldwell Gallery, 1975.
CARR, T. CEMA, 1961.
_____ *New Watercolours*, McClelland Galleries, 1973.
_____ Tom Caldwell Gallery (Dublin), 1975.
COLLINS, W. Arts Council of Northern Ireland, 1971.
_____ Octagon Gallery, 1976.
CONOR, W. CEMA/Belfast Museum and Art Gallery Retrospective Exhibition (introduction by John Hewitt), 1957.
_____ *Belfast of Yesterday* (introduction by Kenneth Jamison), Bell Gallery, n d.
_____ *Memorial Exhibition* Arts Council of Northern Ireland, 1968.
_____ Queen's University Art Gallery, 1969.
EVANS, D. Octagon Gallery, 1975.
FERRAN, D. Social Science Building, Queen's University, Belfast, 1977.
FRIERS, CEMA, n d.
FRIERS, T I. *A Tribute*, Grendor Art Gallery, Holywood, 1976.
GUINNESS; L. Octagon Gallery and Keys Gallery, Londonderry, 1976.
LINTON, R. Arts Council of Northern Ireland, 1963.
McCANN, G G. Old Library Gallery, Queen's University, Belfast (Presented by QUB Festival Society and the Arts Council of Northern Ireland; text by Kenneth Jamison), 1968.
McINTYRE, J. CEMA, 1960.
_____ Bell Gallery, 1967 and 1975.
MACMIADHACHAIN, P. CEMA, 1960.
MILLAR, J. Senior Common Room, Queen's University, Belfast, 1975.
MILLAR, N. Waterside Branch Library, Londonderry, c 1966.
_____ Arts Council of Northern Ireland, 1968.
MITCHELL, C. *Memorial Exhibition*, Rupert Stanley College, Belfast, 1977.
O'NEILL, D. McClelland Gallery (introduction by Mercy Hunter), 1970.
ORR, A D. *People in Conflict — Images of War*, Rose Inn Street Gallery, Kilkenny, 1975.
OSBORNE, D. CEMA, 1962.
_____ Arts Council of Northern Ireland, 1968.
OSBORNE, J. *Memorial Exhibition*, New Gallery, 1967.
PENPRASE, N. *All His Own Work* (introduction by Roy Johnston), Arts Council of Northern Ireland, 1977.
PAKENHAM, J. Tom Caldwell Gallery, 1975.
PIPER; R. *Orchids*, Ulster Museum, 1975.
REED, L. Tom Caldwell Gallery, 1975 and 1977.
_____ Octagon Gallery, 1973.
RITCHIE, A. CEMA, 1961.
ROBINSON, M. CEMA, 1961.
SPENCE, T E. Bell Gallery, 1976.
THOMAS, E. Arts Council of Northern Ireland, 1974.
THOMAS, M. Arts Council of Northern Ireland, 1974.
TURNER, J. CEMA, 1961.
WEBB, K. Bell Gallery, n d.

[*b*] *Two and Three Artist Shows*
ASTON, T and MORRISON, N. Octagon Gallery, 1975.
BOGLE, W. *Corsica* (with Colin Harrison), Arts Council of Northern Ireland, 1971.

BOWEN, G and CAMPBELL, G. *Drawings*, CEMA, 1958.
BRIDLE, K; FLANAGAN, T P and SCOTT, W. Arts Council of Northern Ireland, 1971.
BURCH, L; CARTER, V and SLOAN, R. Arts Council of Northern Ireland, 1971.
CARR, T and CAMPBELL, G. Arts Council of Northern Ireland, 1971.
COLLINS, W; ALLEN, J and BARKER, D. Arts Council of Northern Ireland, 1971.
HOWES, R; McWILLIAMS, B and WEATHERS, C. *Painters of Promise*, Arts Council of Northern Ireland, 1972.
KIRK, B and WATSON, A. *Two Photographers*, Arts Council of Northern Ireland, 1975.
LEONARD, E; REED, L and SELLAR, R G. Arts Council of Northern Ireland, 1967.
LIVELY, R and McBRIDE, D. Arts Council of Northern Ireland, 1967.
MILLAR, J; NORRIS, S K and O'NEILL, W A J. Arts Council of Northern Ireland, 1972.

[*c*] *Group Shows and Collections*
ALICE BERGER HAMMERSCHLAG AWARD WINNERS 1971-1972, Arts Council of Northern Ireland, 1973.
AMERICAN ART OF THE '50s and '60s, Arts Council of Northern Ireland/Ulster Museum/Festival 66, 1966.
ARTE INGLESE OGGI, British Council/Comune di Milano, 1976.
ARTISTS' CHOICE, Ulster Museum, 1973.
ARTISTS FOR PEACE, Down District Council Arts Committee, 1977.
ART SPECTRUM: LONDON, Greater London Arts Association/Arts Council of Great Britain, 1971.
ART SPECTRUM: SCOTLAND, Scottish Arts Council, 1971.
ART SPECTRUM: ULSTER, Arts Council of Northern Ireland, 1971.
ART SPECTRUM: WALES, Welsh Arts Council, 1971.
ASPECTS OF ULSTER LANDSCAPE, Arts Council of Northern Ireland, 1965.
BELFAST COLLEGE OF ART ASSOCIATION EXHIBITION, 1954.
BELFAST SCHOOLS ART COLLECTION, Arts Council of Northern Ireland, 1973.
BUTLIN FOUNDATION FOR YOUNG IRISH ARTISTS, 1967.
CELTIC TRIANGLE, An Chomhairle Ealáoin/Arts Council of Northern Ireland/Scottish Arts Council/Welsh Arts Council, 1970.
CEMA SCHOLARSHIP HOLDERS, CEMA, 1957.
CITY SCULPTURE, Peter Stuyvesant Foundation City Sculpture Project, 1972.
CREATIVE WOMEN, Arts Council of Northern Ireland, 1975.
CUIMHNEACHÂN 1916, Municipal Gallery of Modern Arts, Dublin, 1966.
DRAWINGS, Arts Council of Northern Ireland, 1974.
DÚCHAS: THE COUNCIL OF IRISH TRADITION, Queen's University, Belfast, 1968.
EIGHT NORTHERN IRISH ARTISTS, Third Eye Centre, Glasgow, 1977.
EIGHT NORTH OF IRELAND PAINTERS; New Charing Cross Gallery, Glasgow, 1966.
5 + 1, Project Arts Centre, Dublin, 1975.
GORDON LAMBERT COLLECTION, ULSTER MUSEUM, 1976.
GROUP SHOW (14 ARTISTS), Arts Council of Northern Ireland, 1977.
GROUP 63, no imprimatur, n d.
______ Tom Caldwell Gallery, 1970.
______ Tom Caldwell Gallery, 1971.
______ Arts Council of Northern Ireland, 1973.
HUMAN CONCERN/PERSONAL TORMENT, Whitney Museum of American Art, New York, 1969.
INDEPENDENT ARTISTS, Municipal Gallery of Modern Art, Dublin, 1969.
IRISH EXHIBITION OF LIVING ART, Catalogues of the separate exhibitions from 1947 to 1976.
IRISH PAINTING 1974, David Hendriks Gallery, Dublin, 1974.
IRISH PRIMITIVE PAINTERS, Queen's University, Belfast, 1971.
ITALIAN PAINTING, David Hendriks/Arts Council of Northern Ireland, 1971.
KINETIC ART, Ulster Museum, 1966.
LEWINTER-FRANKL COLLECTION, Belfast Museum and Art Gallery, 1958.
McCLELLAND FINE ART AWARDS, McClelland Galleries, Belfast, 1969.

MacGEOUGH-BOND COLLECTION, Ulster Museum, 1966.
NEW ITALIAN ART, Arts Council of Northern Ireland/David Hendriks, 1973.
OIREACHTAS, An tOireachtas catalogues from 1955 to 1977.
PAINTINGS AND DESIGNS BY ULSTER ARTISTS, CEMA, 1961.
PAINTINGS FROM THE CEMA COLLECTION, CEMA, 1961.
PAINTINGS FROM THE COLLECTION OF THE ARTS COUNCIL/AN CHOMHAIRLE EALÁOIN, An Chomhairle Ealáoin, 1974.
PAINTINGS FROM THE COLLECTION OF THE ARTS COUNCIL OF NORTHERN IRELAND, An Chomhairle Ealáoin, 1974.
PENTA, Octagon Gallery, 1977.
PRINTS FROM THE COLLECTION OF THE BELFAST EDUCATION AND LIBRARY BOARD, Arts Council of Northern Ireland, 1975.
ROSC '71: THE IRISH IMAGINATION, Municipal Gallery of Modern Art, Dublin, 1971.
ROYAL ULSTER ACADEMY ANNUAL EXHIBITION, Catalogues 1955 to 1977.
SCOTTISH REALISM, Scottish Arts Council, 1970.
SOME NORTHERN IRELAND ARTISTS AND CRAFTSMEN, Arts Council of Northern Ireland, 1971.
SURREALIST PAINTINGS FROM THE URVATER COLLECTION, Belfast Museum and Art Gallery/CEMA, 1958.
TORY ISLAND PAINTERS, Octagon Gallery, 1977.
ULSTER FACES, Arts Council of Northern Ireland, 1971.
ULSTER FACES 2, Arts Council of Northern Ireland, 1972.
ULSTER PAINTING '68, Arts Council of Northern Ireland, 1968.
ULSTER PLACES, Arts Council of Northern Ireland, 1971.
WHEN ATTITUDES BECOME FORM, ICA/Philip Morris, 1969.
WOMEN OF ULSTER, Arts Council of Northern Ireland, 1975/76.
WORKS BY SOME FORMER PUPILS OF ANNADALE GRAMMAR SCHOOL 1950-75, Arts Council of Northern Ireland, 1975.
YOUNG CONTEMPORARIES, Octagon Gallery, 1977.
YOUNG IRISH ARTISTS, The Young Irish Artists Foundation, 1965.

INDEX

Page numbers in italics denote illustrations.